RETIRED

Crosscurrents
in the Literatures
of Asia and the West

A. Owen Aldridge.
© Illini Studio

Crosscurrents in the Literatures of Asia and the West

Essays in Honor of A. Owen Aldridge

Edited by

Masayuki Akiyama and Yiu-nam Leung

DELAWARE

Newark: University of Delaware Press
London: Associated University Presses

Associated University Presses
440 Forsgate Drive
Cranbury, NJ 08512

Associated University Presses
16 Barter Street
London WC1A 2AH, England

Associated University Presses
P.O. Box 338, Port Credit
Mississauga, Ontario
Canada L5G 4L8

The paper used in this publication meets the requirements
of the American National Standard for Permanence of Paper
for Printed Library Materials Z39.48–1984.

Library of Congress Cataloging-in-Publication Data

Crosscurrents in the literatures of Asia and the West : essays in honor of A. Owen Aldridge / edited by Masayuki Akiyama and Yiu-nam Leung.
    p. cm.
Includes bibliographical references and index.
ISBN 0–87413–639–3 (alk. paper)
    1. Literature, Comparative—East Asian and Western. 2. Literature, Comparative—Western and East Asian. 3. East Asian literature—History and criticism. I. Aldridge, Alfred Owen, 1915–. II. Akiyama, Masayuki, 1930– . III. Leung, Yiu-nam, 1951–
    PL493.C76   1997
  809--dc21
                                  97–10229
                                    CIP

PRINTED IN THE UNITED STATES OF AMERICA

Contents

Part 1: Ideology and Culture

6   CONTENTS

Part 2: Poetics

Part 3: Genre

Part 4: Themes and Influences

Part 5: Gender

A. Owen Aldridge: A Profile

MASAYUKI AKIYAMA

To honor A. Owen Aldridge, professor emeritus of the University of Illinois, two Festschrifts have already been published: *Deism, Masonry, and the Enlightenment* (University of Delaware Press, 1987), edited by J. A. Leo Lemay, and *Aesthetics and the Literature of Ideas* (University of Delaware Press, 1990), edited by François Jost with the assistance of Melvin J. Friedman. The first of these tributes was inspired by Aldridge's research on early American literature, particularly his books on Benjamin Franklin and Thomas Paine; the second, by his contributions to comparative literature, particularly his work on Shaftesbury, Voltaire, and other European figures of the eighteenth century. The present collection draws attention to the third and most recent segment of Aldridge's scholarly production, his writings on literary relations between Asia and the West. For the last quarter century of his career, tracing the influence of Asian writers in Europe and America has been his paramount activity. As a result, he has had many Asian students at Illinois, including eleven who received their Ph.D. degrees under his direction, ten of whom are now teaching in universities in Taiwan, Hong Kong, and Korea. He has also directed the East-West dissertation of an American, who is now teaching at a Japanese university, one of only two contributors to the present Festschrift who is not Asian. The other is Marián Gálik, an eminent European sinologue.

Oddly enough, Aldridge did not become involved with Asian literature until his middle fifties, when he was invited to attend the first international conference on comparative literature held in the Republic of China, which took place at Tamkang College (now Tamkang University) in August 1971. The city of Buffalo, New York, where Aldridge was born 16 December 1915, although a vibrant multicultural center with distinctive German, Polish, and Italian neighborhoods, had in the early years of the century attracted almost no Asian inhabitants. Before Aldridge's initial visit to Taiwan, the first reference to a Chinese author in his writing appeared in an essay on the French method of *explication de texte* in which he compared a poem by Victor Hugo to verses on a similar theme in a Chinese work, a comparison designed to illustrate the technique of the French comparatist Etiemble, which at the time was just being introduced to the United States. Aldridge had chosen Victor Hugo as the focus of his essay but was not acquainted with a Chinese parallel. Fortunately, he had already forged a warm relationship with the single professor of Chinese at the University of Maryland, where Aldridge was teaching at the time, and this professor provided him with the required text.

Aldridge's first printed reference to Japanese letters came in his contribution to a Festschrift for one of his professors of American literature at Duke University. Here, he cited from an international comparative literature conference a paper on the introduction of American literature to Japan reporting that the empress of Japan had turned into Japanese odes twelve of the virtues Franklin had celebrated in his autobiography, but for some reason omitting that of chastity.

Aldridge's first acquaintance with Japanese nationals also took place at the University of Maryland, where two students on scholarships from the Japanese government, Shunsuke Kamei and his wife, took his graduate seminar on eighteenth-century American literature. He admired the work of both students, and they became fast friends. Kamei is now recognized as the foremost professor of American literature in Japan.

It was a momentous year for comparative literature in America when Aldridge and Melvin J. Friedman founded the quarterly journal *Comparative Literature Studies* in the fall of 1963 at the University of Maryland. In 1967, Aldridge and the journal moved to the University of Illinois, where he was appointed professor of French and comparative literature. He edited the journal until his retirement in 1986, after which he supervised its moving to the department of comparative literature at Pennsylvania State University. He is now listed as editor emeritus. One of its regular issues every two years is devoted to East-West literary relations and is edited in conjunction with members of the College of International Relations at Nihon University.

Aldridge's invitation in 1971 to attend the comparative literature conference in Taiwan, to which I have already referred, came as a result of his friendship with an American comparatist, Claudio Guillén, then teaching at the University of California at La Jolla. One of Guillén's fellow professors at La Jolla was Wai-lim Yip, a specialist in Chinese poetics who had received his literary training in Taiwan. When the organizers of the Tamkang conference asked Professor Yip if he would recommend two or three American comparatists to be invited as participants, he asked the advice of his colleague Guillén, who recommended Aldridge. The paper that Aldridge presented there on the influence of China on Voltaire has been reprinted three times, including a translation in Chinese. Aldridge was also asked to prepare a recapitulation of all the papers of the conference, a task that he then performed and repeated at the next five quadrennial conferences of the Taiwanese organization. Aldridge has participated also in the maiden conferences of the British, the Spanish, and the mainland Chinese comparative literature associations.

On his way to the Tamkang conference in 1971, Aldridge spent a week in Korea during which he lectured at ten universities. He then visited for several days in the home of Mr. and Mrs. Kamei in Tokyo. Kamei arranged for his guest to hold a dialogue with him in the office of his publisher on the methodology of comparative literature. The dialogue was taped and later published in English and Japanese versions, the former in the Canadian journal *Mosaic* and the latter as a chapter in a book by Kamei on the theory of comparative literature. As a result of reading this book, the present writer spent a research year with Aldridge at the University of Illinois, where he established various links between that institution and his own university.

For over fifteen years, Aldridge has collaborated in various research projects with the College of International Relations of Nihon University at Mishima, including special lectures, publications, and joint issues of the journal *Comparative Literature Studies*. He has twice given a series of lectures at the Mishima campus, both of which have been published in book form in Japanese translation. When the College in 1989 held an international symposium with the theme "Toward a New Age of Creativity: Humanity, Cooperation, Peace" to celebrate the centennial anniversary of the foundation of Nihon University and the tenth anniversary of the opening of the College of International Relations, Aldridge was invited as a keynote lecturer. Five of the essays in the present volume are by present or former faculty members of Nihon University.

After his retirement from the University of Illinois, Aldridge occupied for one year the Will and Ariel Durant Chair at Saint Peter's College in Jersey City, New Jersey. In 1987, he went as visiting professor to Penn State University. At about this time, his marriage of nearly twenty-five years broke up, leaving him free to spend long periods out of the country and to pursue his love affair with East Asian culture. In 1988, he served in Korea for four months as Fulbright Distinguished Professor, lecturing at both Seoul National University and Korea University. In the following year he accepted a visiting professorship at National Cheng Chi University in Taipei and the year after that a visiting chair professorship at National Tsing Hua University in Hsinchu, Taiwan.

As the result of his exposure to Asian culture and literature, he has published four books on East-West relations. In the preface to the first of these, *The Reemergence of World Literature: A Study of Asia and the West* (University of Delaware Press, 1986), he heralded East-West studies as a vital part of the university curriculum in the United States.

> From the time of Goethe until the second half of the twentieth century, world literature as represented by printed anthologies and college surveys has consisted almost exclusively of the masterpieces of the Western world. At the present time, however, new technological and political developments . . . have stimulated a revived awareness of world literature and of the need for a new definition, one that recognizes Africa and Asia as equal partners.

Rather than merely theorizing about the desirability of such studies, however, Aldridge has through numerous other publications in the field of East-West comparative studies shown a methodology for the joint study of the literatures of Asia and the West. In the first part of *The Reemergence of World Literature*, he explains his notion of the positive features of what is now called multiculturalism in chapters entitled "The Universal in Literature," "Cultural Pluralism and Criticism," and "The Taiwan-Hong Kong Axis." In the second part of the book, he presents applications of this theory in the form of insightful essays on "Voltaire and the Mirage of China" and a rapprochement study of Western fiction and contemporary Japanese novels.

Comparative Literature: Japan and the West (1979) is a translation into Japanese of a series of lectures that Aldridge gave at Nihon University, some of which are duplicated from his *The Emergence of World Literature*. The later *Fiction in Japan and the West* (1985), although also a translation of lectures given at Nihon University, contains essays which, with one exception, have not appeared in English in any form. This exception is the chapter "The Werther of the Twentieth Century," which appears in *The Comparative Perspective on Literature*, edited by Clayton Koelb and Susan Noakes (Cornell University Press, 1988). The titles of the four other chapters are "From Picaresque to Thingaresque: Western Precursors of Soseki's *I Am a Cat*," "Etiemble and *The Ancient Capital* of Kawabata: a French Critic Interprets a Japanese Novel," "Mishima and Yourcenar: A French Novelist Looks at a Japanese Contemporary," and "Utopianism in World Literature."

Aldridge's most recent book, *The Dragon and the Eagle: The Presence of China in the American Enlightenment* (Wayne State University Press, 1993), combines literary history with analysis of several of the intellectual forces and attitudes of the eighteenth century. Although prior scholarship had concluded that Americans of this period had little knowledge of the Middle Kingdom and hardly more curiosity about it, Aldridge reveals the existence of a widespread interest and a number of direct connections. Benjamin Franklin, Thomas Paine, and Thomas Jefferson each in his own way personally encountered Chinese philosophy and customs. Aldridge also describes the cultivation of ginseng in the New World, parallels between Chinese and Amerindian myths, China in American works of the imagination, and the impact on literature of the burgeoning Chinese trade. Aldridge unearths Franklin's declaration, which has previously been completely ignored, that if he were a young man he would like to go to China. Aldridge's friends are reminded of his similar affirmation, often expressed, that if he were thirty years old or younger he would study an Asian language.

Aldridge's lucid definitions provide both the parameters of East-West studies and a vindication of literary studies in general. I cite the following from *The Emergence of World Literature*:

> *Literature* as such consists of communication by written words or symbols when the purpose of communication involves emotional or aesthetic response in addition to mere transference of information. *Comparative literature* can be considered the study of any literary phenomenon from the perspective of more than one national literature or in conjunction with another intellectual discipline or even several. *World literature* may be said to comprise the great works or classics of all times selected from all of the various national literatures. *Universal literature* in the broadest sense represents the sum total of all texts and works throughout the world, or the combination of all national literatures. In a restricted and more practical sense, universal literature comprises all works that contain elements cosmopolitan enough to appeal to the average person in any literate culture. The study of literature East-West in particular consists in revealing connections between one or more works from one hemisphere with one or more from the other. (55–56)

Throughout his career, Aldridge has remained in the mainstream of literary theory, in a sense tempering the objective rigor of positivism with esthetic and philosophical analysis. At the dawn of his career he remained aloof from the excesses of New Criticism, and today he actively opposes theories that deny the possibility of mutually understood communication through language. He was a pioneer in insisting that criticism must not abandon its function of revealing the relation between the literary work and life. He expressed this opinion forcibly in *Comparative Literature: Matter and Method* when it was by no means a popular point of view: "The most important of all literary relationships is that between literature and life." When Aldridge wrote this in 1969, most of his readers would have understood the word *life* to refer to the atomistic individual rather than to collective groups or communities. He undoubtedly had the first meaning in mind, but readers today, if they wish, may consider life as referring to group entities based on gender, ethnicity, class, or sexual preference.

Despite his concentration on the individual rather than group identities, Aldridge has been wary of the psychological-critical concept of setting the self against various forms of the Other. The universalism he expresses rejects the notions of privilege and hegemony associated with orientalism and Eurocentrism but at the same time invalidates the assumption that discourses from the West inherently embody an attitude of superiority or condescension. His determined opposition to Eurocentrism appears primarily in his insistence that comparative literature studies, no matter where undertaken, should comprise all parts of the globe. Aldridge has made a distinction between two fundamental connotations of Eurocentrism that are almost contradictory. One of these is the view that European culture is superior to that of the rest of the world and should, therefore, be accorded preeminence. This attitude he completely rejects. The other interpretation portrays Western writers as judging everything by their own standards and, consequently, giving a biased portrayal in everything they say about other cultures. Aldridge admits some truth in this interpretation, but he argues that people of both East and West are products of the culture that they have imbibed from birth and that when they compare their own culture with a new one with which they come into contact, they inevitably give preference to the old and familiar. Aldridge disagrees, moreover, with the concept of orientalism, the view that there is an ingrained tendency in Western writers either to see only the trivial and exotic in Eastern cultures or to condemn them as inferior in one way or another to those of the Occident. He has demonstrated that in the eighteenth century, the period of his greatest expertise, a taste for the exotic was balanced by the doctrine of uniformitarianism, which made people look for similarities and resemblances rather than differences between themselves and people of other cultures. Although not touching upon political and economic developments, Aldridge has recently published a number of papers indicating the generally favorable attitude of Western writers of the eighteenth and nineteenth centuries toward China.

The contributors to this commemoration of Owen Aldridge's eightieth birthday are either former students or close colleagues and friends. We take great pleasure in the realization that this book will portray essential characteristics of the literatures of Japan, Korea, and China in relation to the literatures of the European and American continents.

A. Owen Aldridge's Writings on East-West Literary Relations

Books

Comparative Literature: Japan and the West (in Japanese translation). Tokyo: Nan'un Do Co., 1979.

Fiction in Japan and the West (in Japanese translation). Tokyo: Nan'un Do Co., 1985.

The Reemergence of World Literature. Newark: University of Delaware Press, 1986. Reprint. Taipei: Bookman, 1990.

The Dragon and the Eagle: The Presence of China in the American Enlightenment. Detroit: Wayne State University Press, 1993.

Articles

"Comparative Literature East and West: An Appraisal of the Tamkang Conference." *Yearbook of Comparative and General Literature* 21 (1972): 65–70.

with Shunsuki Kamei. "Problems and Vistas of Comparative Literature in Japan and the United States: A Dialogue." *Mosaic* 5 (1972): 149–63.

"Voltaire and the Cult of China." *Tamkang Review* 3 (1972): 25–49.

"The Second China Conference: A Recapitulation." *Tamkang Review* 7 (1976): 481–92. Also in *Yearbook of Comparative and General Literature* 25 (1976): 149–63.

"East-West Literary Relations Conference Revisited." *Yearbook of Comparative and General Literature* 28 (1979): 50–56.

"East-West Relations: Universal Literature, Yes: Common Poetics, No." *Tamkang Review* 10 (1979): 17–33.

Foreword to *Chinese-Western Comparative Literature: Theory and Strategy*, iii-xx. Hong Kong: Chinese University Press, 1980.

Introduction to *China and the West: Comparative Literature Studies*, edited by William Tay, Ying-hsiung Chou & Heh-hsiang Yuan, iii-xiii. Seattle: University of Washington Press, 1980.

"Recapitulation of the Third International Comparative Literature Conference." *Tamkang Review* 10 (1980): 641–58.

"East-West Resonances in New York." *Tamkang Review* 13 (1982): 1–11.

"Balancing Careers or Comparatism Triumphant." *Arcadia. Zeit-schrift fur Vergleichende Literaturwissenschaft. 1983.* (Special issue apart from series volumes. The article is a short autobiography explaining the author's dedication to East-West studies).

"The Universal in Literature." *Neohelicon* 10 (1983).

"Utopianism in World Literature." *Tamkang Review* 24.1–4 (Summer 1984): 11–29.

"Major Themes at the Fourth International Conference in the Republic of China." *Tamkang Review* 24.1–4 (Summer 1984): 31–40.

"The Perception of China in English Literature of the Enlightenment." *Asian Culture Quarterly* 14 (1986): 1–26.

"An Optimistic Perspective on Comparative Literature based on *rapports de fait*—an interview with A. Owen Aldridge." *The Chinese Intellectual* Spring 1987: 3–11.

"The Japanese Werther of the Twentieth Century." In *The Comparative Perspective on Literature*, edited by Clayton Koelbe and Susan Noakes. Ithaca, N.Y.: Cornell University Press, 1988. Reprinted as "Kokoro and Werther," *Contemporary World Literature* (Korea) 18 (1989): 97–118.

"The First Chinese Drama in English Translation." *Asian Culture Quarterly* 16 (1988). Reprinted in Studies in Chinese-Western Comparative Drama., edited by Yun-Tong Luk. Hong Kong: Chinese University Press, 1990.

"A Case of Academic Schizophrenia." (academic autobiography) *William and Mary Quarterly* 45 (1988): 520–26.

"Literature and the Study of Man." In *Literature and Anthropology*, edited by Philip A. Denis and Wendell Aycock, 40–63. Lubbock: Texas Tech University Press, 1989.

"Recapitulation of the Fifth Quadrennial Comparative Literature Congress." *Tamkang Review* 19 (1989): 889–910.

"Utopia and the New Age." In *Toward a New Age of Creativity*, 170–81. Mishima, Japan: Nihon University Press, 1990.

"The Role of Ginseng in Sino-American Trade and Literary Relations." *Asian Culture Quarterly* 18 (1990): 54–64.

"China in the Spanish Enlightenment." *Proceedings of the XIIth Congress of the International Comparative Literature Association* (Munchen, Germany), judicium verlag: 1990: 3:404–9.

"Sex, Sexuality and Utopianism." In *Collected Essays of the Third National Conference of English and American Literature,* 11–31. Taiwan: National Sun Yat-sen University, 1990.

Review of 'La Literatura desde el punto de vista del receptor,' by Franco Meregalli." *Tamkang Review* 20 (1990): 431–38.

"Will Durant as Comparatist." In *International Perspectives in Comparative Literature*, edited by Virginia M. Shaddy, 17–43. Lewiston, N.Y.: Edwin Mellen Press, 1991.

"Benjamin Franklin's Letter from China." *Asian Culture Quarterly* 19 (1991): 62–70.

"Two Court Autobiographers of the Eighteenth Century: Voltaire and Lady Hong of Korea." *Seoul Journal of Korean Studies* 4 (1991): 59–72.

"Irving Babbitt and North American Comparative Literature." In *Comparative Literary History as Discourse: In Honor of Anna Balakian,* edited by M. F. Valdes, D. Javitch, and A. O. Aldridge, 51–65. New York: Peter Lang, 1992.

"Irving Babbitt In and About China." *Modern Age* 35 (1993): 332–39.

"Kien Long and Western Letters." *Tamkang Review* 12 (1991–92): 17–42.

"Yasanuri Kawabata." In *Critical Survey of Short Fiction,* edited by Frank N. Magill, 1317–23. Pasadena, Calif.: Salem Press, 1993.

"Recapitulation of the Sixth Congress." *Tamkang Review* 23 (1993): 819–34.

"The Penetration of Chinese Fiction in the United States." *Asian Culture Quarterly* 22 (Fall 1994): 61–80.

Review of *L'Europe chinoise de la sinophilie à la sinophobie,* by Etiemble. *Yearbook of Comparative and General Literature* 39 (1990–91): 142–44.

Review of *Le Voyage en Chine. Anthologie des voyageurs occidentaux,* edited by N. Boothroyd and M. Detrie. *Yearbook of Comparative and General Literature* 40: 164–66.

"The Introduction of Taoism to America." *Asian Culture Quarterly* 22 (Summer 1994): 43–61.

"American Translations of the *Tao Teh Ching.*" In *Tao: Reception in East and West. Series Euro-sinica*, edited by Adrian Hsia. Bern: Peter Lang, 1994.

"Introduction" to *The Theme of Chastity in Hau Ch'iu Chuan and Parallel Western Fiction*, by Kai-chong Cheung, 9–22. In *Series Euro-sinica*. Bern: Peter Lang, 1994.

"Paradise Lust: Or Sex, Sexuality and Utopianism." In *Proceedings of the XIIIth Congress of the International Comparative Literature Association.* Tokyo, 1995.

"A Regime's Shame and a Human Victory." Review of *Red in Tooth and Claw: Twenty-six Years in Communist China's Prisons,* by Pu Ning. *Modern Age* 38 (Fall 1995): 88–93.

Preface

YIU-NAM LEUNG

Attention to literary relations between Asia and the West is a relatively recent phenomenon in the scholarly world. It is true that sinology emerged in Western universities as an academic discipline early in the nineteenth century, and it has flourished ever since, but despite Goethe's proclamation of *Weltliteratur* at the turn of the century, inspired in great measure by an English translation of a Chinese scholar-beauty romance, Eurocentrism continued for decades to govern Western literary historians, and a parallel insularity existed in China and Japan. The breakthrough toward authentic universalism took place in comparative literature circles in the early 1970s. One of its pioneer manifestations was the first international congress devoted to East-West relations that took place in Taiwan in 1971. Before that time, there had been no recognition of the existence of an East-West component in such organizations as the International Comparative Literature Association, the Modern Language Association of America, or sister organizations in Europe. Today, East-West studies rank among the major concerns of these bodies, as measured by sections devoted to them in annual meetings and articles in official publications. An identical growing awareness throughout the West of Japanese and Chinese literatures may be perceived in the extraordinary increase in the acquisitions of oriental materials in research libraries, more or less in proportion to the proliferation in cities large and small of restaurants with Far Eastern menus.

The extension of the notion of comparative literature to universal literature explains in part the apparent anomaly of the present volume, dedicated, as it is, to an Anglo-American who does not speak a word of any Asian language by a group of scholars most of whom are ethnically Asian and all of whom are professionally engaged in Asian studies. Yet,

21

A. Owen Aldridge has been in the foreground of East-West studies ever since the first Taiwan conference of 1971, which he attended and which he provided with a recapitulation at its close. His book *The Reemergence of World Literature*, which sketches the development of East-West studies as an academic discipline, has been reprinted in Taiwan, and two of his other books have been published in Tokyo in Japanese translation. The contributors to the present volume are either former students or friends and colleagues with whom Aldridge has collaborated. Only two are not Asian, and all except two are professors in Asian universities. One contributor is president of the American Comparative Literature Association and another is president of the Comparative Literature Association of the Peoples Republic of China. Aldridge has taught or lectured extensively in Taiwan, Japan, and Korea, and he has maintained contacts with all the contributors to this volume, residing variously in Taiwan, Japan, Korea, Hong Kong, China, Slovakia, Canada, and the United States.

Milestones in the history of East-West literary relations are sketched in the section of the present book devoted to ideology and culture. Dai-yun Yue analyzes the impact of Western critical theories, chiefly nineteenth-century German and Russian and contemporary French ones, on the more conservative Chinese mainstream. With the optimism for which she is personally noted, she expresses hope for amalgamation of these diverse strands in a "dynamic dialogue" and "new discourse." Heh-hsiang Yuan attempts to answer the perennial question of whether Chinese and Western literatures have enough in common to be treated as parallel artistic products. After seeking a comparable theoretical basis in philosophical discourse that takes him as far as the time of Confucius in the East and Plato in the West, he concludes that despite the constant changes in the notions of canon and genre in both hemispheres, it is possible to discern a genuine foundation of universalism in literature. Adrian Hsia provides a survey of eighteenth-century European attitudes toward Chinese philosophy, moral, religious, and political, with special attention to Germany and Herder. Uncovering the anthropological background of Herder's conception of Tartars and Mongols, Hsia explains the German philosopher's classification of the inhabitants of East Asia as "the ugly peoples," a perspective that he fortunately modified in later life. John T. Dorsey describes the opposite flow, from West to East, in a survey of the influence of Western egalitarian concepts and industrial methods in late nineteenth-century Japan. Shunsuke Kamei portrays the influence of cultural attitudes in his summary of the reception of Mark Twain in Japan, first as a writer of juvenilia, later as a humorist, and finally as a serious literary artist. Instead of presenting a mere chronological account, Kamei reveals that Twain's fiction was originally regarded as alien to traditional Japanese sensibilities, but a contrasting current in the national psyche subsequently warmed to the robust style and feral atmosphere of his writing. Seong-kon Kim adopts a Westward-looking perspective in analyzing the conflicting attitudes represented in Hollywood's portrayal of the highly romanticized and overrated American Dream.

Wai-lim Yip goes back to the time of Ezra Pound, the dawn of the twentieth century, to discuss Pound's concept of the role of natural scenery in the poetic process. After a general analysis of the relationship of language to reality in Chinese culture, Yip shows how Pound used words, both as ideograms and as parts of a linear structure, to portray beauty. He contrasts the Confucian system of naming based on a social hierarchy with Taoist-inspired poetry, which is purposely ambiguous in order to give full play to the perspectives and feelings of the reader while restraining those of the poet. Yip concludes that Pound attempted to follow the Taoist model in principle but failed in practice. Metaphor is usually associated with poetry or at least commonly discussed as an adjunct to verse composition, but, as Eugene Eoyang explains, it has much wider currency. He reveals that in one of the three categories in which it may be classified, the metaphor functions as a component of theory and speculation in a process resembling intuition. After a neat summary of the epistemological premises of the major nineteenth-century-types of literary criticism, Eoyang reveals that metaphor is involved in nearly all methods of acquiring and communicating knowledge.

Goethe, in one of his most profound poems, entitled "Spiritual Yearning," maintains that man's soul aspires toward death and regeneration in the cosmos. Marián Gálik reveals the strong influence of this poem on a modern Chinese poet, Feng Zhi, leading to the latter's composing a sonnet dedicated to Goethe in a volume expressing various manifestations of the concept of spiritual renewal. Koon-ki Tommy Ho, after an original portrayal of the similarities linking utopia and dystopia and the manner in which one may lead to the other, shows similarities in the historical elements in two beast dystopias, George Orwell's *Animal Farm* in the West and Mo Ying-feng's *A Utopian Dream* in the East. Two naturalist novels are treated from the perspectives of both genre and theme in an analysis of Emile Zola's *Money* and Mao Tun's *Midnight*. Several scholars in the past have sought to determine the degree of influence, if any, of Zola upon the Chinese author, but their emphasis has been almost entirely on Tun and his personal declarations on the subject. The study of high finance in the present book reverses this emphasis by revealing the evidence available in the works of Mao Tun's French forerunner himself.

Matoshi Fujisawa's delineation of the inspiration derived by a
Japanese poet, Takuboku Ishikawa, from a novel by Hans Christian
Andersen has much in common with Gálik's account of a Chinese sonnet
inspired by Goethe. Unlike the usual binary studies of influence,
however, Fujisawa's investigation takes into account the translator. A
Japanese novel revealing a considerable degree of influence from the
West is *A Certain Woman* by Takeo Arishima. The female protagonist
embarks on a trip to the United States in order to marry a Japanese
Christian who is living there, but after a short time returns to Japan.
Arishima, as Masayuki Akiyama points out, not only used America as
narrative background but acquired a number of philosophical attitudes
from the works of Walt Whitman. The theme of *A Certain Woman*,
female independence and sexual freedom, is a popular one in our day,
and Arishima's protagonist, Yoko, by experimenting with several men,
has a certain kinship with Edna Pontellier in Kate Chopin's *The
Awakening*, the short novel that has become an American classic almost
overnight. Instead of pursuing this obvious but superficial resemblance,
however, Akiyama probes the theme of feminine cultural identity by
comparing Arishima's protagonist with Henry James's Isabel Archer.
Both follow romantic inclinations, Yoko in seeking sexual gratification
and Isabel in marrying a man who values her only for her wealth. Since
Isabel accepts her lot as an unfulfilled wife, most modern feminists
would place Yoko over Isabel, but Akiyama refuses to do so, adhering to
the connotations in the respective titles of James and Arishima, Isabel a
"lady" and Yoko a "certain woman." The female protagonist of Koyo
Ozaki's *The Golden Dream,* treated by Yoko Matsui is almost the reverse
of Isabel Archer. Unlike James's heroine, she places the values of wealth
and social status over those of respect and romantic love. *The Golden
Dream* illustrates the concept that minor writers in one national literature
may have a direct and profound influence upon a major author in another
national literature. As Matsui reveals, the plot of Ozaki's novel is linked
to two works of American female authors who are now so obscure that
their names do not even appear as footnotes in literary histories.

The two sexes have been standard topics or ingredients in both
Western and Asian literatures since the dawn of imaginative writing. In
recent years, however, feminism and gender have evolved as separate
entities of literary study, even though the meanings of these terms and
the content of studies to which they refer have remained somewhat
ambiguous. In a broad sense, these concerns go beyond descriptions of
bodily appurtenances and functions to a consideration of the political,
economic, social, and psychological consequences of belonging to one
sex or the other. Akiyama's study of female searches for identity

certainly fits one or more of these categories. I-chun Wang focuses on gender in her portrayal of adultery in an English play of the seventeenth century, *Arden of Faversham*, and in a Chinese play of the same period, *Kan Tou Chin* (*Detecting the Hood*), both of which are anonymous. In the politics of gender, according to Wang, the boundaries for females are defined by men. Not making any plea that females be given special consideration on this account, Wang argues that patriarchal authority means perpetual control of women, which leads in these dramas to adultery and murder. Wang suggests that whatever element of guilt exists in the domestic tragedies with which she deals, it is shared by both males and females.

Kai-chong Cheung also goes back in literary history, but only as far as the late nineteenth century, for her first example of female rebellion, *The Revolt of Mother* by Mary Wilkins Freeman. At the time of its original publication, this story was classified under the genre of local color, but it is now hailed as an important document in the feminist movement. Cheung next treats a Taiwanese story of the 1960s by Li-hua Yu that introduces the staples of postmodern feminism, violence, rape, and sexual abuse in the Chinese ambiance of domination by the mother-in-law rather than by the husband. The revolt of the protagonist, however, can hardly be claimed as a victory, especially when contrasted with the outcome in the third story treated by Cheung, Alice Walker's *The Color Purple*. Here the triumph of the heroine is total, comprising ascendancy over the various men who had formerly dominated her life and a quasi-lesbian relationship with a sturdy role model, who serves the like-minded reader in the same capacity. The final essay, a biocritical study of a pioneer Japanese female educator, could fit equally under the rubrics of gender or of ideology and culture. Naomi Matsuoka traces the contributions of Tsuda Umeko, founder of a woman's college in Tokyo bearing her own given name. At a time when few Japanese women received higher education of any kind, Umeko studied at Bryn Mawr College in the United States and, on returning to Japan, worked energetically to promote the process of Westernization at the turn of the twentieth century. In her writings, she placed the problems of women in her own country in the context of the women's movement throughout the world.

This collection of essays follows the example of Owen Aldridge in preferring literary history to abstract theorizing about literature. A consistent theme in his writing has been the difference in style and genre between Western and oriental poetics, a theme taken up in the essay by Heh-hsiang Yuan. The related essay by Dai-yun Yue on the "cultural fever" in mainland China induced by the penetration of Western literary theories is in many ways a replay of Aldridge's many contributions to the

Tamkang Review concerning the importation of Western theoretical fads into Taiwan, especially his essay "East-West Relations: Universal Litera- ture, Yes; Common Poetics, No." Coincident with the current interest in neocolonialism, he has recently quoted the injunction of K. T. Mei in 1914, "China is the dumping ground for all the routine banalities and dubious ideologies of the West."

This collection of essays does not pretend to cover completely any one area of the vast expanse of the East-West literary landscape, but it offers some inkling of the inexhaustible variety in that panorama. Multicultural- ism in the best sense strives to penetrate territory that is unknown, if not exactly exotic, rather than to exalt the known over the unknown. This has been the mission of the voyagers in literary space who have contributed to this volume and who hope that it may encourage others to follow them into this still largely unexplored region.

—Yiu-nam Leung

Acknowledgments

The contributors of this volume gratefully acknowledge a generous grant from Professor Masayuki Akiyama of Nihon University and supplementary amounts from Professors Naomi Matsuoka, Yoko Matsui, and Matoshi Fujisawa of Nihon University, and from John Dorsey of Rikkyo University. Thanks are extended also to Professor Jui-Keng Chen of National Taiwan University for the calligraphy adorning the title page and to the Program in Comparative Literature of the University of Illinois for the photograph of Professor Aldridge.

Crosscurrents
in the Literatures
of Asia and the West

艾德溫教授八十壽慶紀念論文集

一九九五年十二月十六日

黙齋陳瑞華敬題

Part 1
Ideology and Culture

Cultural Discourse and Cultural Intercourse

DAI-YUN YUE

Between the years 1985 and 1989, a heated discussion about culture, including literature and art, took place in mainland China. Commonly referred to as a "cultural fever," it was one of the broadest and most profound currents of cultural reflection since the May Fourth Movement of 1919. The noisy and often hasty discussion during this period produced a flood of miscellaneous theories, ideas, perspectives, and individual voices associated with various scholarly groups and journals. This flurry of discussion inspired a blooming of essays, articles, and conferences on a large range of topics. From the very beginning, the discussion was channeled into two sides: one side advocated the rethinking of the traditional culture, a restoration of traditional values and attitudes; the other side urged the importation of Western theories and discourses. The rapid translation from tradition to innovation and from Western ideas to Chinese ideas led to a dazzling chaos. This essay will focus on the latter aspect.

The influx of Western theories and discourses was overwhelming, composing indeed a world exhibition. Struggling for recognition were new names and methodologies ranging from Max Weber to Daniel Bell; from Nietzsche and Heidegger to Derrida and Foucault; from Russian thinkers like Shestov, Mayakovsky, and Bakhtin to Western Marxists such as Walter Benjamin, Theodor Adorno, Althusser, and Fredric Jameson. Their ideologies vied with concepts such as new historicism, feminism, and postcolonialism. These intellectual currents were designated "new theories." Obviously, it makes little sense to cover under a single title all these various and often conflicting theories. There is little common ground in the highly personalized interpretation of the "poetic tradition" of a Schelling, a Nietzsche, or a Heidegger and the historical, sociological criticism inspired by Lukacs, Walter Benjamin, and Fredric Jameson, or in the elaborate systems of structuralism, narratology, and archetypal criticism. These theories, nevertheless, had a considerable marketability in China during the period under discussion. Although these Western theories originated in different countries, at different periods, and for different purposes, they came to China at almost the same time and consequently had to be considered synchronically. In the process, they inevitably lost their historical context and intellectual aura. As a result, the effort to appropriate Western literary theories is often not as fruitful as people expect, and at the same time it causes critical confusion.

Because of these deficiencies, people began to ask: Is there any valid reason to apply Western discourses to Chinese culture and society? Some critics earnestly insisted that only the Chinese can understand China. They asserted that without native roots, it is impossible to know a native culture. This "only we can understand ourselves" stereotype rejected all discourses from other cultures. For those who held this stereotype, Western theories only make confusion and represent a type of intellectual colonialism. Critics devoted themselves, therefore, to discovering a native (indigenous) cultural discourse. The problem is that it is difficult, perhaps impossible, to find a pure native discourse. Culture is not the fixed "things become" but the developing "things becoming." It is being changed and reformed all the time. Actually, culture exists as the accumulation of different interpretations of different people living in different periods and unavoidably influenced by the current and traditional cultures of other nations. For example, when scholars of the Sung dynasty interpreted Confucianism and created neo-Confucianism, their discourse was formed by the circumstances of their daily lives mixed to a great extent with imported Indian Buddhist elements. In China today, the so-called Chinese native cultural discourse is nothing but the mental impressions of living Chinese people born in this century, educated in a Western-style school, and inevitably affected by numerous Western ideas through different channels. Especially in the past forty years, different generations have been trained by the Western ideologies of Marxism and Russian communism. It is impossible to find a Chinese intellectual with a "pure mind," "unpolluted" by the outside world.

As a matter of fact, in the middle 1980s, a group of talented Chinese writers started a literary movement that they described as "searching the roots." They tried to find a new way to interpret Chinese culture by means of an "authentic Chinese" view. For them, this meant the view of an uneducated peasant living in a highly remote area. But, ironically, the idea of "searching the roots" itself is an idea from Western countries, especially from America in the 1960s, and no doubt the creative works of these Chinese writers will eventually be looked upon as a part of world literature of the time.

Moreover, this "only we can understand ourselves" stereotype is harmful to the development of a broad culture. According to Jurgen Habermas, the process of self-development requires the reexamination of oneself in the light of the alien eyes of the other in order to find a new perspective. This is what he named "inter-subjectivity." He considered this process the only way to surpass self-limitations and to expand oneself. The establishment of a network of communication between one's original system and another system makes it possible for both systems to borrow each other's strong points and to remedy each other's weaknesses. This is the way to rebuild an old system and also to create a new system. No culture can be developed in an isolated, closed situation. The British philosopher Bertrand Russell wrote that exchanges between different cultures in the past have proved many times to be milestones in the development of human civilization. Greece copied from Egypt, and Rome borrowed from Greece. Arabia referred back to the Roman Empire, and medieval Europe in turn imitated Arabia, while Renaissance Europe followed the Byzantine Empire. European culture, in the course of its own development, absorbed all kinds of cultural elements from outside, and not only did it do so without losing its native cultural tradition, but it also greatly enriched the content of this tradition. During the last century, third-world cultures have changed and developed as part of a worldwide cultural discourse. Homi Bhaba spoke profoundly when he stressed that the most distinctive characteristic of colonial culture is its ambivalence. In my opinion, this ambivalence is due precisely to the impossibility of separating the indigenous culture from modern external influences upon its native intellectuals, whose spiritual background is unavoidably mixed with the other's culture.

Obviously, when applying an imported discourse to a native culture, misreading, misunderstanding, and misguiding are inevitable. There is no simple, one-to-one correspondence between knowledge and truth, between reality and the way in which reality is represented, because all representations are embedded first in the language and then in the culture, institutions, and political ambiance of the presenter. These representations, inaccurate as they may be, however, often present a valuable new perspective for exploring and developing an original text. But, on the other hand, it is clear that the imported discourse never can interpret the native culture to a full extent because the unique and most important characteristics of a native culture may not be present in an imported discourse and consequently cannot be interpreted. Therefore, when we try to organize a dynamic mutual dialogue among different cultures for the benefit of each one, it is not sufficient to use merely a single discourse. The exclusive use of a native discourse, moreover, is impossible not only because the native discourse would not be understood by the partner with whom the dialogue is being carried on, but also for the reasons advanced above to show that a pure native discourse does not exist. How can we get through this dilemma? How can we build a new discourse that is neither totally foreign nor totally native to carry out a fruitful dialogue between two different cultures? Perhaps, as the first step, we can raise an important question of interest to both sides, explore it from different cultural perspectives, discover the strong points and the weaknesses of all approaches, and find a new way to resolve the differences. In this process, based on mutual understanding, a new discourse between different cultures may be established.

As an example, let me propose the question of how meaning is to be derived through the reading of a text. What is the relation between meaning and language? Experts in both Western and Chinese poetics have treated this problem extensively. For a long time, Western critics reasoned that since literary texts were created by living writers, it was writers who established the meaning of texts. In the nineteenth century, the biographical approach prevailed, as critics tried to find the meaning of a text according to the writer's life, experiences, and personal characteristics. In the beginning of the twentieth century, the Freudian theory, which highlighted the role of the writer's subconscious, supplemented theories that consider only the writer's ideas and purposes. Later on, new criticism and Russian formalism exalted "literariness," maintaining that meaning is produced only by language itself. After the development of phenomenology as a philosophical concept, critics took note of the reader's role of constructing the meaning of a text. According to the Polish critic Roman Ingarden, words, phrases, and sentences in a literary text contain numerous blanks, which will be filled in by the imaginations of different readers. He divided the process from words to meaning into four levels: the phonics of the words, the smallest units of meaning, the scheme or strategy, and the objective world represented. The process of reading consists in filling in the blanks formed by the four levels with details created by the reader's imagination and finally to present a picture in the reader's mind. Subsequently, one of the adherents to the theories of reader response, Wolfgang Iser, developed the concept of reading process as a dynamic, ceaseless, synthetic, meaning-producing system.

The same question concerning the communication of meaning has occupied Chinese thinkers for many centuries, and we can find several ideas corresponding with those of the West, although they are not identical. Around the fourth century B.C., the famous Confucianist Mencius inquired: "When you recite the poems and read the books, how can you know the meaning without exploring the writers and his circumstances?" But like many ancient Chinese scholars, he also insisted that language is less significant than reality. He taught: "When you talk about poems, never harm the meaning with the sentences, and never harm the sentences with the separate words. You should trace the meaning in the writer's mind with your own mind, and never be limited by the visible sentences and words."[1] At about the same time, one of the creators of Taoism, Tsuang Tze, proposed his theory about gaining meaning through three levels—words, figures, and meaning. According to Tze, words produce figures, but the words are not the figures—they are an instrument to help you reach the figures. In order to grasp the figures perfectly, you should get rid of the limitation of the words. Likewise, figures produce meaning, but it is not meaning itself but an instrument to help you reach the meaning; in order to grasp the meaning perfectly, you have to get rid of the limitation of the figures. Among these three levels, there are enormous blanks that could be filled in by the reader's feeling and imagination. And this is why the critic Wang Fu Zhi in the Ming dynasty (about the sixteenth century A.D.) stressed that what the poet presents in his poems remains unchanged, but that the readers will find different meanings according to their different emotional situations. On this point, the Buddhist idea goes even further: "The Empty is not always Empty; when certain relations form a situation, the meaning will be revealed." In the long history of Chinese poetics, Chinese critics always stress that words could never perfectly reveal the meaning of a poem but merely offer clues to reach it. Chinese poetics, therefore, usually intend to guide the readers to feel and enjoy a poem in a sensitive, synthetic way, comparable to listening to beautiful music. They do not emphasize observing and analyzing, as their Western colleagues do. Ingarden and Iser, for instance, frequently attempted to analyze and discover when and how the blanks made by the different levels of text are filled by readers. Probably we can say that this is the way to enjoy a painting.

A final word about the unsolved "words—figures—meaning" question. We can start a dialogue that is interesting and beneficial for both Chinese and Western scholars, with different cultural perspectives, different historical contexts, and different linguistic systems. Obviously, the common problem and the common interest will push them to find a way better to understand each other. Hopefully, a new discourse including the strong points of both sides may be built up through mutual understanding and consultative conversation. If this kind of dialogue keeps going for a long time, mutual understanding will increase, and a new discourse will be formed. Of course, this does not mean that the differences between different cultures will disappear. On the contrary, when the strong points of a foreign culture have been understood and absorbed, the native culture will have been enriched and developed in its own way. For example, Chinese Confucianism when enriched by Indian Buddhism developed into neo-Confucianism, which is still mainly Chinese and distinct from Indian Buddhism.

When we propose a question and initiate a dialogue around it, the main purpose is to find a suitable answer from both cultures and historical contexts involved. A new discourse may be created, woven by a longitude of history and a latitude of different cultures. The cultural discussion of the 1980s in China can be seen as a beginning of such a dynamic dialogue, and a new discourse can be expected to emerge.

Works Cited

Habermas, Jurgen. *Theory of Communicative Action*. Translated by Thomas McCarthy. Boston: Beacon Press, 1984.

Ingarden, Roman. *The Literary Work of Art: An Investigation on the Borderlines of Ontology, Logic and Theory of Literature*. Translated by George G. Grabowicz. Evanston, Ill.: Northwestern University Press, 1973.

Iser, Wolfgang. *The Act of Reading: A Theory of Aesthetic Response*. Translated from *Der Akt des Lesens*. Baltimore: Johns Hopkins University Press, 1978.

————. *The Implied Reader: Patterns of Communication in Prose Fiction from Bunyan to Beckett*. Translated from *Der implizite Leser*. Baltimore: John Hopkins University Press, 1974.

Mencius. *Mengzi Zhengyi (The Works of Mencius with Exegesis)* Edited by Jiao Xun. In *Mencius*, translated by D. C. Lau. Harmondsworth: Penguin Books, 1970.

Russell, Bertrand. *A Freeman's Worship*. Edited and translated by Hu Pin-qin and Chang Chu. Beijing: Time Literary Press, 1988.

Wang, Fu-zhi. *Ming shi Pingxuan (Commentary and Selected Works of Poems in the Ming Dynasty)*. In *Chuanshan Gushi Pingxuan* (Commentary and selected works of ancient poems), edited by Wang Fu-zhi. Hunan: Huan Guanshu Baoju, 1917.

Zhao Seng. *Three Theses of Seng Zhoa*. Translated and commented upon by Hsu Fan-cheng. Beijing: Chinese Social Science Publishing House, 1985.

Zhuangzi. *Zhuangzi Jishi* (*Variorum Edition of the Zhuangzi*). Edited by Guo Qing-fan. In *The Complete Works of Chuang Tzu*, translated by Burton Watson. New York: Columbia University Press, 1968.

Notes

1. *Mencius*, Book V, Part A.

Genre and Canon:
An Inquiry into the Comparative Study of Chinese and Western Literature

HEH-HSIANG YUAN

A major difficulty confronting one who engages in a comparative study of Chinese and Western literature is the "cultural root" discrepancy between the two bodies of literary works. When comparative literature was first introduced into the Chinese world, it was assumed that a certain sense of universality in literary study, whatever its nature, could be found, whether that sense of universality would cross the boundary of culture being of little significance. The thrill of a new discovery was there to enthuse and to inspire students of a new discipline. Thus the approach usually took the form of *rapport de fait* or influence studies; seldom was it considered essential that this approach be based on a "same cultural root" in order to make valid claims concerning the comparability of two national literatures.

With the coming of the age of theory and cultural studies, it has become clear to many that the early neglect, though unintentional, is a weakness that has created a false phenomenon in East-West literary studies that presumably deal with the idea of "rapprochement." This, of course, does not mean that the comparative study of Chinese and Western literature is impossible. Despite the cultural differences, East-West comparative literature studies still promise the fascinating engagement of minds and cultures in our humanistic discipline. There are, however, restrictions or conditions that more or less limit the "spheres" of possibilities. One of those can be elucidated in a discussion of the relationship between canon and genre in the literature of both the Chinese and the Western worlds.

One approach to canon suggests that "the canon meant the choice of books in our teaching institutions" (Bloom, 15), which immediately ties the concept of canon to education. Taking the word "education" to mean "cultivation" of a national character, "the choice of books" can variably translate into "classics," "standard texts," "required readings," and so on. And what follows is, naturally, the "canonical anxiety," a concern over the "proper basis" for making the appropriate choice. The intimacy in relationship between "set ideas" and "practices of choice" reveals the truth of the variability of the "ideal," whose interpretation in conventional literary study often belies this "reality." A modern-day reaction to this phenomenon is the deconstruction "movement" in theory (which includes many anticanonical concepts). By questioning this attitude, I am not arguing against the partial validity of the speculation that "no canon is canonical," if we are convinced that dogmatism in literary study is as bad as absolutism in politics. But my query is based on skepticism of nihilism for its own sake, particularly in the field of literary studies. In comparative literature studies, this is even more significant, for no comparison of literary texts is possible if we refuse to affirm any comparable ground. By "comparable ground," I mean textual "facts" that bring together two national literatures either culturally, through a common origin, or in other ways in which they can be placed in an influencing and influenced relationship. The latter condition makes it possible to carry out studies in East-West comparative literature, including Chinese-Western comparative literature. However, when none of these "links" can be found, as is often true in the comparative study of Chinese and Western literature, we are forced to "innovate" by appropriating theoretical concepts, in total or in part, and applying them to the study of a single national literature, usually our own. This leads to the heated debate among comparatists, questioning or defending the validity of such a measure. For a Chinese comparatist, this is particularly disconcerting. He can either defend his act by arguing that the study of literature is truly a transnational and transcultural activity, or he can argue that his engagement is "the only possible" way to revive an old sagging literary tradition, by "injecting" into it a new and rejuvenating spirit. In either case, he has to assume that there are "common grounds" for such an endeavor. But many of us cannot so easily accept such an argument, particularly when we look into the cultural differences between the East and the West and see discrepancies in philosophical thinking, political ideas, social practices, and many other areas of our cultural activity, all due to differing attitudes induced by our differing cultural orientations. However, we can study the results effected by these "differing cultural orientations." And, in literary study, such effects are usually found in canonical concepts governing the creation of literary works and their generic forms. This makes possible a comparative study of certain major Chinese and Western abstract ideas as the moving force behind their respective creative processes. After all, these creative processes are in a sense interpretive processes too; they "interpret" a thought-formation development described by an author as the evolving theme of his or her work. And such an evolving theme argues either for or against an accepted idea (canon), resulting in affirmation or denial of a literary convention (genre). In either case, it speaks for the close relationship between literary canon and genre.

The very fact that intimacy between canon and genre cements a relationship between idea and form does not, however, automatically suggest an unchanging genre. Temporal and spatial factors do affect the constitution of a literary category; other factors related to the framework of mind, such as the thinking process and social practice, also influence literary expressions. Alastair Fowler cited two examples to initiate and prove this argument, one regarding the sixteenth-century concept of the epigram, the other that of the nineteenth-century romance. The term "romance" was resurrected by the Victorians to represent the "non-naturalistic novel," as the Victorians seemed to favor a return to "historical authentication" (Fowler, chap. 8), correspondent to the Aristotelian description of epic as history fictionalized. Thus, the term may simply be "another old bottle for the new wine." The other example cited by Fowler was the epigram. Epigram, according to Samuel Johnson's definition, is " a short poem terminating in a point," with its subject matter (theme) being a great variety of things, from epitaphs to encomia, from fortuitous events to anecdotal narrations; the structural constitution always suggesting a witty closure, which oftentimes comes suddenly. By pointing out the conceptual differences between the epigram of the sixteenth century and that of the twentieth century, Fowler suggested that, unless generic terms "carried a *radix* showing the relevant date," a reader would not be aware of the particular "traits" of a particular work under a generic term label that otherwise may remain undistinguished and thus lack formal characters.

In the medieval period, Fowler further argued, the focus of literature was less concerned with the concept of genre than with the idea of rhetoric, its cause being the concerted attention paid to sermons and homilies. Dante explicated the practical aims of the medieval grammarian in *De Vulgari Eloquentia* as correspondent to Aquinas's two levels of "signification" in *Summa Theologiae*. This indeed altered the whole literary concern.

According to Wimsatt and Brooks, the allegorical and etymological meanings present in poetic texts in the Middle Ages, though of the ancient heritage, were "differently slanted," as "grammar was" in this case "allied as a method to a view" that was noted "in ancient philosophers, in Church fathers as exegetes of the Scriptures, and in medieval theologians" (147). Aquinas suggests that the concept of the world as the "cortex" (shell or cover) of a "nucleus" (inner meaning) argues for an interpretive process that entertains two levels of signification and that the Holy Scripture signifies not only by words but also "by things themselves":

> Therefore the first signification whereby words signify things belongs to the first sense, the historical or literal. The signification whereby things signified by words have themselves also a signification is called the spiritual, which is based on the literal, and presupposes it. (I.1.10)

As symbolism became a way of "medieval thinking," it further manifested itself in literary expressions across the generic line. Whether it appeared as the "allegorical conflictus" entitled *The Owl and the Nightingale*, as a fictional pilgrimage named *Canterbury Tales*, as "an allegory of theologians" portrayed in the *Divine Comedy*, or as a more rudimentary form of folk allegory found in the *Second Shepherd's Play*, the concern apparently was not of the generic modes but rather of the canonical intentions, focusing on the didactic, moral, and religious. This shift in generic concern demonstrates what Fowler called the impossibility of imposing generic labels as terms of classification since classification shows "genera grouping," which in this case no longer seems adequate. Fowler recommended the term "types" in place of "genre" to avoid the difficulties arising from the tendency to subdivide literature unavoidably brought about by the passage of time, which in turn induced the change of the dominant concept governing a literary movement. Thus we see two types of definitional attempt involved in the act of labeling; one regards genre as a permanent abstraction, the other treats it as a continuously evolving "entity" that shows the developing history of a particular group of literary works. Brian Stock considered the two speculations as polarities suggestive of the conflict between the literary study of "synchronicity" and that of "diachronicity," one embracing the idea of fixity, the other that of change (*NLH* 1977.8.2). Fowler, however, felt that the best way to deal with the question is to combine the two, but instead of providing a detailed "plan" he leaves us only a statement of "truth" to contemplate:

Each individual kind is continually, inexorably changing, all the time adding
further extensions, new transformations; so that the terminology, even when
it remains outwardly the same, changes internally without our noticing"
(141).

A similar dilemma exists in the study of genre in Chinese literature.
Take, for instance, the genre of novel. The Chinese term for the novel
originated with *Chuang-tzu: "wai wu p'ien"* (chapters on things without).
Its literal translation, "little talks" (*hsiao-shuo*), sheds light on the contextual suggestiveness found in *Chuang-tzu*—trivia. The "incident" in which
the term appeared has nothing to do with fiction in the modern sense,
meaning a well-developed plot that not only has a beginning, a middle,
and an end, but also contains the growth of characters and the intricate
evolvement of adventurous actions. The event in *Chuang-tzu* tells a
simple story of the nature of a fable. It narrates how the Prince of *Jen*
made himself an extraordinary fishing rod with a huge hook, a very thick
rope, and a bait of fifty oxen. He then used the rod to catch a big whale
by sitting on the seashore for a whole year. He finally caught the whale,
which he carved to pieces and fed to the villagers far and near. The event
became a legend for later generations. What makes the story unique is
not the plot itself but the commentary made by Chuang-tzu, the author:
"Depending on the trivial to reach far and beyond is indeed far from
reaching the Truth."[1]

In another classical work, *Yieh Chou Shu* (*The History of Chou*), one
finds three narratives that fit the conventional definition of *hsiao-shuo*
comfortably; all three, *Wang Huei* (*The Gathering of the Nobles*), *Tai-tzu
Chin* (*Prince Chin*), and *Yin Chu* (*The Exile of Yin Chu*), tell of historical
incidents, using fictionalized plots and characters described in well-
structured detail. But the term *hsiao-shuo* is never used. The stories were,
in fact, regarded as histories, not as fiction. The intention was obvious: to
match moral teachings with supposedly historical events to achieve a
didactic purpose that would influence both the ruler and the ruled. In a
later development, in the Wei Chin period (A.D. 220–420), such a genre
of fiction was called c*hi kuai hsiao-shuo* (tales of strange events). And
still later, in the Tang Dynasty (A.D. 618–905), it was labeled *ch'uan ch'i*
(legendary tales, or strange tales). We need not go into the specifics of
the circumstances under which such terms were adopted to address
generic issues, but one thing is clear, that the concept of genre does vary
with time, whether it may or may not point toward the same thing. One
can only agree with Fowler that the problem of precision in generic
definitions is a major hurdle, as new terms keep emerging. The attempt to
"resuscitate" generic labels according to traditional categorizations is no

longer possible unless one "restricts" the "conditions" for such an act to the historical and intellectual contexts of the specific works being considered. This is an area, I believe, in which the comparative study of Chinese and Western literature is possible.

Literature can be described as either lyrical or dramatic. This is amply evidenced in the histories of classical Greek and classical Chinese literature. According to Northrop Frye, the lyrical must be considered narrative because it narrates the poet's inner self. With the lyrical, there is no distance between the poet and what he describes (or discusses); the written lines are the direct expression of the inner soul of their creator. The dramatic, however, is somewhat different; it "conveys" more of the substance of a discourse than the "person's inner self." The very fact that it is of an imitative nature creates a problem, regardless of whether imitation means "a process of imitation, representation, creation, or fiction." Any answer to the question implies a new interpretation and thus a new definition. Others may argue for a formal-expressive or stylistic-linguistic definition based on speculations on "identical relations translated into languages of communication," and consequently name the direct intervention but nonparticipation of the poet "narrative," and the nonintervention but direct participation of the poet, "dramatic," that is, the poet as "representative" does not speak as the poet but as a character and evokes emotions through action."[2]

In the Chinese scene, the concepts of "outer form" and "inner form" can be found in Liu Hsieh's treatise on literature *Wen Hsin Tiao Lung* (*Carving of the Dragon*), where generic labels were given to "the regulated verse" of the pentasyllabic or septasyllabic lines. Hsieh did not seem to bother much with the "form" of literature in his critique of literary works, though he did list many "kinds" of literature according to their "contextual suggestiveness," which seems to imply a preference for the "inner form" concept. Regulated or patterned verse, however, suggests another story. The very fact of placing emphasis on the "syllabic and tonal" arrangement of the lines brings out conspicuously the concept of "outer form."

Adrian Marino suggests that the only solution to the problem of literary genre is to make definition represent "types of creativity, identified within the very process of creation as the most specific attitude of the creative self, which is self-reflection and detachment." This makes genre "typological"; therefore, he defines the lyrical genre as "the self which contemplates itself in the act of self-expression," the epic genre as "the self which reflects itself for the whole duration of the subjective or objective narrative," the dramatic genre as "the self which reflects itself in its internal tension or external conflicts," and the comic genre as "the self which reflects itself in critical, ironical, ridiculous attitude."[3] The Chinese poetic "types" in *fung, ya,* and *sung* parallel Marino's concept most closely. *Fung,* by nature of its reflective mood, is a contemplation of self-expression; it is "melic," and if we take away the fallacious inter- pretation given to it by P'u Shang (a Han critic), it truly is "the self which contemplates itself in the act of self-expression." If we take the inclusion of the poem *Sheng Ming (Nurturing the People)* in the *ya* group (of poems) as indicative of the nature of the collection of these verses, the *epica* nature of *ya* becomes obvious. And *sung* is the *scenica* and, as Liang Ch'i-ch'ao (1873–1929) commented, is close to the dramatic in its literary character.

Henri Bonnet regards fiction and poetry as the two fundamental "artistic genres." Such consideration treats genre in the sense of form varieties "which are nothing but species or hybrids."[4] This makes drama but a mode of presentation of fictional or poetic substance, a point that reminds one of the Chinese *sung* mentioned earlier. Bonnet further sug- gests that history is not a genre, certainly not a literary genre, but a nar- rative that aims at authenticating "a form of scientific truth." The historian Jules Michelet adds to the veracity of facts a poetic charm, creating a sort of "admixture" that, transplanted to the Chinese soil, brings to mind the Chinese version of historical novels (*yien-yi*). *The Romance of the Three Kingdoms, Water Margin,* and *The Chronicles of the States of Eastern Chou* all belong to this grouping. One can also think of Walter Scott's tales in the nineteenth century, though Bonnet did not think that Scott's works belonged to the group.

Bonnet's concept of the two "fundamental" genres is formulated on the basis of the mode of expression, comprised of four principles.

1. Both fiction and poetry are dominated by "the preoccupation with the process of creating a work of art which translates their feelings or their *weltanschauung* (philosophy of life)" (p. 8).
2. Novelists and poets may also be preoccupied with the public to whom they address themselves. The danger of this is, of course, that the artists either tend to appeal to or to influence the public and thus lose the independence of expression of the individual and the particular. Literature of political propaganda provides a good example.
3. Poetry and fiction share a common purpose, namely, "the expres- sion of the individual (work) in its quality or its originality" (p. 8). Poetry and fiction, nevertheless, differ in their particular objects and means of expression. For the poet, the individual element is pre- sented in a subjective manner, that is, the poet attempts to translate

the inner self, while the novelist "gets away from the self in order to reach the individual in the others" in an objective manner.

4. In method, the poet relies on the cadences attached to words, the choice of sonorities and images, and the use of abstract language subjectivised. The novelist, on the other hand, relies on means of historical but fictionalized characters and events in a world of imagination. The value lies, therefore, in objectivised characters and in the world that surrounds them (p. 10). Thus, Bonnet suggests that art is dualistic in nature, as we are dualistic in character, being both corporeal and spiritual. (However, Bonnet did suggest that in music and painting such duality disappears.)

In the classical concept of generic (literary) origin, the fictional and the poetical modes are differently interpreted. Aristotle discussed only two genres, the epic and the tragic, though he also mentioned the comic drama, but whatever texts are available to us do not seem to enlighten us theoretically. For Aristotle, the epic is broad in scope and variable in subject; its mimetic purpose is less focused, perhaps, as compared with that of the tragedy. Tragedy takes its theme from the epic and personalizes it to effect a "purging result." But such identification, though individualistic in the beginning, eventually "sublimates" to a higher realm and becomes universalized; the cathartic effect of tragedy in classical times thus affects the "audience" (reader) in both personal-subjective and social-objective ways. We need not look far to find examples in Aeschylus's *Agamemnon*, Sophocles' *Antigone,* and Euripedes' *The Trojan Women*.

A similar case can be found in the Chinese concept of genre in the early period (pre-Han). Three genres constituted the literary corpus of early Chinese literature (to ca. 100 A.D.)—the sagacious sayings (the *Analects), shih (The Book of Poetry),* and history (*The Spring and Autumn Annals*). The first comprised recorded sayings of the ancient sages; the second, lyrics and poems collected from various parts of the nation; the third, histories of different nation-states, presumably compiled and edited by Confucius. The modes of expression may differ with each; the given interpretations, however, converge on one point—moral edification. In *Kuo-Yu Chou Yu* (*Histories of Nations*), one finds the earliest appearance of the poet as sage in the record of the Duke of *Shao,* who advises the emperor not to take punitive measures against those who gave him good counsel:

It is said that Emperor *Li* (Emperor of *Chou*, reigned 878–828 B.C.) was cruel to his subjects and threatened to execute those who dare to offer admonishing words. The Duke of *Shao* heard of this and said, "It is unwise to forbid people to give sound advice; it is better to induce them to speak out freely through poetry." He further said, "When a (good) emperor reigns,[5] he makes the nobles offer poetry, decrees the blind bards to compose songs, orders the imperial scribes to record events, and encourages the royal tutors to give words of admonition; he also instructs the court officials to persuade in rhythmic prose and decrees that all youths should recite the proverbs."[6]

One can discover here that the division between poetry (*shih*) and rhythmic prose (*fu*) lies less in the differences between their technical construct, though these do count for part of it, than in the senses of their contextual implication. The actual separation between *shih* and *fu* appeared in the works by Ch'ueh Yuen, Hsun K'uan, and Sung Yu, where the emotive and the didactic elements first distinguished themselves.

In retrospect, the traditional (Chinese) definition of poetry appearing in such terms as *fung, ya, sung, fu, pi,* and *hsin* addresses only content and style. But the multiplicity in terms does present a problem, namely, that the definitive constraint of a genre depends on many factors that converge on one single element, the canon. Liang Ch'i-ch'ao (1873–1929) presented an intriguing argument in his interpretation of *fung*. He suggested that the genre was neither a term for poetic works setting "emulative examples by the ruler for his subjects" nor "the parabolic advice offered by the subjects to their lord" (*shang I fung hua hsia, hsia I fung tz'e shang*); rather, according to Liang, it indicated the recitations by the blind bards. Here, an interesting comparison can be drawn between the Chinese way of the bards and the Greek way of the "singers of songs," a point that may explain why an early generic form possessing some universal character could lead to two very different literary traditions. The Chinese bards in *Shih Ching* (*Book of Poetry*) did not sing "of the anger of Achilles," "of arms and men," or "of the disobedience of one man"; they sang of the customs of the land. Such, according to Liang, was the content of *fung* until Confucius turned it into a literary genre of edification. Liang further posited the view that the didactic nature of the two genres of *fung* and *fu* actually showed a common origin, despite the fact that the two possessed different technical constructs, with one emphasizing musical form and the other ritualistic propriety. This confirms the view that Confucius's desire to set didactic examples in every literary work and in every historical event has set the tone for literature in China. The canon has decided both the form and the content of literature. One is easily reminded of Plato's expulsion of the poets (the didactically nonconforming ones) from the Republic.

It is also interesting to note that the only place where the poetic expression of an epic nature ever occurred in early Chinese literary works was in the *ya* (elegant lines) genre, not in the *nan* (works presumably about the *Chou* empire proper), which were songs sung by the blind bards. In *Ta Ya, Sheng Ming* (*Songs of Grand Elegance*, "The Origin of the People"), the ancestry of the *Chou* people was given in a miraculous birth story, out of which an epic poem could easily have evolved. Yet this did not happen. The accepted didacticism of all literary works, though setting a tradition, seems to have hindered the development or the acceptance of drama and fiction as legitimate literary expressions conforming to a canonical demand. This led to a later division of high- and lowbrow literature found in the distinction between poetry, drama, and the novel.

In the West, the canon concept can be traced to the classical Greek education curriculum that included the Homeric epics as essential textbooks. When Plato separated Homer's heroes in the *Iliad* from Hesiod's gods in the *Theogony*, he was advocating an educational concept that had been prevalent before and preserved after his time. It is, therefore, no surprise to those who are familiar with the Greek concept of culture and nobility in antiquity to read about Petroclus, Glaucus, Diomede, Hector, and Achilles going to war exalted by the idea "to win," which meant to the Greeks a demonstration of the quality of prowess, marking one's possession of the essential virtue of manhood. This concept of *arete* outlined an entire way of life or portrayal of character of the Greek nation in ancient times, just as in *Shih Ching*, the idea emulating virtue, formed the Chinese notion of *chun-tze* (gentleman) in the early days. Plato's admonition against the wrong kind of imitation was aimed at training the good guardian-citizen, who was to perform his civic duties in the most satisfactory manner. The culmination of this virtue appears in *Gorgias* as happiness, in the *Dialogues* as "the proper order of the soul." Of course, one also realizes that the doctrine of ideas as expressed in the *Symposium, Phaedo, Phaedrus,* and the *Republic* points to two levels of truth—the aesthetic and the intellectual. On the aesthetic level, idealism is "the recollection" of an absolute, as the love of beauty "passing by prescribed ascending steps from single beautiful bodies to all beautiful bodies, from bodies to souls, and to the ultimate" (*Symposium* 211). Such ascendancy leads to intellectual idealism, a state in which "reality" becomes attainable by the philosophical soul. If poetry is aimed at achieving that goal, as the *Symposium* seems to imply, a parallel exists between the Greek and the Chinese concepts regarding the intimate relationship between the canon and the genre.

The Chinese poetic genre of *ya* prescribes the "correct sound" reflective of the moral condition of a people, according to the annotation by
P'u Shang (Han dynasty). Here, *ya* also reflects a condition, "the rise and
fall of a reign" due to its "proper rule." The interesting stress in the syn-
onymity between the "sound" (music) and "sense" (thinking) of poetry
reminds one again of Plato's idea of the function of poetry. Though the
implication is not exactly the same as Gibbon's in *The Rise and Fall of
the Roman Empire*, a certain sense of suggestiveness of the moral character of a nation, particularly of its ruler, affecting the prosperity or depri-
vation of the state cannot be missed. In the poetic genre of *sung* (praising
utterances), the human character described solicits a Socratic impression
of the wise in search of moral goodness as the ultimate goal in life. It
dignifies life with an existential nature of reality and a philosophical
idealism of the mind. In affirming the canonical status of *shih*, as P'u
Shang's *The Grand Preface to Poetry* indicated, the formal distinction
between poetry and history as a generic distinction was set. However,
this distinction, which is different from that between the Homeric epic
and the Thucydidian history, is blurred by a shared intention, to instruct.
Thus, in Homer, when old Phoenix counseled Achilles "to be both a
speaker of words and a doer of deeds," the narration presents a fictionalized "reality" that, as self-evident, needs no verification; its purpose is to
encourage the hero to be a man of both prowess and nobility.

The Chinese concept somehow is slightly different. History has to
consist of recorded events with moral implications. Thus, in the historical
incident of moving the imperial capital from its original site in the west
to the east of the country, P'ing Wang (Emperor P'ing of *Chou*) was
admonished by the recitation of the poem *Kuo Luei*, in which a definitive
tone of disapproval was voiced. Here, history is not fictionalized but
analogized; thus it retains its historicity despite the fact that the intended
purpose is to be didactic. The Greek example suggests a process evolving
from the epic to the dramatic, as Aristotle stated in the *Poetics*; the
Chinese one, from the historical to the poetic. This perhaps explains why
in the West the epic genre does not monopolize the literary field, while in
China the poetical has become the "established," if not the only, literary
tradition of canonical statue. The restrictive factor of mimesis has made
all the difference; the intimacy between the canon and a literary genre is
too clear to deny.

One need not rely too much on any explanatory annotation to appreciate the poetic beauty of Homer's description of early morning as "the
rose-tip dawn," or the ocean as "the swan's way"; imagination connects
and fills all the gaps between the real and the ideal, the concrete and the
abstract, the descriptive and the suggestive, the expressive and the emo-

tive. But the translation of the bird *kuan tsuei* in *Shih Ching* as "osprey" requires explication. The bird, as translated, not only signifies "majesticalness" and "dignity" but also a certain sense of "ferocity," which betrays a character flaw, being somewhat at odds with the personality of a majestic ruler. Thus, some people argued for the "identity" of the bird as a species akin to the turtle dove. The focus of attention is not on which is the right translation, though the correct one is important, but rather on which gives the best representation. The concept of *pi* (comparison) and *hsin* (analogy) as poetic genres explains this. To convert the concrete image of the bird to an abstract idea of virtue necessitates a "metamorphosis." The "parabolic" signification of *hsin* consists of both a comparison and an analogy; the end result is a combination of the "object-thing" and the "object-event," functioning metaphorically and metonymically at the same time. This combined effect results from the didactic intention of the poetics. Thus, if imitation is the proper name for such a didactic concept of poetry in the classical literary tradition of China, the dominance of poetry as the "only" genre proper is quite explainable. This being a point of departure in Chinese literature as compared with the traditional Western sense of the genre, one can indeed find in it a topic of interest for Chinese and Western comparative literature studies.

Works Cited

English

Aquinas, St. Thomas. *Summa Theologica*. 3 vols. Trans. Fathers of the English Dominican Province. New York: Benziger Brothers, Inc., 1947. 1:7–9.

Bloom, Harold. *The Western Canon: The Books and School of the Ages*. New York: Harcourt Brace & Co., 1994.

Bonnet, Henri. "Dichotomy of Artistic Genres." Trans. Arnolds Grava. *Theories of Litrary Genre*. Ed. Joseph P. Strelka. University Park: The Pennsylvania State University Press, 1978. 3–16.

Fowler, Alastair. *Kinds of Literature*. Oxford: Oxford University Press, 1982.

Marino, Adrian. "Toward a Definition of Literary Genres." In *Theories of Literary Genre*. Ed. Joseph P. Strelka. University Park: The Pennsylvania State University Press, 1978. 41–56.

Stock, Brian. "Literary Discourse and the Social Historian." *New Literary History: A Journal of Theory and Interpretation* 8.2 (Winter 1977): 183–94.

Wimsatt, W. K., and Cleanth Brooks. *Literary Criticism: A Short History*. Vols. 1 and 2. New York: Routledge & Paul, 1957.

Chinese

Ch'i-ch'ao, Liang. *Chung Kuo Wen-hsueh-yien-chiu*. N.p. N.d.

Chuang-tzu. *Chuang-Tzu Chi Shih*. 4 Vols. Edited by Kuo Ch'ing-fan. Beijing: Chung Hwa Book Co., 1961.

Hsieh, Liu. *Wen Hsin Tiao Lung (Carving of the Dragon)*. Taipei: Chung Hwa Book Co., n.d.

Kuo Yu Chou Yu. Beijing: Chung Hwa Book Co., n.d.

Kuo, Shao-yu. *Chung Kuo Li-Dai Wen-lun-hsueh*. 3 Vols. Hong Kong: Chung Hwa Book Co., 1979.

Notes

1. In the original, the term "trivial" means "little talks," an expression of "insignificance."

2. See Marino in Strelka, 43.

3. Marino 47.

4. See Bonnet, 8.

5. Literally,"listens to sound political advice."

6. See also *Carving of the Dragon*, the chapter "On Annotating Poetic Prose," for similar discussions.

The *Zeitgeist*
and Herder's Reconstruct of China

ADRIAN HSIA

When we encounter something novel or strange, or a new culture, we usually react in one of two ways. We can either de-alienate it—this is usually a simple process of appropriation—or demonize and animalize it. Either way, we reconstruct it to fit it into our own worldview.

Chinesia—i.e., the other China—can be the result of both possibilities. In the encounter with China through the Jesuits, Europe received China on three levels: religion, philosophy, and the arts.[1] In the first area, we are reminded of the extent of Jesuit accommodation to Chinese culture. When Matteo Ricci entered China, he assumed the appearance of a Buddhist bonze, believing that he could reach the Chinese in this disguise (Buddhism will be ridiculed in later Jesuit relations). He later changed his habit to that of a mandarin, and other Jesuits carried their accommodation to the realm of theology by means of what was known as Chinese figurism. Like the Egyptian figurists, some Jesuits in China believed that the coming of Christ was prefigured in ancient Chinese books, thus depriving Europeans of the exclusive right to the true God and the revealed religion. Inevitably, a reaction in Europe started against the Jesuits and their construct of China.

Nicole Malebranche (1638–1715), a forerunner of ontology, for whom cognition without God is impossible, can be considered a typical case. In 1708 he published *Entretiens d'un philosophe chrétien et d'un philosophe chinois sur l'existence et la nature de Dieu* as a continuation of the polemics of his friend Artus de Lionne, then archbishop of Rosalie. Lionne was for some time the archbishop of Sichuan and took part at the deliberation of the Curia on the question of Chinese rites within the

53

Catholic Church under Pope Clement XI. Later he joined the entourage
of Cardinal Carlo Tomaso Maillard de Tournon to the court of Kang Hsi.
The emperor received de Tournon twice, in 1705 and 1706. According to
Chinese sources,[2] Kang Hsi told the envoy in no uncertain terms that
decisions concerning China and the Chinese should not be reached by
people who were not familiar with the country and its culture and customs. De Tournon promised to send a "China expert" to present the matter. Carol Maigrot, de Tournon's expert, knew only a Chinese dialect and
required an interpreter for the audience. Kang Hsi asked Maigrot to read
four Chinese characters. The latter could decipher only one. Thereupon,
the emperor disqualified him—as an illiterate!—from being a China
expert because he could not legitimately take part in discussions concerning Chinese canons and rites. When de Tournon reaffirmed in 1707 the
prohibition of Chinese rites, Kang Hsi had him banished to Macao,
where he died in 1710.

In the book by Malebranche,[3] who had been previously convinced by
Lionne that only his philosophy was able to prove the superiority of the
Catholic doctrine, the Christian philosopher wins the debate without
losing much breath, and the Chinese philosopher is kept very quiet. Since
Malebranche had never read Chinese philosophy, not even in translation,
he used the cosmic theories of Spinoza as representative of Chinese
views. By condemning the impiety of Spinoza, he was also censuring the
atheism and materialism of his fictional Chinese philosopher.[4] In such a
Cartesian book, the Chinese philosopher has no chance. Malebranche left
no doubt that Chinese rites should be prohibited in China and everywhere
else.

In the field of political and moral philosophy, China held an eminent
position in the writings of Gottfried Wilhelm Leibniz (1646–1716),
Christian Wolff (1679–1754), Pierre Bayle (1647–1706), Voltaire (1694–
1778), and the Physiocrats, particularly François Quesnay (1694–1774).[5]
As long as political reality embraced arbitrary despotism, and Europe
longed for enlightened princes, China fared quite well in the cultural and
political philosophy.[6] However, when enlightened absolutism was no
longer an ideal, as in Montesquieu, China appeared in an unfavorable
light, even though Voltaire continued to defend his perception of China.[7]
Two years after Montesquieu's l'Esprit des lois (1748), Rousseau began
to tear down the ideal of the early Enlightenment in his discourse to
answer the question of the Dijon Academy: "Si le rétablissement des
sciences et des arts a contribue à épurer les moeurs." Rousseau was of the
opinion that the sciences and the arts lead to decadence, and that China
was the perfect example of his thesis. Despite its ancient and manifold
achievements, China was unable to defend itself against the uncouth

barbarians, the Manchus. Obviously, in the final analysis it is military prowess that counts, not cultural accomplishments. The nonmilitancy of the Chinese was emphasized and criticized in nearly all Jesuit relations concerning China, including Matteo Ricci's. Military skill was considered a part of masculinity, and Chinese men were perceived as effeminate. Rousseau followed the line of an anti-Jesuit perception of China: the British Admiral Anson had depicted the Chinese, in contrast to the "popists," as false, corrupt, and deceitful, while Montesquieu had "proved" that climate and natural inclination gave the Chinese a permanent slave mentality. Rousseau's contribution was to argue that the Chinese were now established as corrupt and decadent, therefore, weak. He glorified the noble savage, and the Chinese were, according to him, neither noble nor savages. When Rousseauism swept over western Europe, his China construct became part and parcel of his doctrine.

In Germany, Rousseauism became the backbone of the new literary movement titled "Sturm und Drang," the major literary production of the 1770s. Its mentor was Johann Gottfried Herder (1744–1803), while its leading figure was the young Johann Wolfgang Goethe (1749–1832). Goethe, however, did not pay much attention to China during the Sturm und Drang years. The only evidence we have that he took notice of China at all is one single scene in the light comedy *Triumpf der Empfindsamkeit*.[8] The netherworld is transformed into an Anglo-Chinese or Chinese-Gothic garden in which pagodas, *tings* (i.e., pavilions), and Chinese temples are mentioned. Goethe opposed the artificial state of these kinds of decorative gardens. His distaste for the *tings* is easy to understand and explain; he was against the rococo culture of which chinoiserie is one of many elements. Before 1800, he had borrowed from the public library of Weimar only three general travelogues that contain some description of China. It was only much later that he became interested in China.[9] Herder's severe judgment of China in his *Ideen zur Philosophie der Geschichte der Menschheit* (1784–91) is more difficult to explicate. A traditional explanation is that exponents of the younger generation emphasized spontaneity and Nature and rebelled against the rationalism of the older generation. This explanation is valid for the young Goethe, but it is inadequate to explain Herder's attack on China, especially because his philosophy of the history of mankind is written in a humane and open spirit. It seems that Herder singled out China as a major example of his theories.

In his philosophy of the history of mankind, Herder follows the climatology of the "great" Montesquieu.[10] He uses a second determining element, however, which, according to him, also formed the human species: the "genetic force" (*die genetische Kraft*), which he sometimes calls "inner climate" but never fully explains.[11] For Herder, both factors determine the nature of peoples of different regions. The combination of climate and the "genetic force," which sometimes is equated to genius, produces cultural elements such as mythology, customs, and tradition. Herder knows no superior climate. Therefore he recognizes different peoples, but no people are a priori superior or inferior. Besides, Herder believed that mankind, including Europeans, Africans, and Amerindians, originated in Asia. Furthermore, he thinks that monosyllabic languages are the oldest in the world, and Hebrew and its related languages were developed from a monosyllabic language![12] Nevertheless, Herder does distinguish between handsome and ugly peoples. Relying on available travel and anthropological literature of his time, he placed the handsome peoples in the cradle of Western civilization, i.e., the plains of the Tigris and Euphrates, [13] although he calls Kashmir the "Paradise of the World" and its inhabitants, especially the women, the most handsome of the world. The farther removed from the Tigris and Euphrates, the uglier the people are. However, this rule seems applicable only to north and north-eastern Asians. Europe, in general, is perceived to be close to the cradle of civilization, especially ancient Greece, which Herder admired. He does not seem to be very impressed by the Romans,[14] whose main contribution to European culture constitutes the free spirit. This, however, is not unique and can be found again in the "heroic" Germanic tribes. These are perceived as strong, tall, and handsome people with intensive blue (*fürchterlich-blau*) eyes. They are filled with the spirit of loyalty and temperance, obedient to their superiors, brave in action, and tenacious in dangerous situations.[15] Although their campaigns led them all through Europe and even North Africa and they imposed—not unlike the Mongols—their rules on other people, Herder glorifies only the Germans. The Mongols he condemns.

In the eighteenth century, the Kalmucks and Mongols were considered proverbially ugly and primitive. Herder calls them "predators" among human beings. They have the eyes, ears, teeth, neck, and foreheads of beasts of prey.[16] According to Herder, the Chinese are descendants of these "vultures" and are ashamed of their physical deformations, especially of the ears and feet. The deformed organs have impacted their taste and mentality, consequently their government and wisdom smack of despotism and rawness. It is the law of causality. The other ugly peoples, such as the Turks and the Persians, are transformed by moving to a more favored climatic and topographic zone. This natural transformation, however, is denied the Chinese. They remain, in essence, Mongols even though they moved to milder climates millennia ago. The Japanese also belong, according to Herder, to the exception to the natural law. They are perceived to be a people of Chinese culture and Mongolian descent. Therefore, they are extremely ugly: they have a thick head, small eyes, a stubby nose, flat cheeks, practically no beard, and crooked legs. There-fore, their form of government and wisdom is full of violent coercion. Herder lists still a third despotism in northeast Asia: Tibet, without describing it further.[17]

It is obvious that Herder's perception of China must be viewed in the light of his conception of Tartars[18] and Mongols, the ugly people who can never be ennobled like the Turks and Persians. Climate and topogra-phy alone, therefore, do not determine the nobility of a people; there must be another more decisive factor. The one common denominator of these ugly peoples is that they are outside the sphere of the Bible, that is, entirely beyond the Judaic-Christian culture and anthropology. They are the ulterior "others." Ever since the Jesuits had openly proclaimed the antiquity of the Chinese, Europe was in a state of perplexity. When the Chinese figurists even threatened to take away Europe's religious supremacy by advancing the thesis that China knew the true god, prefig-ured in ancient Chinese writings, even before Christ was born, Europe rose in indignation. The Chinese rites were suppressed, the heresy discredited, and eventually even the Society of Jesus was dissolved in 1773, a few years before Herder began to write his *Ideen.* I think Herder was still reacting to the "Jesuit heresy" when he trampled mercilessly on the Tartars and Mongols, perceiving the Chinese as the representative of these man-beasts. This seems to be a more acceptable explication than merely asserting that the younger preromantic generation was reacting against the despotic goddess of reason of the older one. Such an explica-tion cannot explain why Herder singled out China for vitriolic and mali-cious attacks in the twenty books of his *Ideen zur Philosophie der Geshichte der Menschheit.* In the same work, he praises the Arab disposi-tion and contribution to culture despite Montesquieu, whom Herder admired, and his theory of oriental despotism. He defends Africans by ridiculing the notion that their "monstrous appearance" was the punish-ment of God (being the cursed sons of Cham). He even turns to the other sides of the coin on behalf of the Africans by declaring Europeans, as Albinos, to be inhuman robbers and white Satans. And he condemns with the uttermost sincerity the crimes that Europe still continues to perpetuate on the Continent. Thus the iconoclast of Eurocentrism still adhered to a part of it. He had to repudiate the Jesuit heresy first before he could enter into a more normal relation with Chinese culture.

In his *Ideen,* Herder describes the Chinese as a people of small eyes, stubby nose, flat foreheads, little beard, large ears, and big bellies who are incapable of important inventions and excel only in paltriness.[19] This "nook-people" (*Winkelvolk*) with the slave culture who sleep on warm ovens and drink enervating warm tea from morning to night, try to corrupt Europe by selling to its merchants millions of pounds of tea.[20] Furthermore, the Chinese have no notion of manly vigor and honor; they are hypocrites who can do nothing good because of their natural corruptness. Even their filial piety is a sham. Herder compares China to an embalmed mummy painted with hieroglyphics and shrouded in silk. If Europe were a noble steed, then China would be a domesticated mule that occasionally assumed the role of a fox.

Günther Debon describes Herder's subsequent transformation by comparing it with the metamorphosis of Saul to Paul[21] because he retranslated into German about half of the Confucian canon *Zhongyung* from Latin, printed in 1687,[22] and recapitulated in German some Chinese segments originally published in French.[23] Herder may not have become St. Paul for China, but he did change his attitude toward it and toward the Jesuits. All these changes appeared in 1802, a year before his death, in *Adrastea,* a journal that he edited.[24] Now he no longer ridicules the Jesuitical fiction regarding China but pays tribute to the Jesuits for introducing Christianity to China and for their role as intermediary between the two cultures. Particularly he recognizes the achievement of the Jesuit missionaries by their reputation as "learned mandarines." The emperors Kang Hsi, Yung Chen, and Chien Lung no longer appear as arbitrary despots but reasonable sovereigns. He blames the failures of the China Mission on the ignorance, jealousy, and bigotry of the Mendicant Orders. Because of Eurocentrism and the stupidity of the pope in prohibiting Chinese customs in China, Emperor Chien Lung became rightfully indignant and consequently forbade any European cult in China. Herder called the situation "despotism against despotism." Today we might wish to say that it was Eurocentrism against Sinocentrism. These two mutually exclusive centers held the balance of power in the seventeenth century. However, in the following century, especially in the latter half, Europe was well on its way to becoming the sole modern power of the world. Parallel to this physical and economic development, Eurocentrism grew accordingly. Even Herder, an advocate of accepting cultural differences of other peoples and a critic of Western expansion, could not extricate himself from the dynamics of the new *Zeitgeist*. This new spirit reaches its zenith in the nineteenth century. In the words of Karl Marx, Europe had recreated the remainder of the world for better exploitation by European powers. After two world wars in the twentieth century, the direction of historical development has shifted again, bringing along a more equitable *Zeitgeist*. In accordance with this new spirit, a new framework of perception has been developing. Value judgments of other peoples and cultures based on differences are gradually, although very slowly, weakening. The contour of a multicultural and intercultural globalization is becoming more visible.

Notes

1. In this essay, we shall not concern ourselves with the arts. This field requires a separate analysis.

2. Cf. Yang Senfu, *Zhongguo jidujiao shi* (The history of Christianity in China) (Taipei: Taiwan Shangwu yinshuguan, 1991), 134 ff.

3. Étiemble discusses Malebranche's position toward China in detail; cf. *L'Europe chinoise I* (Paris: Édition Gallimard, 1988), 335–69.

4. Cf. "Et il me paroit y a beaucoup de raport entre les impiétés de Spinoza et celles de notre philosophe chinois. Le changement de nom ne changeroit rien dans ceu qui es essentiel à mon écrit." Virgile Pinot, *La Chine et la formation de l'esprit philosophique en France (1640–1740)* (Paris: Librairie Orientaliste Paul Geuthner, 1932), 331.

5. Willy Richard Berger has discussed succinctly the position of China in the works of these thinkers in his detailed study titled *China-Bild und China-Mode im Europa der Aufklärung* (Köln/Wien: Böhlau Verlag, 1990), 52–85.

6. Great Britain, the home of constitutional monarchy and supremacy of commerce, was the first to reverse the trend of enthusiasm for China. Daniel Defoe (1659/60–1731) was one of the very first to paint China in black. In the second part of *Robinson Crusoe* (1719), he depicted China as a land of idolatry, barbarism, ignorance, and poverty. He opined that China could be conquered with "30,000 German or English foot, and 10,000 French horse."

7. Ingrid Schuster blames the decline of China in the European perception on China's obstinate resistance to trade. This seems to be a simplistic, Eurocentric explication. To trade—including in opium—and to colonize are perceived to be the God-given right of European powers. Any resistance is construed as a punishable act. See Ingrid Schuster, *Vorbilder und Zerrbilder. China und Japan im Spiegel der deutschen Literatur 1773– 1890* (Bern: Peter Lang, 1988), 151.

8. Cf. Erich Chung, "Chinesisches Gedankengut in Goethes Werk," diss., Johannes Gutenberg Universität, Mainz, 1977, pp. 110–20, and Schuster, *Vorbilder und Zerrbilder,* 143–61.

9. See Erich Chung's thesis for details. See also Katharina Mommsen, "Goethe und China in ihren Wechselbeziehungen," in *Goethe und China, China und Goethe,* ed. Günther Debon and Adrian Hsia, Euro-sinica 1, (Bern: Peter Lang Verlag, 1985), 15–33, for the research history on Chinese elements in the work of Goethe.

10. I am using the 1985 edition of *Ideen zur Philosophie der Geschichte der Menschheit* published by Fourier Verlag in Wiesbaden, Germany. Here, chap. 3, bk. 7.

11. Cf. chap. 4, bk. 7.

12. Chap. 3, bk. 10.

13. Cf. chap. 3, bk. 6.

14. Herder devotes a whole book each to the Greeks (bk. 13) and the Romans (bk. 14).

15. Cf. chap. 3, bk. 17.

16. Cf.chap. 2, bk. 6.

17. Cf. ibid.

18. It is conventional to write Tartar. However, the Tartars themselves write "Tatars."

19. The thought that the Chinese might find Europeans, with their body hair, to be ape-like never entered his mind.

20. The first opium ship of the British East India Company arrived in China in 1781. Herder uses such terms as "opium of the spirit" (*Opium des Geistes*) in his *Ideen*. He knew, therefore, the damaging effect of opium. It can, therefore, be assumed that trading in whatever commodity was considered good.

21. Cf. Günther Debon, *China zu Gast in Weimar* (Heidelberg: Verlag Brigitte Guderjahn, 1994), 127.

22. Phillipe Couplet, *Confucius Sinarum Philosophus sive scientia sinensis latine exposita, studio et opera prosperi Intocetta* . . . . (Paris, 1687).

23. The French translation is in vol. 12 of *Mémoires concernant l'histoire, les sciences, les arts, les moeurs, les usages etc. des Chinois* (Paris: Nyon, 1776), 91.

24. The introductory part is reprinted in Adrian Hsia, ed., *Deutsche Denker über China* (Frankfurt am Main: Insel Verlag: 1985), 135–40.

Shades of Enlightenment:
Concepts of Modernization and Westernization
in Meiji Japan

JOHN T. DORSEY

In Meiji Japan, enlightenment, as translated in the motto *bunmei* and in
the word *keimo*, meant different things to different people. For many, it
meant rapid Westernization, and the more extreme proposals to accomplish this end included adopting the English language and marrying
Westerners. Indeed, Westernization was the most visible aspect of the
enlightenment movement in Meiji Japan but often not the most profound:
eating meat, wearing suits, cutting one's hair, and waltzing. This shade of
enlightenment soon became the object of satire in the Meiji period itself.
Others saw enlightenment as a matter of dispelling the darkness by
ridding Japan of what they thought were feudalistic customs and beliefs.
But one central meaning of enlightenment was the goal of advancing and
developing the country, although the means of reaching it were disputed.
It was generally agreed that Japan had to modernize, had to develop and
improve its society in order to establish its place in the world order, after
more than 250 years of keeping the world at bay with the policy of
sakoku (closing the country). However, with the Meiji restoration as a
central force (the word *Meiji* can be translated as "enlightened government"), there was a strong movement to change, develop, and improve
the social system.

What concerns us here is a group of Meiji thinkers, writers, statesmen,
scholars, and educators such as Fukuzawa Yukichi (1834–1901) and the
members of Japan's first Western-styled learned society, the *Meiroku-
sha* (formed in the sixth year of the Meiji period), including Fukuzawa,
Nakamura Masanao, Nishi Amane, Mori Arinori, Kato Hiroyuki, and

Tsuda Mamichi. In *The Japanese Enlightenment*, Carmen Blacker compares these Meiji thinkers with European counterparts: "Like the *philosophes* of the French Enlightenment of the eighteenth century, they set out to educate their countrymen to an entirely new kind of learning, a new view of man and his place in nature" (xi–xii). This is an appealing analogy, but we should keep in mind that what is called the enlightenment movement in Japan took place nearly a century after the European Enlightenment, so although there were direct influences from Enlightenment writers and thinkers, contemporary thought and society in the Europe and America of the 1870s and 1880s had changed considerably. Thomas Havens, in a study on the Meiji philosopher and enlightenment figure Nishi Amane, reminds us of this difference:

> By enlightenment, however, the Japanese did not mean simply the philosophy of the European enlightenment; they intended a semi-scientific developmental process whereby ignorance would be progressively transformed into cosmopolitan understanding of this world through rational, empirical investigation. (83–84)

Consequently, I have chosen to use the lowercase "enlightenment" in this essay to refer to an intellectual, social, and cultural movement in Japan that is analogous to the uppercase Enlightenment in Europe, in the same way that lowercase "romantic" and "romanticism" are often used to describe tendencies similar to those that characterized the uppercase Romantic Movement.

In a highly ambivalent relationship to the overall goal of bringing civilization and enlightenment to Japan were the sudden, strong influences *from* the West that came with the opening of the country. There had certainly been steady, if controlled, contact with the West through the Dutch in the Edo period, but suddenly in the latter half of the nineteenth century, the Japanese were confronted with the military, economic, and cultural power of Europe and America. They admired and feared these powers, welcomed and tried to limit or to prohibit them. Sandra Davis in a study on the legal scholar, politician, and enlightenment figure Ono Azusa, writes: "The dominant concept propelling intellectual and political developments in the early Meiji period was the dramatic realization that Japan was unable to resist Western incursions and demands and that drastic changes were necessary if the country was to survive as an independent state" (13). Finally, the focus shifted to imitating the West in order to come up to its level or surpass it. Fukuzawa hoped that through civilization and enlightenment it would be possible "to form a great nation in this far Orient, which would stand counter to Great Britain of the West, and take an active part in the progress of the whole world" (334). Thus, the sudden rush to increase contact with the West was undertaken ambivalently by many as a means of defending Japan against the West, indeed as a means of keeping the West at bay.

First let us look more closely at the motto *bunmei kaika*, civilization and enlightenment, which pointed to the development, the flourishing state of a civilization. The latter word was taken as a goal, in the sense that a country develops *toward* civilization. The first part of this expression, *bunmei*, a translation of the word civilization, is composed of two characters. The first, *bun,* refers to writing and learning, as in the words *bunka* (culture) and *bungaku* (literature), while the second, *mei*, is one of the central images common to enlightenment in Japan and in the West: brightness, light, and clarity, with the implication of reason, understand-ing, knowledge, and even wisdom. The image of light is central, for this was a period of bringing "light" to a "dark" culture. And this light was the light of understanding, of seeing, of reason, and of science, very much as in the West. It was to a large extent light from the West, but recognized as universal. We have already encountered *mei* in the word *Meiji* (enlightened rule or government), and there are related words, such as *meigetsu* (bright moon, full moon), *meikai* (clear, lucid), *meihaku* (clear, evident, obvious), and *meisatsu* (insight, discernment).

To many in the West at this time, civilization was an idealistic concept—it meant an advanced stage of social and cultural development. Caroline Blacker writes:

> The scholars of the Enlightenment were fortunate in discovering a school of western historiography admirably suited to their needs. Buckle's *History of Civilization in England* and Guizot's *General History of Civilization* in Europe were examples of the supremely optimistic school of positivist histor-ical writing which grew up in Western Europe during the second half of the nineteenth century. Both these writers were convinced that the underlying process of history was one of progress, and that it was discoverable in the same way as were truths of natural science. (92)

Western societies aimed at becoming great civilizations, and through historical investigations they created narratives of the great civilizations of the past that served to guide them in approaching that goal. They believed in progress toward civilization and held those countries that were not marching in the same direction as "uncivilized," even as we do now. This value-centered, hierarchical concept of civilization was intro-duced to Japan.

Thus, the first word of the motto, *bunmei*, the translation of civilization, was used as a goal, sometimes as a proximate one, that is, of reaching the same stage of social development as Europe and America, other
times as a distant goal that all strove to attain, both Westerners and
Japanese. In the latter sense, then, civilization was not a Western
phenomenon; it just happened that Western countries had progressed
further along the road. But it was a road open to all. Fukuzawa was clear
about this point in his *Outline of a Theory of Civilization*:

> When, several thousand years hence, the levels of knowledge and virtue of
> the peoples of the world will have made great progress (to the point of
> becoming utopian), the present condition of the nations of the West will
> surely seem a pitifully primitive stage. Seen in this light, civilization is an
> open-ended process. We cannot be satisfied with the present level of attain-
> ment of the West. (15)

The other component of the motto, *kaika*, implies opening, flourishing, enlightenment. The first character, *kai,* contains the image of opening up, blossoming like a flower, and this part of the expression *bunmei
kaika* is a kind of semantic doubling that is common in Japanese, especially in dealing with combinations of Chinese characters and concepts,
for by itself *kaika* means civilization and/or enlightenment. The image of
opening is related to the discourse of *sakoku/kaikoku* (closing the
country/opening the country), which was central to early Meiji thought.
Fukuzawa wrote in his autobiography, "After all, the purpose of my
entire work has not only been to gather young men together and give
them the benefit of foreign books but to open this 'closed country' of
ours and bring it wholly into the light of Western civilization" (246). It
was a matter of opening to the West, opening the country after more than
250 years. Opening the country, opening the society, opening the mind
suggested defenselessness or lack of control to many who opposed *bunmei kaika*, for the image of "closed" suggested safety, containment, and
order.

But to the enlightenment thinkers in Japan, opening was directly
related to flourishing, as a flower opens up to the light, as the mind
develops in the light of reason and knowledge. Enlightenment thinkers
such as Fukuzawa Yukichi, Mori Arinori, Nishi Amane, and Tsuda
Masamichi saw themselves as working to bring about civilization and
enlightenment, actually one concept not two, in Japan. Many of them
were convinced of the superiority of the West, that is to say, of the fact
that the Western nations had developed their societies to an advanced
stage of civilization. This led opponents to claim that *bunmei kaika* did

not mean civilization and enlightenment but merely Westernization, a superficial process, and that Eastern culture and tradition, whether Shinto, Buddhist, or Confucian, had much more to offer in terms of true or inner enlightenment in a spiritual sense, as well as in terms of civilization, than these visitors from the West with their guns, crosses, and treaties.

The enlightenment thinkers countered with the thought that traditional Asian culture in the forms of Shintoism, Buddhism, and Confucianism was precisely the darkness that needed to be enlightened or dispelled, the obstacle to civilization and enlightenment in Japan that had to be removed. Of these three, the most secular and social was Confucianism, and as it was foreign to boot, it was perhaps most openly criticized. Naturally, although there had long been tolerance or at least attempts at peaceful coexistence among these religions, there was a certain amount of aggressive jockeying among them, especially in the Meiji period, for Confucianism had been the most pervasive in the Edo period, while the history of Buddhism reached back to the sixth century in Japan, but Shintoism, the most closely tied to the Imperial System, with the "restoration" of the emperor, reached back to the beginning of the world, i.e., Japan. So, in a sense, enlightenment thinkers in Japan often found themselves in opposition to traditional religions, which they in turn blamed for the backwardness and lack of progress toward civilization in Japan.

This opposition was naturally heightened with the reappearance of Christianity in Japan. The latter had been proscribed during much of the Edo period because of its ties to Western imperialism and colonialism, but it went underground, and a number of "hidden Christians" emerged in the Meiji period. But far more important, there was an influx of Christian missionaries, teachers, and foreigners in general. And there were also the Japanese enlightenment thinkers, many of whom were Christian, most of whom admired aspects of Christian thought, and all of whom were suspected of being Christians. Tsuda Mamichi, for example, wrote in the *Meiroku zasshi*,

There is no religion in the world today that promotes enlightenment as does Christianity. Nevertheless, since all Christianity is not an unmixed blessing, the best way at present to promote enlightenment is to adopt the Christian ideas that are most liberal, most civilized, and most advanced. (Braisted, 39–40)

At first, this suggestion that Christianity and enlightenment are closely linked may seem an odd turn of thought when we consider that Enlight-

enment thinkers in Europe were, when not openly skeptical of Christian
beliefs, at least of the view that the discourse of religion was subject, as
were all other things, to the discourse of reason. But we should keep in
mind that the same thinkers were fascinated by Eastern thought, culture,
philosophy, and religion, and without much detailed knowledge, idealized them as "natural" and "rational" in opposition to the artificial and
irrational beliefs of Christianity that stultified thought and arrested social
development. The enlightenment criticism of Shintoism, Buddhism, and
Confucianism in Japan was based in part on rational assessment, in part
on the imported Christian view that such religions were primitive idola-
tries, but in most part to the commonsense speculation that such religions
were responsible for the keenly felt civilization gap with the West.
Accordingly, Christianity was seen as socially progressive, and since the
Japanese attitude toward religion was not marked by absolute thinking or
exclusivity—for Japanese, even now, belonging to, believing in, or par-
ticipating in the rites of several religions poses no intellectual or spiritual
conflict—Christianity in its post-Enlightenment, American Protestant,
progressive stage was seen as a liberator, even by those who did not for-
mally embrace it.

Christianity was considered an intellectual's religion, an attitude that
exists even now. This attitude was reinforced by the founding of schools
and universities by foreign missionaries, Japanese Christians, or what
might be called Japanese Christian fellow-travelers, including Japan
Women's College, Rikkyo University, Doshisha University, Tsuda
College, and Tokyo Christian Women's College. It is worth noting that a
number of these colleges were devoted to providing higher education for
women, an important social development in the Meiji period. Thus, even
to study English, already perceived by many as the *lingua franca* of
Western civilization, was to come in contact with Christianity in the form
of a missionary or merely a Christian foreigner. Reading the Bible in
English in order to study English was as common as reading Shakespeare, a custom that continues in a number of schools today. And visits
by Japanese to America in particular immersed them in a family-centered
Christian society that goes to church on Sunday, something that continues to impress exchange students today. Again, more than 100 years
later, one is much more likely to run into a Mormon, Quaker, Baptist, or
Methodist in an English lesson here than a Buddhist Japanese teacher in
America, and the Buddhist would not be likely to talk about religion.

The other word often used at the time for enlightenment is *keimo,*
which literally means opening up or dispelling the darkness. It is composed of two Chinese characters, the first, *kei,* meaning to open, teach,
and guide; the second, *mo,* meaning darkness in the sense of ignorance.

In this sense, *keimo* meant bringing knowledge, wisdom, and reason to those who were kept in the darkness of ignorance. Carmen Blacker writes that "*keimo* meant, in fact, 'enlightening the darkness' of the masses, educating them not merely to a knowledge of new facts, but to an entirely new outlook on the universe, to a rethinking of some of their most unquestioned assumptions about man, nature and value" (32). Those who pursued the ideal of *keimo* wanted to spread knowledge by writing simply, by encouraging public education, by creating newspapers and magazines, by lecturing, and by founding universities and libraries. There was a democratic feeling here that the people who lived in darkness were not inferior but deprived, and the aim was to restore their dignity to them. Indeed, this is one important theme of Fukuzawa's writings, especially in his autobiography and in his *Encouragement of Learning*: education as the great equalizer in postfeudal Japan, a belief that is central to the contemporary Japanese equivalent of the American Dream. In Europe, one central aim was to enlighten the darkness remaining from the dark ages, specifically those traces of a feudalistic church and state that had not merely survived but flourished in the Renaissance. In the Meiji period, there was great political change that involved "restoration" of the emperor, civil war, rebellion, and forced contact with the West, as well as the end of a long feudalistic system. Thomas Havens writes:

> Enlightenment in the early Meiji context meant infusing the literate public with certain political, social, economic, and intellectual values of contemporary European civilization. Although there was no complete agreement among *keimo* scholars on exactly which European values should be inculcated, the consensus was that the European spirit of rationality, practical experience, personal profit, and self-awareness of individual rights must accompany the technological and institutional revolution that was taking place. (81)

Fukuzawa Yukichi (1834–1901), whose portrait now graces the 10,000-yen bill, is widely regarded as a great educator, the founder of Keio University, and one of the foremost Meiji enlightenment thinkers. The historian Hane Mikiso sums up Fukuzawa's contribution in this way: "Fukuzawa Yukichi was one of the leading private proponents of 'civilization and enlightenment.' Through his enormous publications he contributed more than any other individual toward the education of the people about the West" (105). Fukuzawa used the words *bunmei kaika* and *keimo*, being particularly fond of *bunmei* (civilization), and his books were best-sellers in his own time and are now revered if not often read: *Seiyou jijo* (*Conditions in the West*), *Gakumon no susume* (*An Encour-*

agement of Learning), *Bunmeiron* (*An Outline of a Theory of Civilization*) and *Fukuo Jiden* (*The Autobiography of Fukuzawa Yukichi*). The first introduces various sights and sounds, things and institutions from his visit to the West. Fukuzawa wrote essays on public schools, public libraries, schools for the dumb, schools for the blind, institutions for retarded children, museums, education in the United States of America, and education in Holland, England, Russia, France. He gives precise statistics on the number of schools, students, districts, books, etc. The second, *Gakumon no susume*, affirms that education plays a central role in civilization and enlightenment, and that education in particular disregards class distinctions in forming the elite who will manage the country. "We must avail ourselves of the opportunity of the present moment to encourage learning and guide the public mind to higher levels of civilization. Since it is precisely we scholars who at the present time are presented with this opportunity, we must work very hard" (61). *Bunmeiron* defines and discusses the concept of civilization as an advanced stage of society in which individuals freely participate in the social and cultural fields of society. He outlines three stages of civilization and highlights the third as the common goal:

> Thirdly there is the stage in which men subsume the things of the universe within a general structure, but the structure does not bind them. Their spirits enjoy free play and do not adhere to old customs blindly. . . . They cultivate their own virtue and refine their own knowledge. . . . Not resting with small gains, they plan great accomplishments for the future and commit themselves wholeheartedly to their realization. . . . Today's wisdom overflows to create the plans of tomorrow. This is what is meant by modern civilization. It has been a leap far beyond the primitive or semi-developed stages. (14)

Fukuzawa has been compared with the American Enlightenment figure Benjamin Franklin for various reasons, including his very popular autobiography, which tells how a young man of humble origins became the highly respected Fukuzawa, a tale intended to be an inspiration to young people. Occasionally, however, Fukuzawa's direct, ironic, and even sarcastic tone and attitude seem quite different from that of the humble tone and attitude adopted by Franklin. We might say, however, that Franklin adopted a humble, meek, moderate tone as a mild sedative for individualistic, revolutionary America, while Fukuzawa prescribed a bracing tonic for conservative, conformist, and, in his view, feudalistic Japan. But what they share is the desire to inform, indeed to enlighten, their contemporaries in a new nation. Especially in his autobiography, Fukuzawa's attitude of showing his humble beginnings and as an old man of instructing the young, the next generation, does indeed remind us of Benjamin Franklin:

> Since the active business of human life begins from about one's tenth year when a person attains to the use of reason, people should endeavor daily to make a precise balance of accounts and not to suffer losses in the attainment of knowledge and virtue. When a person examines his account books, he will always find some troublesome areas in regard to past or present actions. He should inquire: What have been the losses and gains in the past ten years. What business are you now engaged in, and how is it going? (89)

It should also be noted that in many of his writings, including the autobiography, Fukuzawa tried to write as simply and as clearly as possible in order to reach a large audience, and since his books were bestsellers that were in addition passed from hand to hand, it would be difficult to overestimate their influence. He urged Western studies, but he was very proud of Japan; in fact, he believed that only through Western studies could Japan survive and prevail politically, economically, and socially.

Fukuzawa was also a founding member of the *Meiroku-sha* (named after the sixth year of the Meiji period), a learned society, a discussion group in some ways reminiscent of Franklin's Junto Club, which included such members as Nakamura Masanao, Nishi Amane, Mori Ari-nori, and Kato Hiroyuki. They published a journal, *Meiroku zasshi* (*Meiroku Journal*) lasting for not much longer than a year (1874–75), in which the debates and speeches were made public. From the first, however, Fukuzawa seems to have kept his distance from the society and the journal, humbly declining to be its leader and then publishing in the journal infrequently. He seems to have insisted on the importance of the individual and of maintaining his independence, on the one hand, while on the other, he was actually very busy with his numerous publications and with the school he founded and to which he devoted himself. Also, he was openly skeptical of the choice by many members of the *Meiroku-sha* to work for and in the government.

The object of the *Meiroku zasshi* is explained in the February 1874 announcement of its publication:

> We companions have recently gathered together, sometimes to discuss reason and sometimes to discourse on foreign news. On the one hand, we have pol-ished our scholarly faculties while, on the other, we have refreshed our minds. The transcriptions of these discussions have mounted to become a volume that we are printing and distributing to gentlemen of like mind. We shall be happy if, its small size notwithstanding, the volume promotes enlightenment among our countrymen. (xvii)

In the issues of this short-lived journal we can see the living cultural debate of the enlightenment in Japan. The contributors examined serious social problems, took positions, examined the views of others, and, most important of all, made their views public in a form that would be accessible to a large audience.

The members of this learned society wrote about a surprising variety of matters. There were articles concerning education, the good life, the rights of women, the English language, the advantages and disadvantages of a representative form of government, and of course civilization. Certainly a number of these articles appear innocent, especially in their admiration for the West. For example, here is Nishi Amane's expression of keenly felt sorrow at the civilization gap with the West: "My colleagues and I have often drawn comparisons with the various countries of Europe. . . . Envying their civilization and mourning our own unenlightenment, we have suffered unbearable sorrow, having finally concluded that our people seem indeed to be incorrigibly ignorant" (3). In an article entitled "Methods for Advancing Enlightenment" in the third issue of the magazine, Tsuda Mamichi wrote in a similar vein:

> We may call a society truly civilized when the reason of each individual has been illumined by the general circulation of practical studies through the land. Progress by the people as a whole to the area of civilization, however, cannot be expected for a very long time even in the West. How much more is this the case in the regions of the south and Eastern Seas! Ah, when can our people reach the area of civilization! When I contemplate the matter, I am in despair. (38)

Nevertheless, the writers were not uncritical. Indeed, they insisted that the level of civilization attained in the West could be reached by the Japanese, and they devoted themselves to that end.

What is most interesting, though, in this journal is the spirit of open debate and discussion that we encounter here and there. The writers for the most part wrote in order to be understood by many people. They felt that they were doing a service in contributing to the enlightenment of Japan. Also, the use of logic and rhetoric strikes us perhaps as somewhat formal, but this type of discussion was as new and as important as the contents themselves. To state your opinion clearly, to cite the opinions of others, to examine them, and to refute them by producing examples, reasons, and other evidence—all of this helped to set the discourse of reason in Meiji culture, and, as in the European Enlightenment, it was in many ways anti-authoritarian in that it tacitly recognized the supremacy of reason.

What 100 years later strikes the reader of Meiji enlightenment writings is, nevertheless, their freshness, their openness, their excitement. Perhaps such qualities are responsible for the various shades of enlightenment, the multiple meanings associated with this concept, which were due to the strong emotional commitment to making a new country. Some of the shades in retrospect look rather dark. We noted at the outset that there was much foolish and slavish imitation of Western habits and customs, which may account for Japan's ambivalence toward both Asia and the West. In addition, many have come to look back at this movement skeptically, assuming that the enlightenment in Japan led to the rise of nationalism and militarism. In particular, a number of the leading figures, including Fukuzawa, have been subject to revisionist analysis that reevaluates their enthusiasm for the greatness of Japan in light of Japan's subsequent militarism and imperialism. Clearly, a number of their pronouncements on Japan's place in the world order, for example, seem foreboding, considering Japan's history in the first half of the twentieth century. If these darker shades of enlightenment exist, however, I believe that the Meiji enlightenment thinkers, writers, statesmen, scholars, and educators also introduced those values and concepts that helped Japan survive the disasters of war and create a safe, prosperous, highly educated, and peaceful society.

Works Cited

Blacker, Carmen. *The Japanese Enlightenment: A Study of the Writings of Fukuzawa Yukichi.* Cambridge: Cambridge University Press, 1969.

Braisted, William Reynolds. *Meiroku Zasshi: Journal of the Japanese Enlightenment.* Tokyo: University of Tokyo Press, 1976.

Davis, Sandra T. W. *Intellectual Change and Political Development in Early Modern Japan: Ono Azusa, A Case Study.* Rutherford, N.J.: Fairleigh Dickinson University Press, 1980.

Fukuzawa, Yukichi. *The Autobiography of Fukuzawa Yukichi with Preface to the Collected Works of Fukuzawa.* Translated by Eiichi Kiyooka. Tokyo: Hokuseido, 1981.

———. *An Encouragement of Learning.* Translated by David A. Dilworth and Umeyo Hirano. Tokyo: Sophia University/Monumenta Nipponica, 1969.

———. *An Outline of a Theory of Civilization.* Translated by David A. Dilworth and G. Cameron Hurst. Tokyo: Sophia University/Monumenta Nipponica, 1973.

Hane, Mikiso. *Modern Japan: A Historical Survey.* 2nd ed. Boulder, Co.: Westview Press, 1992.

Havens, Thomas R. H. *Nishi Amane and Modern Japanese Thought.* Princeton, N.J.: Princeton University Press, 1970.

Kiyooka, Eiichi, trans. and ed. *Fukuzawa Yukichi on Education: Selected Works.* Tokyo: University of Tokyo Press, 1985.

Mark Twain in Japan, Reconsidered

SHUNSUKE KAMEI

In 1959–61, while I was a graduate student at Washington University in St. Louis, I met an old gentleman named Cyril Clemens. Probably having heard of me as a Japanese student intent on studying Mark Twain, he got in touch with me. After a pleasant conversation, he asked me to contribute an article concerning Mark Twain's reputation in Japan to the *Mark Twain Journal*, which he had been editing for many years. I was totally unprepared to do such a work, but I had no power to decline the request. I hastily procured a few reference books from Japan and wrote an essay anyway. "Mark Twain in Japan" was printed in the Spring 1963 issue of the *Mark Twain Journal*.

Needless to say, the information I could offer in the essay was very limited and my observation narrow. Yet, nearly a quarter of a century later, I found in *The New Mark Twain Handbook* by E. Hudson Long and J. R. LeMaster (1985) that the essay had been used as virtually the only source of information about Mark Twain's place in literature in Japan. I decided I should rewrite it. As a matter of fact, I had written a better-prepared article, "Mark Twain and Japanese Fiction," in *From Meriken to Amerika: Essays on Cultural Relations between Japan and America* (1979). There are also two voluminous books in this field by Professor Yoshio Katsuura, *Mark Twain in Japan, A Survey and Bibliography* (1979) and *Mark Twain in Japan, Continued* (1988). These three books, however, are all written in Japanese.

The present essay, however, does not pretend to be a full-scale attempt at treating this topic. It tries only to make good the deficiencies of my previous essay. It will offer more information and widen the range of observation. It will advance the discussion of the meaning of Mark Twain in Japan. Yet, it will be again what I would call an essay rather than a treatise. Perhaps the spirit of Mark Twain induces me to write in this kind of personal style.

The year 1868, when the Tokugawa feudal regime collapsed and the Meiji centralized government succeeded it, is widely considered the starting point of modern Japan. During the two decades after that, the *Bunmei Kaika* (civilization and enlightenment) movement flourished. In the literary world, Western literature and thought were eagerly imported, although mainly through rough translations.

Benjamin Franklin, naturally, was the first American writer to be introduced to this newly rising nation. He commanded high respect as a model of a "modern," self-made man. Henry Wadsworth Longfellow, the poet of "A Psalm of Life" and "The Village Blacksmith," was also welcomed, mainly for his teachings of "act" and "labor." Ralph Waldo Emerson was likewise held in high esteem as an experienced moral teacher.

In the 1890s, the literary Romantic movement started in Japan. Emerson began to be appreciated in a new way: Tokoku Kitamura, Doppo Kunikida, and Homei Iwano, all young Romantic rebels, admired him as an inspirational prophet of "nature" and "self-reliance" rather than as a teacher of "civilization." Washington Irving, sentimental author of *The Sketch-Book*, also became popular, especially among students who yearned after Western life. Particularly high esteem was given to Edgar Allan Poe, whose writings began to be translated in 1887. Probably his tales and poems appealed to the Japanese for their aestheticism. A welcome to Walt Whitman followed, but I will discuss it later.

Generally speaking, however, literary men in Japan tended to find their model in English and European literature, which seemed to them more easily adaptable to the traditionally refined Japanese expression and sentiment. They thought American literature was rather coarse and vulgar.[1]

Mark Twain, hardly a writer of refined expression and sentiment, was slow to come into the Japanese literary world. The first appearance of his work in Japanese was probably *The Prince and the Pauper*, "translated orally" by Kawa Sanjin, "written down" by Ko Sanjin, and "complemented" by Sazanami Sanjin. It was serially printed in 1898 in the magazine *Shonen Sekai* (*Young People's World*), which Sazanami Iwaya (Sanjin's real surname) edited, and the next year in book form. Sazanami Iwaya was a popular novelist and the virtual originator of Japanese juvenile literature. Probably he let his two disciples, Kawa and Ko, render the English into Japanese and himself elaborated the Japanese style. *The Prince and the Pauper* is the most "refined" among Twain's works, and so it was the most accessible to the Japanese. Yet the style in translation is even more elaborate and decorative than the original.

The first image of Mark Twain in Japan was thus that of a writer of juvenile literature, and this image continued to be dominant. But, soon after, Mark Twain as a humorous storyteller was to be introduced. In 1903, Hoichian Hara translated half a dozen of Twain's short stories in various periodicals, and in the same year, he included three of them, all published in the *Asahi Shinbun* (*The Asahi Newspaper*), in his book of translations, *Western Strange Stories*. Hara was a well-known but conceited translator of Western fiction, and Isoo Yamagata, one of the best writers of English in Japan at the time, bitterly criticized him. In the *Asahi Shinbun*, he pointed out some defects in Hara's understanding of Twain's writings. Hara, for instance, in translating "The Killing of Julius Caesar 'Localized'," completely ignored the meaning of "localized" and failed to convey the very "American" character of Twain's humor. Yamagata, in addition, emphasized that Twain's humor was never flippant but was linked to a strong "sense of justice." Hara, in his answer to Yamagata's criticism, insisted that Mark Twain was merely a writer of "strange" (fanciful) talent. Hara was soon to die mad in the hospital.

In spite of Yamagata's repeated efforts to present Mark Twain as "a rare moralist and righteous man," it was mainly the humorous writings and episodes of Twain that continued to be presented to the Japanese. And he was not widely regarded as a major writer. In 1907, Kyushiro Honma, a scholar in English, published a translation of *Adam's Diary*, probably at his own expense. After an interval of two decades, in 1926, Rinnosuke Kagaya published *Witty Stories That Let the World Laugh*, in which he collected his translations of fifteen short stories, as well as humorous lectures, of Mark Twain. These two books were probably the only notable translation books of Twain at this period, except for those by Kuni Sasaki.

In my previous essay, because of a lack of information, I did not mention that some writers received a literary impetus from Mark Twain's writings. As early as 1901, Fuyo Oguri, a novelist who belonged to the same literary group as Iwaya, published a short story entitled "A Story of a Skeleton." It was an adaptation of "A Curious Dream." It, however, had completely erased the element of tall-tale humor of Twain's story and was much closer to the traditional ghost story of Japan. Oguri's two other stories published in 1907, "A Haunted House" and "Unripe Plums," were again adaptations of "A Ghost Story" and of "Experience of the McWilliamses with Membranous Croup," respectively. But they too were never successful in reproducing the literary charm of the original.

Takeo Arishima, who later became a major novelist in modern Japan, also made an adaptation of "Is He Living or Is He Dead?" and wrote a

short play entitled "The Death of Domo Mata," Domo Mata corresponding to François Millet in Twain's story. But here again the hilarious
vitality that abounds in Twain's story was lost, and the sentimental
friendship and simple antiphilistinism of the young artists were emphasized. Arishima was a sincere idealist, but he did not have the stout mag-
nanimity of Twain.

Probably, in what I would call the first phase of Mark Twain in Japan,
Kuni Sasaki played the most important role. He says he first learned of
Twain through the disputes between Hoichian Hara and Isoo Yamagata.
After graduating in 1906 from Meiji Gakuin, a Christian college traditionally strong in English education, he started his career as a translator
of Western humorous fiction. Later he became a professor of English at
his alma mater. From his love of humor, he translated even *Don Quixote*
merely as a funny romance.

In July 1909, Sasaki's lifelong work on Mark Twain started, the first
product being a translation of "Luck," which appeared in an aesthetic
literary magazine, *Subaru* (*The Pleiades*). In 1912, we find his translation
of "The Celebrated Jumping Frog" in the magazine *Bungei Kurabu*
(*Literature and Art Club*). In 1916, he collected his translations and published *Ten Humorous Stories* (by Mark Twain).

After this book, Sasaki's efforts to introduce Mark Twain to the
Japanese public never lost their vigor. Especially noteworthy was his
translation of *The Adventures of Tom Sawyer* and *The Adventures of
Huckleberry Finn*, which were published in 1919 and 1921, respectively.
In 1929, he translated *The Tragedy of Pudd'nhead Wilson*. In my previous essay, I called them "adaptations . . . rather than faithful translations," but I think now that that was an overstatement. It is true that they
were translations primarily for children and done at the translator's own
free will. Sasaki, for instance, frequently omitted sentences and para-
graphs that he supposed would be difficult for his readers to understand.
Nevertheless, they were the first full-scale translations of Twain's major
works, and they ran through several editions from various publishers.

Sasaki's work was not limited to translation. In 1909, he made his
debut as a novelist with the publication of *A Bad Boy's Diary*. This book
pretended to be a translation of an anonymous novel, but I have not yet
located the original. Probably this was Sasaki's own creation, getting
ideas from Thomas Bailey Aldrich's *The Story of a Bad Boy* or the like.
After this book, Sasaki wrote many humorous novels for juvenile
readers.

Mark Twain's influence on them is obvious. I dare repeat here what I
wrote in my previous essay:

For instance, if my memory is correct, he published, just before the outbreak of the war between America and Japan, a novel entitled something like *Tom-boy and Sam-boy*, in which the American twin children living in Japan became friendly with the Japanese children of the neighborhood and with them have Tom Sawyer type adventures. In another novel, two children chase a robber into a cave and, after a time, find the robber dead of famine there. This too, of course, is a Japanese version of *Tom Sawyer*.[2]

I must only add that *Tom-boy and Sam-boy* (the Japanese title is *Tom-kun, Sam-kun*) was actually published in 1933, but probably I read it just before the outbreak of the war. I have not yet located what I called "another novel."

Sasaki's novels, however, were primarily based on the urban social life of the middle class. And, although he pointed out in his introduction to *Ten Humorous Stories* that "under Mark Twain's humor there is vehement indignation at the falsehood of society," his own humor was always light, warm, and optimistic, as he later proudly admitted. Evidently he felt more affinity to Tom Sawyer than to Huck Finn. And probably the wild atmosphere of the American West was beyond his realization. Nevertheless, through Sasaki's efforts, Mark Twain as a humorous and juvenile author finally established his fame in Japan.

Around 1930, Mark Twain in Japan entered a second phase: scholarly studies of him began to appear. Eizo Ohashi, who edited the first critical edition in Japan of *The Adventures of Huckleberry Finn* in 1923 with 188 pages of notes and a glossary, published in 1936 a book entitled *Mark Twain*. Though a small book of only 158 pages, it was the first Japanese critical biography of Mark Twain. Since then, many other annotated editions of Twain's works, mainly college textbooks, have been published. And a large number of scholarly articles have been printed in academic journals.

Translation of Twain's major works with accuracy and faithfulness began, probably, with Tameji Nakamura's complete translation of *The Adventures of Huckleberry Finn* in 1941. Nakamura was one of the earliest Mark Twainians in Japan to be professedly attracted by "American society, especially the life of the people in the Mississippi Valley, vividly described in this novel." In the postscript to his translation, he further says: "People call Mark Twain humorist, but I would not. He loved liberty and hated falsehood. Humor was something like a smoke screen to hide his true nature."[3]

After the end of the Second World War, several other translations of *Huckleberry Finn* appeared. The most difficult problem for any translator must have been how to render Huck Finn's vernacular into Japanese without losing the original power. Nakamura's Japanese was too standard in this respect. Some other translators let Huck Finn speak and write a middle-class boy's Japanese. In the previous essay, I wrote: "The best among them, I think, was Kinichi Ishikawa's . . . published in 1958. . . . His translation of *Huckleberry Finn* reproduced very well the imaginative and yet real world of the original." Takashi Nozaki's translation, published in 1971, however, surpassed it in his free and bold use of the vernacular Japanese of a rustic boy. We have now two more dependable and enjoyable translations of this masterpiece: Minoru Nishida's (1977) and Shozo Kajima's (1995).

In addition to the works mentioned above, translations of *The Innocents Abroad, Life on the Mississippi, A Connecticut Yankee in King Arthur's Court*, and other major works of Twain also appeared, one after another. *The Complete Short Stories of Mark Twain,* edited by Charles Neider, was translated and published twice, first in 1959 and then in 1993–94. Since 1994, the "Mark Twain Collection" in Japanese has been in the process of publication. This "collection" is scheduled to consist of ten volumes, including such works as *Personal Recollections of Joan of Arc* and *Letters from the Earth.* It will not be an exaggeration to say that virtually all the major works of Twain will soon be available in Japanese. My observation in the previous essay, that "indeed, Twain is now one of the most popular American novelists among the Japanese, young and old," might be confirmed.

As I said in the same essay, however, "it is one thing to be translated and get popularity and another to have literary influence." It is true that novelists such as Fuyo Oguri and Takeo Arishima took hints from Twain's stories in writing their short works. It may also be said that some juvenile and humorous writers, including Kuni Sasaki, were under the influence of Twain. But it will not be easy to find any major Japanese writer who learned directly from Twain the immediacy of expression, bitter criticism of society, and keen insight into human nature.

Masajiro Hamada, in his fine little book *Mark Twain: His Character and Works* (1955), explains why Twain has been less influential than he should have been:

Since they determined to absorb Western civilization in the 1850s and 60s, the Japanese have most highly respected English culture and have learned foreign literature mainly from the English point of view. Accordingly, they have not favored Twain's rustic, contradictory, and continental character. Moreover, the Japanese from their country's start have hardly experienced a frontier life, so they have not felt sympathy with the life of wandering and strife which Twain describes.[4]

This opinion is perfectly legitimate. As I remarked earlier in this essay, Japanese literature has traditionally set value on refinement in expression and sentiment, and many readers have tended to regard American literature as coarse and vulgar. And Mark Twain is very much "American" in this respect. Poe, exceptionally aesthetic for an American writer, has had a far wider and deeper influence in Japanese literature than Twain.

On the other hand, it may be ingrained in our literary instinct to find in foreign literature what we don't have, enjoy it, and try to absorb it in order to enrich our own literature. With such a feeling and thought, the Japanese in the *Bunmei Kaika* period eagerly read Franklin, Longfellow, Emerson, and others. Later, Walt Whitman, the most "American" poet, with a "rustic, contradictory, and continental character," was even more enthusiastically introduced into Japan, although traditionalists fervently opposed him. Around 1919, the centennial year of his birth, when a democratic movement happened to be flourishing in this country, Whitman almost changed the trend of Japanese poetry.[5]

Thus, beneath their apparent affinity to refined literature, it is likely that some (or many) Japanese have a longing for rough and vigorous literature. In the case of Mark Twain, however, the overemphasis on him as a humorist and juvenile writer might have prevented Japanese readers from taking him as a serious, great writer. In this respect, perhaps, it must be admitted that Japanese scholars and critics did not satisfactorily succeed in realizing Twain's total achievement and explaining it to the Japanese. Although they discussed various aspects of it, they rarely attempted to present it in its entirety.

When I wrote the previous essay, Ohashi's and Hamada's were nearly the only notable books on Mark Twain available in Japanese. But after some interval, in the 1970s, books on Mark Twain began slowly to reappear. And in recent years, an increasing number of titles have been published. Although the greater part of them treat some specialized topics, studies of Mark Twain may be said to be rapidly accelerating. I personally think that because we are studying Mark Twain distantly from abroad, we should rather make the most of the distant view; we should try, and we might be able, to observe the whole figure of Mark Twain.

There is, I think, another impetus that might help us develop our studies of Mark Twain. In an essay entitled "Huckleberry Finn going to Hell," published in the September 1966 issue of *Sekai* (*The World*) magazine, Kenzaburo Oe, the Nobel Prize winner for 1994, wrote about his experience with *Huckleberry Finn*. I read it very recently and found his experience to be, in a way, similar to mine. In his school days, he says, Japan was defeated by the United States and was occupied by the U.S. army. Naturally, he had "the strongest fear" of America, and that fear continued, but when he actually saw American soldiers, who gave chocolate and milk to the onlooking children, he felt the existence of "the generous, good-natured America." Since then, he had been obsessed by an intricate "complex" in regard to America. In 1965, just a few years later than the time of my stay in St. Louis, Oe was at Harvard as a member of an international young writers' conference, or something like that. One day, he happened to be "ridiculed" by four young Americans who shouted at him "yellow peril" and other mocking words. Oe says he had read Nakamura's translation of *The Adventures of Huckleberry Finn* some two decades before, but at this instant he realized the inner experience of Huck Finn. He continues:

> Unlike Tom Sawyer who is within the system of society, Huckleberry Finn, freely staying outside of society, chooses hell for himself. Hence the Japanese youth, whether he is in fear and hatred of America, or he is dependent on and submissively influenced by America, could observe from his own point of view the meaning of this free hero standing aloof from America.

Oe says that he sees Huckleberry Finns in "the civilized world of today's America" also. I grew up likewise in the devastated Japan during and just after the war with a strong "complex" in regard to America, and, somehow owing to this "complex," I think I can sympathetically trace and realize the widely swaying feelings and attitudes of Huck Finn and, further, of Mark Twain.

Recently I published a book entitled *The World of Mark Twain* (1995), probably the first full-scale treatment in Japan of the development of Mark Twain's inner and outer world. A review of this book by Takayuki Tatsumi in the *Tokyo Shinbun* (11 November) said: "Probably Mark Twain's frontier spirit itself is the most pressing problem to this author who himself pioneered in (culturally) cultivating the wilderness of postwar Japan." I believe, then, that Mark Twain is a profoundly meaningful writer still to be greatly explored, from the Japanese point of view too.

Notes

1. For further details on American literature in Japan, see Shunsuke Kamei, "Japanese Reception of American Literature until World War II," *Comparative Literature Studies* 13.2 (June 1976): 143–59.

2. "Mark Twain in Japan," *Mark Twain Journal* 12.1 (spring 1963): 10–11.

3. Iwanami Shoten, *Huckleberry Fin no Boken* (Tokyo: Iwanami Shoten, 1941), 1:6 n.

4. Masajiro Hamada, *Mark Twain: Seikaku to Sakuhin* (Tokyo: Kenkyusha, 1955), 213.

5. For a detailed discussion of Whitman in Japan, see Shunsuke Kamei, *Kindai bungaku ni okeru Whitman no Unmei* (Walt Whitman in modern literature: a comparative study of Japanese and Western receptions). (Tokyo: Kenkyusha, 1970). An English summary of a part of this book is "Whitman in Japan," in *Eigo Seinen* (The rising generation), Walt Whitman Special Number (June 1969): 29–36.

Through Asian Eyes:
American Culture on the Silver Screen

SEONG-KON KIM

"In dreams begin responsibilities," once said Delmore Schwartz. As David Madden has pointed out, to most Americans this has meant only a responsibility to transform the dream into reality (xvii). But to others it has meant a responsibility to expose ways in which the dream has failed to include nonwhite Americans in its official feast and has provided a green pastoral vision of the gray "Valley of Ashes"(Fitzgerald, 29) in which we now live.

What, then, is the American Dream and why does it sometimes evolve into a nightmare? How can the complexities of American Dreams and nightmares be expressed through motion pictures? This question has preoccupied the Hollywood cinema for the past few decades. Since the early days of moviemaking, Hollywood has produced many movies directly or indirectly dealing with the American Dream and the nightmare, starting with D. W. Griffith's silent movie *The Birth of a Nation* in 1915. *The Birth of a Nation* immediately provoked large-scale protests by the N.A.A.C.P. (National Association for the Advancement of Colored People), which believed that the movie seriously distorted the nature of the American Dream.

The American Dream, then, is perhaps nothing more than a nightmare for the colored man. African Americans and Native Americans, for instance, do not believe in the American Dream because the American Dream doesn't believe in them. And as a result, in our collective field of vision today, we perceive mainly the nightmare landscape of the defunct American Dream.

Hollywood movies from the beginning have projected visions of dreams and nightmares onto the silver screen. In their projection, American movies and TV dramas have often tried to dream the impossible dream of reconciliation between white and nonwhite Americans, and they envision the green pastoral vision of restoring the (American) western garden currently invaded by the (American) eastern machine.

It was Leslie A. Fiedler who first pointed out that there has been a recurrent idyllic mythos in both American literature and film—"a lifelong love, passionate though chaste, and consummated in the wilderness, on a whaling ship or a raft, anywhere but 'home,' between a white refugee from 'civilization' and a dark-skinned 'savage,' both of them male" (*What Was Literature?* 15, 1982). Fiedler continues:

> It is clear, at any rate, that deep in the mind of America, if not actually below, at least the lowest level of consciousness, there exist side by side a dream and a nightmare of race relations and that the two together constitute a legend of the American frontier, of the West (when the second race is the Indian), or of the South (when the second race is the Negro). (*Waiting for the End*, 113)

Indeed, that archetypal American mythos of "male bonding homoerotic love" between white and nonwhite Americans persistently recurrs in American movies such as *The Defiant Ones*, *One Flew Over the Cuckoo's Nest*, *48 Hours*, *Diehard*, *Lethal Weapon*, *Beverly Hills Cop*, *The Last of the Mohicans* and *The Unforgiven*, as well as in numerous TV shows, including *StarTrek*, *Hill Street Blues*, *C.H.I.P.s.*, and, more recently, *Renegade*.

In these adventure movies and TV dramas, and especially in westerns, the male protagonists, who are mostly "men without women," always leave town and the woman who wants to get married, firmly refusing to settle down at the end. Home is what they know they ought to want but can't really bring themselves to accept. The dream of home for this mythical American male is not so much a home for anyone but a wish whose attraction depends on its lack of fulfillment. For home is a sort of nightmare for the mythical American male, and an oblique justification for all the wandering that keeps him away from it for so long. Stanley Cavell writes in *The World Viewed*:

> When the man goes home to his wife, his life is over. In a thousand other instances, the marriage must not be seen, and the walk into the sunset is into a dying star: they live happily ever after—as long as they keep walking. (49)

Rhetorical exaggeration, to be sure, but this is a remarkable insight into and a keen perception of the relationship between men and women in American movies. Indeed, Hollywood films characteristically assert community not through the family but through male companionship. The American hero seems to assert the myth of community, the idea that society is man's natural state. It is an all-male community for lonely wanderers and long riders. As soon as women enter the community, however, these idylls end and the paradise turns into a nightmare. Leslie A. Fiedler writes in *Waiting for the End*:

> His wigwam represents the earthly paradise of the American imagination, a Garden of Eden, be it noted, for men only—and for one chosen out of many, to boot. Once the female enters the wilderness, it ceases to be heaven and becomes hell, since she brings with her the nurse, the child, the homestead, the family, the courts and bounties on scalps: all, that is to say, the compounded evils bred of sex and money. In her presence, the dream of reconciliation between the races turns into the nightmare of miscegenation, not a promise but a threat. (113)

It is not men but women who in fact assert the myth of community in American movies, in which they propose a world of homes and churches and schools—everything the American hero is running from. Perhaps men secretly dream of a wishful exemption from this grim destiny. That's why, in the American men's world, community is often replaced by corporate masculine adventures.

When community is asserted in American movies, therefore, it is asserted by women as a form of entanglement, a dark snare almost always eclipsed by the glamor of loneliness and wandering. Again, women in American movies are the undisputed representatives of society and civilized life, and marriage is the emblem of many entangling alliances. Philip French, too, provides a profound insight into the relationship between men and women in American movies:

> The hero secretly fears women and the civilization, compromise and settled life they represent; he sees them as sources of corruption and betrayal, luring him away from independence and a sure sense of himself as well as from the more comforting company of men. (66)

In many westerns, indeed, deciding to get married simply ruins the American hero as a cowboy. That is, in order to settle down, the American protagonist has to abandon his lonely and wandering career of outlaw or sheriff, whose job requires constant movement and peril in the wilderness.

Thus the protagonist in American movies continues to ride on to another frontier in search of another colored male companion and another adventure. To all the girls' dismay, the lonely American protagonist always disappears beyond the horizon in total silence. Even Scarlett O'Hara (Vivien Leigh), the tough and aggressive heroine of *Gone with the Wind*, is finally deserted by the scamp and gambler Rhett Butler (Clark Gable). (Perhaps it is the destiny of the American hero, then, to return to the womanly embrace only just before death. Until then, he will continue his journey in the wilderness, whether physical or spiritual.) The frontier can even be expanded to deep space, where the American protagonist encounters his first alien. It is delightful to notice, as Leslie Fiedler points out, that even in deep space, the old American mythos continues, embodied in the relationship of the white Captain Kirk and his green-blooded Vulcan companion, Mr. Spock, as portrayed in *Star Trek*.

Today, however, the American hero seems to have finally exhausted frontiers and thus returned to the East, where dreams are realized more easily (*The Great Gatsby* comes to mind). As the American hero has lost frontiers and been reduced to a helpless city slicker merely watching sports on TV at home, American women are now beginning to leave town instead and go west, searching for their own adventures and pastoral visions. In *Kramer vs. Kramer*, for instance, the wife (Meryl Streep) leaves home on the day her husband (Dustin Hoffman) receives a promotion at work. It is symbolic that her journey is westward, from New York to Los Angeles.

In *Thelma and Louise*, too, it is not men but women who leave their home in New York and begin a cross-country journey to the West. In Hollywood films, strong women have replaced the strong cowboys and taken the perilous journey to the West, the wild territory that once belonged to men. Naturally, men feel threatened by these bold, adventurous women. In *Thelma and Louise*, therefore, Texas and cowboys, which are a quintessential emblem of the all-male community, are presented as a threatening force that intimidates the two American women traveling west. In this film, Thelma and Louise have to cross Texas, a cowboy territory for "men without women," in order to reach their ultimate destination, Mexico. It was in Texas that Louise was once raped, and it was also a scamp in a cowboy outfit that ripped off Thelma. Throughout the movie, the two women are constantly harassed and haunted by the cowboys, truck drivers, and police officers on the road. The American men's dream, then, can be a nightmare for American women, just as the white Americans' dream can be a nightmare for nonwhite Americans.

Hollywood movies have also attempted to delineate America as a Garden of Eden rapidly turning into the Valley of Ashes, hopelessly losing the original European vision of the "fresh, green breast of the new world." *Rain Man*, for instance, is an excellent Hollywood film that vividly portrays the predicament of modern Americans who have lost their original pastoral dream while pursuing the distorted American Dream of material success. Charles Babbit (Tom Cruise) in *Rain Man* is an easterner who went west in pursuit of the distorted American Dream of being rich and famous. He is a car dealer whose everyday life is surrounded by machines such as telephones and automobiles. Neither pastoral dream nor green light seems to exist in his inhumane mercantile life. One day, while driving, he is informed by mobile phone of his father's death. Charles decides to return to the East to inherit his father's wealth.

Back in the East, however, Charles is dismayed at finding that his father has left him only a Buick and a rose bush, whereas all the money has been donated to a certain Health Institute. At the institute, Charles happens to find his autistic brother, Raymond (Dustin Hoffman), who has been institutionalized ever since he was a child. Charles decides to kidnap Raymond and take him to California, hoping that by doing so he can retrieve his rightful inheritance from the Health Institute. Traveling west in his father's car, Charles comes to realize the importance of his long-lost brother, as well as the true meaning of his father's will; the Buick symbolizes the machine, and the rose bush the pastoral garden. Charles has always preferred the machine, but he now realizes the impor-tance of "the pastoral green light" that Gatsby saw at the end of Daisy's dock a long time ago.

In *Pretty Woman,* the protagonist (Richard Gere) is an easterner who goes on a business trip to Los Angeles, where he meets a western girl (Julia Roberts). The western girl reminds the eastern man of the pastoral dream and the green light that he has completely lost during his blind pursuit of material success. (Note that the protagonist dances barefoot on the green lawn after he decides to save a company suffering from finan-cial difficulty). Now the easterner has restored his long-lost pastoral dream and green light thanks to the fresh, green, "pretty western" girl he happens to meet during his sojourn in the West.

Restoring the lost pastoral vision is always achieved during the pro-tagonist's journey to the West, whether symbolic or actual. A recent attempt in film to restore the frontier spirit and the pastoral dream of Americans can be found in *City Slickers*, a Hollywood tribute to the last cowboy—the cowboy is played by Jack Palance, an actor with a tough-guy image who writes poems in his real life. In this movie, a few timid and clumsy city slickers decide to leave the city (and also women and home) and once again assume the guise of the cowboy whose job is to drive cattle to the country. It is a boring film but an excellent depiction of the predicament of contemporary Americans who have completely lost the once flourishing cowboy spirit and have been reduced to the gray denizens of the Valley of Ashes.

Often, indeed, Hollywood movies fail to perceive the "foul dust" floating in the wake of the dream and the hideous nightmare hidden beneath the gorgeous patterns of the American Dream. And often they tend to blame the other (nonwhite) Americans for the nightmare realities and prospects. In *Diehard*, for instance, a film about the crisis of contemporary America, Hollywood blames Japanese businessmen for the economic crisis of America and German terrorists for its political crisis. In Hollywood movies, the American hero fights to protect his home whenever he thinks his home is threatened by foreign powers (Gary Cooper in *High Noon* comes to mind). To protect home, then, is to protect America, and to protect America is to protect home. During the process, however, the American hero often blames the "other," represented by foreigners, for the decline of America. All in all, it seems that Americans tend to think that it is always a foreign or alien force that threatens the stability of peaceful America.

In a recent controversial film, *Falling Down*, the down-and-out protagonist (Michael Douglas) blames Asian Americans and Latin Americans for the failure of the American Dream. Once again, Asian Americans are portrayed as an economically threatening force to jobless white Americans, and Latin Americans as another intimidating force that invades white Americans' territory. The only comfort for the audience is that the protagonist of *Falling Down* is no "hero" but an irresponsible madcap who has recently been laid off from his job.

The misrepresentation of Asians and the prejudices against them can be found also in war movies such as *Apocalypse Now*, *The Deer Hunter*, and even *Platoon* (not to mention *Rambo*). In those films, the enemy is rarely seen, just referred to as the "Vietcong," as if they were too horrible to visualize. American soldiers cannot trust anything in the environment since they do not know where the enemies are lurking. Although it might have been the reality of the Vietnam War, the representation of Vietnamese enemies on the Hollywood screen is still problematic.

Perhaps Hollywood has found that the allies and the enemy are difficult to differentiate in Vietnam War movies, for all Asians look alike to Western eyes. How could Hollywood produce movies about a war when the enemies and the allies look the same? As Daril Chin points out, the Vietnam War and the Korean War have nicely defied American simplifications of good and evil, right and wrong simplifications based on the Cold War ideology that has flourished since World War II. ("Hollywood Melodrama and the Representation of Vietnamese and Korean Enemies," 199).

When Vietnamese and Koreans are shown in war movies, they are usually presented in the most outlandish and dehumanized of stereotypical terms. The Vietnamese in the above movies, for instance, are portrayed as exotic and unreal, so remote that they seem to be aliens from another planet. It is regrettable that whatever Francis Ford Coppola or even Oliver Stone is saying about war has often nothing to do with the specificity of Asia and American involvement in the political conflicts in Asia.

Films have served one of the purposes that literature has always served. They are faithful and reliable documents about our social life. Likewise, Hollywood movies can be seen as an excellent text for a rather special kind of social history of America. Sometimes they succeed in reflecting and recording the American ethos and mythos as well as contemporary American society. There are times, however, when American movies set out with good will to excavate a text in social history but come up only with frivolous entertainment at best, and an affront to the victims at worst, of whatever predicament they tried to expose.

Of course, it is undeniable that films are primarily mass entertainment. And often entertainment is not as comforting as it looks. Entertainment is neither a full-scale escape from our problems nor a means of forgetting them completely. Nevertheless, Hollywood entertainment often rearranges our social problems into shapes that disperse them to the margins of our attention. In that sense, it may not be going too far to say that Hollywood movies have served as a means of keeping discontented voices silent, as an effective anesthetic for troubled minds. As Nathanael West once said, the business of films is the business of dreams. And the Hollywood studios have always been a manufacturer of dreams to keep America content through hard and stressful times (the Great Depression movies come particularly to mind).

It is undeniable, indeed, that Hollywood has been a comforting heaven for Americans who think they inhabit a nightmarish hell. At the same time, however, Hollywood has often been an artificial paradise for those who pursue the heavenly dreams portrayed on the silver screen. Since the 1930s, a large number of serious American writers of the highest rank have gone off to Hollywood either to become scriptwriters for, or to sell their work to, the American movie industry.

What, then, drives them to the most artificial of paradises? First, under the pressure of market forces on literary works, we have to agree that film is the most powerful market factor of them all. Hollywood is a treasure island. In America, the health of fiction has often depended on the motion picture industry. Film saves fiction by bringing back audiences. Mark Shechner writes:

Contrary to popular myth, film has been the salvation of fiction, not its down-fall. I would go farther and say that the current health of American fiction is dependent almost entirely upon the motion picture industry. I don't know the figures, but it ought to be clear that fiction in itself is not a money-making venture without subsidiary rights. There just aren't enough readers to go around in America. . . . [W]riters require audiences, and there is no writer who is wholly unaffected by the pressure of contemporary taste, or lack of same. (36–37).

Secondly, The yearning for highbrow culture, prevalent among makers of successful commercial movies, beckons American writers to Holly-wood. Out of a sense of duty, condescension, and even clandestine hostility to art, the movie mogul invites the writer to help him produce "good movies" with the money he has made on "bad ones." Again, Fiedler writes:

And while he is salving his conscience, he may be convinced that he is also doing a favor for the largest public, and for the serious author as well. . . . He believes, therefore, that by translating them into the language of the images, he has benefited not only that audience but also the writers, living and dead, who do not—for the best of reasons—know how to communicate as well as he. (*Waiting for the End*, 55)

Under the circumstances, literary works have emerged that read like studio treatments and thus could be easily converted into film. Those literary works are so sketchy and vacant in their language that they just seem to wait for a filmmaker to fill in the blanks with appropriate images (Michael Crichton's *Jurassic Park* and Thomas Harris's *The Silence of the Lambs* come to mind). It is the writers of such frivolous literary pieces that are actually exploiting and selling out the dream of virtually all. And it is also the "studio novels" that suit the taste of the movie mogul.

The dream recedes. And once again, we wake up in the landscape of nightmare. It is precisely in this sense that the sociology of Hollywood movies becomes a question of the contribution of American films to ideology. It is not a question of the one-way influence of movies but of a complicated transaction and interplay between movies and society. The actual effect of films may be hard to determine. But the range and ubiquity of the effect seem quite clear. Today, nobody can escape the influence of movies or be completely free from it. Meanwhile, American movies will continue their projections on the silver screen.

Projections can be misleading. American films have often succeeded in recognizing the difference between what Americans dream and what

they can expect to achieve. It was precisely these dynamic tensions that
have produced both dreams and nightmares, and what Americans achieve
or fail to achieve happens within the tensions and conflicts of these polar-
ized conceptions of the American experience. American projections on
the screen will continue, as we live in the age of electronic multimedia
and high-tech projection television. And so will the dynamic clashes and
reconciliations between the American Dream and the American nightmare, and between the peaceful garden and the powerful machine.

Works Cited

Cavell, Stanley . *The World Viewed*. New York: Basic Books, 1968.
Fiedler, Leslie A. *Love and Death in the American Novel*. New York:
    Stein and Day, 1960.
———. *Waiting for the End*. New York: Stein and Day, 1964.
———. *What Was Literature?* New York: Simon and Schuster, 1982.
French, Philip. *Westerns: Aspects of a Movie Genre*. London: Seckes &
    Warburg, 1973.
Fitzgerald, F. Scott. *The Great Gatsby*. New York: Penguin Books Ltd.,
    1956.
Madden, David, ed. *American Dreams, American Nightmares*. Carbon-
    dale: University of Southern Illinois Press, 1970.
Marx, Leo. *The Machine in the Garden*. New York: Oxford, 1964.
Shechner, Mark. "American Realisms, American Realities." In *Neo-Real-
    ism in Contemporary American Fiction,* edited by Kristiaan Versluys.
    Amsterdam: Rodopi, 1992.
Wood, Michael. *America in the Movies*. New York: Delta, 1975.

Part 2
Poetics

Ezra Pound's Tensional Dialogue with the Chinese Conception of Nature

WAI-LIM YIP

Abbreviations

Cantos	*The Cantos of Ezra Pound* (New York: New Directions, 1970).
SR	*The Spirit of Romance* (New York: New Directions, 1953).
SP	*Selected Prose 1909–1965*, ed. William Cookson (New York: New Directions, 1973).
PD	*Pavannes and Divagations* (New York: New Directions, 1958).
L	*The Letters of Ezra Pound 1907–1941*, ed. D. D. Paige (New York: Harcourt, Brace & World, 1950).
F	E. Fenollosa, *The Chinese Written Character as a Medium for Poetry*, with forward and notes by Ezra Pound (San Francisco: City Light Books, 1963).
Y/I	Wai-lim Yip, *Ezra Pound's Cathy* (Princeton: Princeton University Press, 1969).
Y/II	Wai-lim Yip, *Diffusion of Distances: Dialogues between Chinese and Western Poetics* (Berkeley & Los Angeles: University of California Press, 1993).

Editors' Note: This essay came with excellent pictures Mr. Yip obtained from Ezra Pound's daughter Mary de Rachewiltz of Brunnenburg, Dorf Tirol, Italy, but due to technical difficulties they cannot be reproduced here.

93

Y/III   "The Daoist [Taoist] Theory of Knowledge, " *Poetics East
           and West* 4 (1988–89): 55–74.
Chuang   Kuo Ch'ing-fan's edition of *Chuang-tzu Chih-shih* (Chuang-
           tze: collected annotations) (Taipei: Ho Le, 1974). (Lao Tzu's
           Tao-te-ching will be referred to by chapter).
Surette   Leon Surette, *A Light from Eleusis: A Study of Ezra Pound's
           Cantos* (Oxford: Clarendon Press, 1979).

Pound's concepts are rarely one-dimensional. In fact, they constantly
evoke a mirage of subtexts, often "botched" together like a huge conceit.
In spite of the brief Imagist period during which he postulated the need to
call "a hawk a hawk," in spite of the Taoist, Ch'an-Buddhist source of
the "Seven Lakes Canto" (Canto 49), which I will presently examine in
greater detail, his concept of Nature rarely approaches the Taoist, Ch'an-
Buddhist, achieved awareness of "mountains are mountains, rivers
rivers."[1]
    "Mountains are mountains, rivers rivers." "To see Nature as Nature
sees itself." "View things as things view themselves." "Mountains and
rivers are Nature's Way, Tao." "What we see is where the Tao is." These
proverbial statements echo loudly in Chinese poetry and poetic theories.
While the total intellectual horizon of China is definitely more than
Taoist, everybody agrees that, in aesthetic matters, in particular, in aesthetic consciousness of Nature, Taoism plays a pivotal role. In Pound's
elation over Chinese poetry, poetics, and culture, how well did he understand the full implication of this perceptual horizon? We remember that
in his crusade for the Rectification of Names (*Cheng Ming*, or Pound's
Ching Ming) of Confucius, he blatantly attacked the Taoists and the
Buddhists; and when he allied Eleusis with Confucius in salvaging Nature from the whoring consequences of Usury, he seemed to suggest the
Chinese perception of Nature in the context of the *"Yueh-ling"* (monthly
commands) chapter of the *Li Chi* (Pound's *Li Ki*), allegedly Confucian,
in Canto 52, rather than the Taoists' conception. What are we to make of
this? To complicate matters, it could be argued, on one hand, that
Pound's strategies of representation via syntactical innovations matured
from his contact with those of Chinese poetry, despite his lack of awareness of the Taoist contribution to the latter (Y/I; Y/II, chap. 2); on the
other hand, it must be pointed out that he never understood the Taoist
deeper critique of the Naming System as a form of linguistic violence
upon both human and phenomenal nature. It may be useful, therefore, to
provide here a brief cartography of the Taoist project, covering both its

aesthetic and political dimensions, as a prism through which to gauge Pound's ambivalent appropriation of the Chinese intellectual horizon.

* * *

Since I have written extensively on the Taoist project (Y/II, chap. 3 & Epilogue; Y/III), I will simply highlight some of its relevant features. The Taoist project began with a critique of the dominating and exclusionary functions of language and those of human subjectivity on Nature. Aesthetically and philosophically, the Taoists are of the opinion that no conceptions or linguistic formulations will be able to comprehend the totalizing process of the great composition of things in phenomenon, which is changing and ongoing. Between "the world as it is (self-so)" (the object-pole, the world) and "the world as it is believed to be" (the subject-pole, human consciousness), the Taoists turn their attention toward the former because they understand that naming, meaning, language, and concept are restrictive acts, none of which can fully authenticate the very original state of things and all of which will, in one way or the other, distort it, and that the real world, quite without the supervision and explanation by us humans, is totally alive, self-generating, self-conditioning, self-transforming, and self-complete, and that we, humans, being only one form of being among a million others, have no prerogative to classify the cosmic scheme. We must, therefore, give it back its original forms, understanding that "ducks' legs are short; lengthening them means pain. Cranes' legs are long; shortening them means suffering" (*Chuang*, 317). We must leave them as they are by nature. Each form of being has its own nature, has its own place; how can we take *this* as *subject* (principal) and *that* as *object* (subordinate)? How can we impose "our" viewpoint upon others as the right viewpoint, the only right viewpoint? White clouds are white; green mountains are green. White clouds cannot blame green mountains for being green. Green mountains cannot blame white clouds for being white. All things are what they are without knowing why and how they are. Although things are different, yet they are the same in that they produce themselves and exist spontaneously as they are. They are not created by others (*Chuang,* 55). This is the Way of Nature (*Chuang*, 10). And hence, we should not put *I* in the primary position to dominate and determine the forms and meanings of things, but instead, we should allow consciousness and the million things freely to exchange positions so as to coexist, to answer one another, to illuminate mutually, and to be totally transparent.

But the Taoist distrust of language goes deeper and can be traced to its clearly historically grounded response to the territorializations of power in the naming activities in the feudalistic Chou dynasty. As Lao Tzu puts it: "With the beginning of Institution, there emerge Names" (Chuang, chap. 32).

In the Chou dynasty, before the rise of Taoism, names or norms were invented to delineate hermeneutic structure and activity out of the need and desire to legitimatize and solidify a power structure by circling out determinable attributes such as privileges and duties. In order to facilitate the feudalistic rule, the clan system was rationalized according to various class stratifications with well-defined duties and rights. Hence, the concept of the "Son of Heaven"; various orders of manors and dukes; relationships between lords and subjects, fathers and sons, husbands and wives; the investment of special privileges in first males whose power over other males, not to mention females, came in complex forms and matrixes as well as clearly demarcated sets of rituals and directives. The system of names or norms (which Confucius took over and Pound later adopted) was invented as the cement that held the feudalistic power structure together. As a result, the birthrights of humans as natural beings were restricted and distorted. Lao Tzu began his project with full aware-ness of this restrictive and distortive activity of names and words and their power-wielding violence. It was this awareness that opened up the Taoist reconsiderations of language and power, both a political and an aesthetic project.

Politically, when Lao Tzu said, "The speaking Tao is not the Constant Tao. The nameable Name is not the Constant Name" (Chuang, chap. 1) and proposed to return to the *Su P'u* (uncarved block) or the "Great Undivided Institution" (chap. 28), he intended to implode the so-called "Kingly Tao," the "Heavenly Tao" as well as the Naming System of the feudalistic ideology of the Chou dynasty so that memories of the repressed, exiled, and alienated natural self could be fully reawakened. The Taoist project, from the parameters of the Naming System, is a negating, abandoning, and even escapist act; but from the parameters of "No Naming" (that is, before the territorializations of power) and of the "Uncarved Block," it helps to break the myth of the reductive and dis-tortive naming activities, to affirm the concrete total world that is free from and unrestricted by concepts, and to move onto reclaiming the natu-ral self as well as Nature as it is. Thus, we can say that the Taoist project is a counterdiscourse to the territorialization of power, an act to disarm the tyranny of language; it is not, as most superficial readers believe, a passive philosophy.

Aesthetically, by questioning the limits of language, the Taoists suggest a decreative-creative dialectic to repossess the prepredicative concrete world by dispossessing the partial and reduced forms that the process of abstract thinking has heaped upon us.

Underlining the Taoist project is the primary idea of nonintrusiveness into and noninterference with Nature's flow. As reflected in poetic language, it has engendered a freedom from syntactical rigidities. For example, although the Chinese language also has articles and personal pronouns, they are often dispensed with in poetry, opening up an indeterminate space for the reader to enter and reenter for double to multiple perception rather than being locked into some definite position or guided toward one direction by one parent subjectivity. Then, there is the absence of connective elements (prepositions, conjunctions), and these, aided by the indeterminacy of parts of speech and no-tense declensions in verbs (which give us back a sense of time before artificial demarcations), afford the reader a unique freedom to consort with the real-life world. The words in a Chinese poem quite often have a loosely committed relationship with the reader, who remains in a sort of middle ground between engaging with and disengaging from them. The asyntactical and paratactical structures promote a kind of prepredicative condition wherein words, like objects (often in coextensive and multiple montage layout) in the real-life world, are free from predetermined closures of relationship and meaning and offer themselves to us in an open space. Within this space around them, and with the poet, so to speak, stepping aside, we can move freely and approach them from various vantage points to achieve different shades of the same moment. We are able to witness the acting-out of objects and events in cinematic visuality, and stand, as it were, at the threshold of various possible meanings.

Similarly, in almost all Chinese landscape paintings, we see scenes not only from the front but also from the rear; not one moment from one specific perspective but many moments from many spatial viewpoints. The viewer is not restricted to seeing the landscape from one static location selected arbitrarily for him by the painter. The viewer revolves, as it were, with the multiple perspectives available to him. In order to preserve this flexibility, the Chinese painter sometimes makes use of an emptiness, which is at the same time a space of thingness, such as mists and clouds, to diffuse the distances, or to facilitate the curving lines of mountains or other natural objects to camouflage the change of perspectives, subtly returning to the viewer his freedom of mobility.

In Chinese poetry, especially in Chinese landscape poetry, language is used to punctuate the vital rhythm of things in their natural measure as

they emerge and act themselves out in the real world. What we call vital
rhythm or atmosphere is often what we can feel but not see, and so it is
even more important that poetry be free from the fetters of words. Thus,
the Taoist artist stresses also the emptiness of language. What is written
is fixed and solid; what is unwritten is fluid and empty. The empty and
fluid wordlessness is the indispensable cooperator of the fixed and solid
word. The full activity of language should be like the copresence of the
solid and the void in Chinese paintings, allowing the reader to receive not
only the words (the written) but also the wordlessness (the unwritten).
The negative space, such as the emptiness in a painting and the condition
of silence with meanings trembling at the edge of words in a poem, is
made into something vastly more significant and positive, and indeed,
has become a horizon toward which our aesthetic attention is constantly
directed.

It must be clear by now that the Taoist noninterference with Nature is
also an affirmation of the immanence of things in Nature. The whole art
of landscape poetry in China aims, therefore, to release the objects in
Nature from their seeming irrelevance and bring forth their original
freshness and thingness—return to their first innocence, so to speak—
thus making them relevant as "self-so-complete" objects in their coextensive existence. The poet focuses attention upon them in such a way as
to allow them to leap out directly and spontaneously before us, unhin-
dered. Let us look at two poems by Wang Wei.

> Man at leisure. Cassia flowers fall.
> Quiet night. Spring mountain is empty.
> Moon rises. Startles—a mountain bird.
> It sings at times in the spring stream.

> (Wang Wei, "Bird-Singing Stream")[2]

> High on the tree tips, the hibiscus
> Sets forth red calyces in the mountain.
> A stream hut, quiet. No man.
> It blooms and falls, blooms and falls.

> (Wang Wei, "Hsin-i Village")

The scenery *speaks* and *acts*. There is little or no subjective emotion or
intellectuality to disturb the inner growth and change of the objects in
front of the poet. He does not step in, or rather, having opened up the

scene, he has stepped aside. The objects spontaneously emerge before the reader-viewer's eyes—in most Nature poems in the West, the concreteness of the objects gives way to abstraction through the poet's analytical intervention, or his symbolic, transcendental impulse, when an apple cannot be viewed purely as an apple. In both of these poems, Nature rules as an ongoing entity unrestricted by human makeover. "No man. / It blooms and falls, blooms and falls."

It is no accident that a Taoist should stress the Fast of the Mind (*Chuang*, 14) or Sitting-in-Forgetfulness (384), for it is by emptying out all traces of intellectual interference that one can fully respond, as does a mirror or still water to things in their concreteness, to their spontaneous, simultaneous, and harmonious presences, to arrive at a sense of infinity without the burden of having constantly to struggle to match a set of assumed permanent forms.

Looked at from another angle, the Taoist "Fast of Mind," "Sitting-in-forgetfulness," and removal of one's conscious self ("Loss of Self"), resemble a trance-like consciousness:

> Empty mountain: No man.
> But voices of men are heard.

> (Wang Wei, "Deer Enclosure")

In this consciousness, free from the burden of thought, from the unrest of metaphysics, the poet has another hearing, another vision, so to speak, hears voices that we (that is, our conscious thinking selves) normally do not hear and sees activities that we are normally not aware of.

This state of stillness, emptiness, silence, or quiescence is ubiquitous in the landscape poems of Wang Wei and his contemporaries. The "voices" one hears are those one hears in absolute silence—voices from unspeaking, self-generating, self-conditioning Nature outside the world of language. In this poetry, discursiveness is out of place; each object discloses its original spatiotemporal extensions and relationships, luminous, fresh, and pictorial as in T'ang poets like Wang Wei, Liu Tsung-yuan, and Wei Ying-wu and in Japanese haiku poets like Basho.

As we can see, The Taoist project has brought forth a special type of nonmediating mediation by way of a continual decrease in discursive, analytical, and explanatory procedures leading toward an art of pure landscape poetry of noninterference, that is, *tzu-jan* and self-so-completeness.

* * *

It is not difficult to detect immediately how Pound's project converges with and diverges from the Taoist dimension. Risking gross simplification, one may say that, aesthetically, Pound longs for the kind of language strategies engendered by Taoism, but being unaware of the full implication of the Taoist project politically, he departs *significantly* from it.

Partly suggested by a different form of indeterminacy and multidimensionality of the French symbolists and the futurists, partly spurred by what one may call a Taoist impulse (i.e., the impulse to liberate oneself from straitjacket framing), Pound, as early as 1911, before he came into contact with Chinese poetry, argued:

> The artist seeks out the luminous detail and presents it. He does not comment. (SP, 23)

After his contact with Chinese poetry, he wrote:

> It is because certain Chinese poets have been content to set forth their matter without moralizing and without comment that one labors to make a translation.[3]

Early in 1901, Pound advised William Carlos Williams in similar terms, and in 1916 he wrote to Iris Barry emphatically about

> the necessity for creating or constructing something; of presenting an image, or enough images of concrete things arranged to stir the reader. . . . I think there must be more, predominantly more, objects than statements and conclusions, which latter are purely optional, not essential, often superfluous and therefore bad. (L, 90–91)

Following the footsteps of Mallarmé's dislocation and even destruction of syntax in order freely to transpose objects and words for a pure state of the poetry of essences, Pound began his adjustment of conventional English in his poem "The Coming of War: Actaeon" by breaking the traditional lines into small units graphically arranged; he attempted to promote the visuality of the images, to isolate them as independent visual events, to force the reader-viewer to perceive the poem in spatial counterpoints, to enhance the physicality of objects, and to activate the poem through phases of perception (as does the spotlighting effect or the mobile point of view). These effects, modified and refined, dominate the entire *Cantos*.

In "The Coming of War: Actaeon," Pound used a space break to occasion a time break; he had not yet dealt actively with syntactical breaks. The latter aspect started with the "Metro" poem, which was modeled after Japanese haiku. Like the structure of haiku and like the paratactical and montage technique of Chinese lines, Pound took away possible conventional connective phrases such as "are like" and thus disrupted syntax, giving prominence and independence to the two visual events, letting them coexist to interdefine one another:

> The apparition of these faces in the crowd:
> Petals on a wet, black bough.

Space breaks and syntactical breaks now dominate much of Pound's *Cantos*.

> Rain; empty river, a voyage
> . . . .
> Autumn moon; hills rose above lakes
> . . . .
> Broad water; geese line out with the autumn.

(from Canto 49)

> Prayer: hands uplifted
> Solitude: a person, a Nurse

(from Canto 54)

> Moon, cloud, tower, a patch of the battistero
> all of whiteness.

(from Canto 79)

Two more moves in Pound's poetic development seemed to promise a possible path to the Taoist perceptual horizon. First, at about the time of his Imagist period, Pound proclaimed that

the proper and perfect symbol is the natural object, that if a man use "symbols," he must so use them that their symbolic function does not obtrude; so that a sense . . . is not lost to those who do not understand the symbol as such, to whom, for instance, a hawk is a hawk. (L, 9)

This seems to suggest, along with Kafka's questioning of metaphoric function of language, the possibility of retrieving the immanence of objects as objects. If this were to be explored further, it is not impossible that Pound could conceivably be thinking in a Taoist mode. Second, at about the same time, Pound, following Fenollosa, was ecstatic about the structure of the Chinese character as the embodiment of a whole poetics that seems to contain all the aesthetic dimensions he had been arguing for: simultaneity, montage, and visual perspicuity, which happen to be also the staple of the Taoist aesthetic. One might also recall this important passage from Fenollosa's essay:

> Chinese poetry . . . speaks at once with the vividness of painting, and with the mobility of sounds. It is, in some sense, more objective than either, more dramatic. In reading Chinese we do not seem to be juggling mental counters, but to be watching *things* work out their fate. (F, 9)

"Not to juggle mental counters, but to watch things work out their fate" can easily be taken to be within the Taoist horizon.

Following this line of development in Pound, Canto 49 seems to emerge as a possible culmination of Pound's "Taoist " impulse. Here are the first two stanzas:

> For the seven lakes, and by no man these verses:
> Rain; empty river; a voyage,
> Fire from frozen cloud, heavy rain in the twilight
> Under the cabin roof was one lantern.
> The reed are heavy; bent;
> And the bamboo speak as if weeping.
>
> Autumn moon; hills rise about lakes
> against sunset
> Evening is like a curtain of cloud,
> a blur above ripples; and through it
> sharp long spikes of the cinnamon,
> a cold tune amid reeds.
> Behind hill the monk's bell
> born on the wind.
> Sail passed here in April; may return in October
> Boat fades in silver; slowly;
> Sun blaze alone on the river.

It is necessary to point out here the visual source of the first three-fourths of this canto. It is a version of the famous Chinese landscape motif of "Eight Views of Hsiao-hsiang or Lake Tung-t'ing," done by an unknown Japanese painter, inspired probably by the Chinese Ch'an-Buddhist painters Mu-ch'i and Yu-chien (most revered in Japan) on an album that Pound obtained in Italy. The eight motifs in eight paintings (often accompanied by poems) are: "Lake Tung-t'ing: Autumn Colors," "Mountain Town: Clear Sunlight," "River-sky: Evening Snow," "Rivers Hsiao and Hsiang: Night Rains," "Fishing Village: Evening Glow," "Distant Shore: Returning Sails," "Smoke-mist Monastery: Evening Bells," and "Sandbar: Descending Geese." A quick perusal of the written source—i.e., the rough draft translation of the Chinese poems that accompany these frames by a Miss Tseng, then living in Italy—for example, this portion, will betray clearly Pound's adoption of the asyntactical structure of the Chinese:

RAIN ///

       Chinese book reads as follows, rough trans.
Rain, empty river,
place for soul to travel
     (or room to travel)
Frozen cloud, fire, rain damp twilight.
One lantern inside boat cover (i.e., sort of
     shelter, not awning on small boat)
Throws reflection on bamboo branch,

      Causes tears

       ///

AUTUMN MOON ON TON-TING LAKE

West side hills
screen off evening clouds
                     flowers.
Ten thousand ripples send mist over cinnamon tttttttt/
Fisherman's flute disregards nostalgia
Blows cold music over cotten bullrush.

Monastery evening bell
/////
Cloud chuts off the hill, hiding the temple
Bell audible only when wind moves toward one,
One can &&&&&&&&&&&&&
    &&&&&&&&&&&&&   whether
        not tell ////////&&&&&&   the
summit, it is near or far,
Sure only that one is hollow of mountains

///////////
Autumn tide,
AUTUMN TIDE, RETURNING SAILS
Touching green sky at horizon, mists in suggestion of autumn
Sheet of silver reflecting /// all that one sees
Boats gradually fade, or are lost in turn of the hills
Only evening sun, and its glory on the water remain.

But, even without knowing these sources, one can still detect easily the Taoist tinctures. Aside from the Chinese asyntactical structures, the things in Nature seem to by playing themselves out before our eyes rather than being locked into or guided by the subjective interests of the poet. "And by no man these verses" reinforces the autonomous existence of these elements in Nature "working out their fate," in spite of the fact that Pound coined this phrase most probably because he did not know who did the paintings and wrote the poems. The Taoist idea of nonintrusive-ness of humanity into Nature's flow will be even clearer when we resur-rect the visual history of this motif from its relationship to Chinese landscape painting tradition in general and its development from Sung Ti through Mi Yu-jen to Mu-ch'i and Yu-chien in particular.

Pound seemed to have intuited, if not known consciously, the Taoist theme of noninterference, for he has added to the landscape set a rather famous (presumably) anonymous poem from ancient China that evokes a kind of primitive Taoism.

Sun up; work
Sundown; to rest
dig well and drink of the water
dig field; eat of the grain
Imperial power is? and to us what is it?

Here, living according to one's natural bent is pitched against the distort-ing imperial power.

But this canto is strategically placed between the Usury Canto and the Chinese History Cantos. The concluding line, "the dimension of stillness / And the power over wild beasts," which, taken in isolation, can be con-sidered Taoist and quite in keeping with the overtones of the landscape paintings and poems, is, in Pound's mind, Confucian because the state-ment is made in direct relation to Geryon in this canto, which immedi-ately brings us back to the master narrative built around Usury.

The master narrative within which Pound's concept of Nature is subsumed can be constructed between two passages. The first appears in Canto 45; it represents the strongest restatement of the evils of Usury,

Pound's version of Dante's hundred-legged beast, Geryon, "that fouleth all the world" (SR, 133), which prevents the human race from creating a paradise on earth, being a destructive force of the generative and produc-tive energy of the world (Canto 5), leading to the disorder of modern society.

> Usura slayed the child in the womb
> It stayeth the young man's courting
> It hath brought palsey to bed, lyeth
> between the young bride and her bridegroom
>
> CONTRA NATURAM
>
> They have brought whores for Eleusis
> Corpses are set to banquet
> at behest of usura

(45/23)

Usury is a sin against Nature because it affects not only the stonecutter (no good house or architecture, "no paradise on his church wall"), the weaver (craft), and husbandry and agriculture ("the peasant does not eat his own grain," "Usury is against Nature's increase") (45/23 and 51/44), but also the church, which is riddled with tendencies to fanaticism, with sadistic and masochistic tendencies such as asceticism, which are counter to creativity (SP, 58, 273), and to art. (Pound once said, in his eclectic way

> "With Usura the line grows thick"—means the *line* in painting and design. Quattrocento painters still in morally clean era when usury and buggery were on a par. As the moral sense becomes as incapable of moral distinction . . . painting gets bitched. I can tell the bank-rate and component of tolerance for usury in any epoch by the quality of *line* in painting. Baroque, etc., era of usury becoming tolerated. [Letter to Carlos Izzo, 1938; *L*, 303])

Indeed, this theme has been emphatically pronounced: "We can see more clearly the grading of Dante's values, and especially how the whole hell reeks with money. The usurers are there against nature, against natural increase of agriculture or of any productive word" (L, 211). "They have brought whores for Eleusis"; they have destroyed the *natural* bond and the generative energy of marriage.

If Usury represents the dark, withering power in civilization, then Eleusis, or Eleusian Mysteries, in which Demeter, the goddess of corn and fertility, was worshipped in a series of rituals before ploughing, would represent harmony and abundance of Nature, including the sacramental marriage, new birth, family, and renewal of life in Nature. Only through reviving Eleusis can we resurrect a *paradiso terrestre*. Here, I would like to point out that, for Pound at this stage, Nature is conflated with Myth. Indeed, one may want to go so far as to say, as will be clear later, that Pound has never abandoned the mystical theory of myth of his early poems. He has never abandoned the second half of his statement concerning no commentary in poetry: "The artist seeks out the luminous detail and presents it. He does not comment. *His work remains the permanent basis of psychology and metaphysics* (1911)" (*SP*, 23; italics mine). Except for his brief wooing with the *real* as real during his Imagist period and some sporadic flashes in the *Cantos*, Pound has never taken the step that Williams takes in affirming that "a life is here and now is timeless, . . . a new world that is always 'real,'" and that "no symbolism is acceptable"[4] Pound continues to take on some form of Platonism and continues to relish some transcendental light and delight rather than allowing things in Nature to assume their immanent emergence.

As we wade through Canto 49, which provides, as it were, a moment of stillness in the brilliant beauty of Nature, almost an artistic example of *paradiso terrestre* (to Pound, a Chinese-Confucian vision), a contrast to the whoring activities of Usury, which continue to evolve in the next two cantos, and come to the *Li Ki* (*Li Chi*) Canto (52), another dimension of the master narrative is introduced in the phrase "Between Kung and Eleusis." One immediately recalls Canto 13, which is constructed of quotations, or Pound's "luminous details," culled from Confucius's *Four Books*, at the heart of which we find this important rewriting from *The Great Learning*: "If a man have not order within him / He cannot spread order about him; / and if man have not order within him / His family will not act with due order; / And if the prince have not order within him /He cannot put order in his dominions." And Pound underlines the word *order*. Kung represents, then, the other alternative to retrieve an earthly paradise, order, according to the Confucian Rectification of Names, *Cheng Ming* (Pound's *Ching Ming*), the Chinese ideograms for which appear at the end of Canto 51, in the midst of the Usury theme. In the Chinese History Cantos that follow, the Confucian order is played out in the various dynasty histories, in which, as can be expected, the destructiveness of Usury is shown to have been artfully avoided. But by allying Kung with Eleusis, Pound also means to see such an order growing out of a process similar to that of the Eleusian Mysteries. Accordingly, he grafts a section from the "Monthly Commands" of the book *Li Chi* to the beginning of the Chinese History Cantos, and by doing so he shrewdly highlights the echoing theme of ritualistic sacrifices to heaven and earth

as acts to achieve natural measure and abundance. It is worth quoting a
portion of this section:

> In red car with jewels incarnadine
> > to welcome summer
> In this month no destruction
> > no tree shall be cut at this time
> The empress offers cocoons to the Son of Heaven
> > Then goes the sun into Gemini
> Virgo in mid heaven at sunset
> > indigo must not be cut
> No wood burnt into charcoal
> > gates are all open, no tax on the booths.
> . . . .
> > this is the third moon of summer. . . .
> To this month is SEVEN,
> > with bitter smell, with odour of burning
> Offer to gods of the hearth
> > the lungs of the victims
> Warm wind is rising, cricket bideth in wall
> Young goshawk is learning his labour
> > dead grass breedeth glow-worms.
> . . . .
> > This month is the reign of Autumn
> Heaven is active in metals, now gather millet
> > and finish the flood-walls
> Orion at sunrise.
> . . . .
> > This month winter ruleth.
> The sun is in archer's shoulder
> > in crow's head at sunrise
> Ice thickens. Earth cracks. And the tigers now move to
> > mating.
> Cut trees at solstice, and arrow shafts of bamboo. . . .
> The fishing season is open,
> > rivers and lakes frozen deep
> Put now ice in your ice-house,
> > the great concert of winds
> Call things by the names. Good sovereign by distribution
> Evil king is known by his imposts. . . .

The theme of correspondence between human/governmental actions and
natural activities is repeated over and over again. This observance of
Nature's way, through proper ritualistic offerings and emulation of its
rhythm and measure, will lead to Nature's increase and an abundance of

art—a perfect match, as it were, with the Eleusian Mysteries. Lifted out of the larger historical context, these activities may even be defined as not deviating from the Taoist emphasis on following Nature. Here, Pound is careful not to include many of the restrictive, repressive, and distortive practices done to humans' natural being in general, and to women in particular, under the grand scheme of correct moral codes and Rectification of Names found in the *Li Chi* and Confucian texts.[5] Although the line "the great concert of winds / Calling things by the names" seems to suggest that the institutional and societal structures created by the Naming System are an outgrowth of the Measure of Nature, it cannot hide the fact that it was invented to legitimatize existing power hierarchies that called the emperor the "son of Heaven" (or that called the prince "God-ordained," as in Western medieval cosmology), and that the explanations of and justifications for subjugation of subject to lord, wife to husband, and son to father, both in China (witness, in particular the practices in the feudalistic Chou dynasty and the large-scale rationalizations of Confucius's Rectification of Names, in cosmic terms, by Tung Chung-shu in the Han dynasty) and in the West (witness similar messages in the "Homilies" in medieval and Renaissance times) are nothing but language strategies to territorialize the domains of so-called appropriate rights and duties under the grand pretexts of proprieties (*li*) so that a whole range of privileging can be instituted and so that a whole range of repressive hierarchies can go unquestioned. Pound's nostalgia of the medieval age is as problematic as his understanding of Confucianism.

While it is true that the inner order advocated by Confucius and brilliantly explained by Mencius as "intuitively known innate goodness" continues to be an important dimension for idealistic Confucians to launch an effective educational program leading to a personal cultivation of goodness in humans, Confucianism as it operates or as it is operated in institutional and societal structures has unfortunately been brutally repressive. Pound wants to cast everything in light of the idealistic Confucians and has purposely looked past the implied repressions in *Cheng Ming* (probably in the same way that he looked past those of Mussolini). It is no accident that Pound went on to define, in his eclectic way, *Cheng Ming* (rectification of names) as "precise definition," which he shrewdly joined with Flaubert's almost style-exclusive "mot juste." The fact that the all-mystical concept of light ("divine light in all things") of the neoplatonic Erigena can be merged with the transparency (*ming*—literally, light, brightness) through reason and understanding of the inner workings of things of the neo-Confucians, despite many essential metaphysical differences, is another such eclectic botching. Eleusis, Kung,

Erigena, etc. are only various spokes toward an extremely complex and often opaque hub (or to use Pound's own image, an opaque, heavy "crystal ball of light") where Pound's concepts of Eleusian/Confucian Nature must be played out.

Clearly, this is no place to allow all the subtexts, with all their accords and discords, that enter into the making of Pound's master vision that is supposed to lead to a *paradiso terrestre* to play themselves out. Let us focus on Eleusis, since it is "a light [that] persisted throughout the Middle Ages and set beauty in the song of Provence and of Italy."[6] Here, Leon Surette's account of Eleusis in light of Pound's unique obsession with the cult of Amor as a beatific and illuminated vision attained through the agency of sexual love is most revealing. Nature is seen not only through the essence of the Eleusian Mysteries, which involve a ritual encounter with Death (Persephone) by the worshippers, who are in a psychological state of both joy and sorrow, which fact helps to explain many of the cantos that deal with the descent to the Underworld brimming with illuminated dark images—but also through the union of man and woman in the form of divine beauty. Pound's obsession with Cavalcanti's "Donna mi Prega," which Pound incorporated into the beginning cantos and in which he purposely changed two lines to fit his vision, represents his attempt to give Eleusis a philosophical expression. "The ritual expression of Eleusian religion . . . is the sacred marriage of man and goddess, as between Odysseus and Circe, or Anchises and Aphrodite; that is to say, a union of perceiving intellect and perceived beauty in epistemological terms, or of Mind (male) and Thought (female)" (Surette, 77). Or witness Pound's own confession: in a response to a query, he says, "Eleusis is very elliptical. It means that in place of the sacramental_ _ _ _ in the Mysteries, you'ave the 4 and six penny 'ore. As you see, the moral bearing is very high, and the degradation of the sacrament (which is the coition and *not* the going to a fat-buttocked priest or registry office) has been completely debased largely by Xtianity, or misunderstanding of that Ersatz religion" (Letter to Carlo Izzo, 1938; *L*, 303). The subtle tripling of Eleusis, Amor, and Nature now affords a new reentrance into the cantos. According to Surette, "It is Amor that reveals the rose in the steel dust, and conveys godlike power of grasping to the human intellect. Amor is manifest in the Divine Mind" (Surette, 78). "CONTRA NATURAM / They have brought whores for Eleusis / Corpses are set to banquet / at behest of usura" now should be read in this vein: "It is through the power of Amor that death is conquered as with Odysseus and Circe, or Persephone and Zagreus" (76). "Usura is the antitype of Amor; the prostitute replaces the priestess" (79).

"The corpses set to banquet are those of Itys, Tereus' son and Cabestan, Seremonde's lover . . . where the essentially contractual and economic marriage vows interfere with the over-weening power of Amor" (80).

It is now all too clear that Pound never approached, or rather never intended to approach, Nature as it is. Whereas, for Mallarmé, everything exists eventually to end up in a book, one may perhaps say that, for Pound, everything exists to help eventually to complete his own Dantean vision of beautific Beauty. It is therefore both puzzling and revealing to read the following annotation by Pound of the line from Propertius, "Ingenium nobis ipsa puella facit" (My genius is no more than a girl):

> [In that line] is the whole of the XIIth century love cult, and Dante's metaphysics a little to one side, and Gourmont's Latin Mystique; and for image-making [Note: he might be thinking of *Phantastikon* rather than image-qua-image of the Chinese] both Fenollosa on "The Chinese Written Character," and the paragraphs in "Le Probleme du Style." (PD, 214)

Such is the intricate eclectic "botching" of Pound's vision at work.

Notes

1. Witness this famous *kung-an* (koan) in the Ch'an (Zen) Buddhist *Transmission of the Lamp*:

> Thirty years ago before I was initiated into Ch'an, I saw mountains as mountains, rivers rivers. Later when I got an entrance into knowledge, I saw mountains not as mountains, rivers not as rivers. Now that I have achieved understanding of the substance, mountains are still mountains, rivers still rivers.

(See *Wu-teng Hui-yuan*, vol. 17, in *Ching-yin Wen-yuan-ke Ssu-k'u Chuan-shu Tzu-pu*, no. 359 (Taiwan: Shang-wu, 1983), 1053 che, p. 735.)
2. This and subsequent translations of poetry by Wang Wei are my own.
3. Ezra Pound, "Chinese Poetry," *Today* 3 (April 1918): 54.
4. William Carlos Williams, *Paterson* (New York: New Directions, 1946), 6; *Selected Essays* (New York: New Directions, 1954), 213.
5. In leafing through Pound's copy of S. Couvreur's *Li Ki* while visiting Brunnenburg recently, I found that Pound put pencil marks on many examples of forms of repressive acts rationalized in the *Li Ki*, including the question of women's confinement (I.ii.33). In other words, Pound *knew* that these were repressive acts.
6. Reply to Eliot, "Credo," *Front* 1 (December 1930): 11.

Metaphor in the Sciences and in the Humanities: Logic, Rhetoric, or Heuristic?

EUGENE EOYANG

In this essay, we will deal with what Max Black calls "implicative" metaphors that have resonance, descriptive metaphors that are useful, and instrumental metaphors that engender new thoughts, new ideas. Special emphasis will be placed on the third use of metaphor, which can be sub-sumed in the familiar notion of "intuition," where the value, fecundity, or validity of a metaphor occurs inductively and not deductively. In a sense, these metaphors say more than the conceiver of the metaphor is fully aware of. These mental constructs are akin to speculations and theories, which venture forth from what is known to what is unknown, and they are—unlike the truths of science—far from conclusive. Richard Boyd characterizes these metaphors as "theory-constitutive."

Boyd makes the intriguing contrast between the effect of repeated use of literary metaphors as opposed to scientific metaphors. "When the same metaphor is employed often, by a variety of authors, and in a variety of minor variations, it becomes either trite or hackneyed, or it becomes 'frozen' into a figure of speech or a new literal expression," whereas "theory-constitutive scientific metaphors, on the other hand, become, when they are successful, the property of the entire scientific community, and variations on them are explored by hundreds of scientific authors without their interactive quality being lost" (Ortony, 361). In other words, literary metaphors lose their novelty with repeated citation, whereas scientific metaphors gain in meaning when more and more researchers share them.

We may then separate the various uses of metaphor and establish different kinds of "validity" in metaphoric thinking. The first, and most

111

common, is the syllogistic, or logical, mode of metaphor. Examples include "language is a code," "thought is a kind of information process-
ing," and "the brain is a sort of computer." A second kind of metaphor is
the suasive, or hortatory, mode of metaphor, where the effectiveness of
the metaphor is proportionate to the degree to which the speaker and
audience agree on the same point of view. The metaphor "I cannot but
conclude that the bulk of your natives to be the most pernicious race of
little odious vermin that nature every suffered to crawl upon the surface
of the earth" depends on a particular—decidedly negative—view of "the
bulk of your natives."[1] The metaphor here resounds in "truth" only in the
sense that individuals agree with the proposition and indicate their
agreement with an acknowledgment of its "truth." But it has no bearing
on those who believe better of "the bulk of your natives." The persua-
siveness of the metaphor is in the strength of its descriptiveness rather
than in the logic of its formulation.

A third kind of metaphor would be the catalytic, the heuristic: this
mode of metaphoric thinking, which Coleridge, among others, has characterized as "creative," has the propensity of stimulating thought rather
than merely eliciting admiration or agreement. The catalytic metaphor is
open-ended, whereas the others are conclusive, either logically or
rhetorically. Theoretical constructs are a form of paradigmatic metaphor,
with the power to engage other minds to stimulate thinking for heuristic
reasons. As Katherine Hayles puts it: "Overlaying a heuristic onto a
theory is never merely an inert transposition of concepts, for it generates
a surplus of signification that can lead to interpretations not intended by
the person who proposed the theory or, for that matter, the heuristic"
(Peterfreund, 211).

The nineteenth century contributed three scientific models of thought,
each of them with ramifications for literary study. The first, the positivism of Auguste Comte, which established sociology and social science
research, provided a paradigm for study that stressed empirical or experimental proof. That this method, which tends to be statistical, is little
suited to the study of the humanities, is by now obvious. Its dead end was
reached, I suppose, in the statistical, stylistic studies a generation ago that
tried to determine authorship in texts of the Bible. The theoretical mis-
take in applying this mode of research to literature is that, where deter-
minations of norms is amenable to quantifiable research, literature is
precisely about the abnormal and the inexplicable. The failure of this
model derives from a mistaken premise: the techniques to determine and
describe the ordinary are used to evaluate and to analyze the extraordinary. It further misconstrues the nature of the data measured, which are
not words but meaning. One cannot count on frequencies of usage and

have an accurate fix on meaning because frequencies take no account of such literary tropes as irony, allusion, anaphora, and satire, none of which is subject to quantifiable analysis.

The second model of thought that the study of literature adopted from nineteenth-century science was evolution. Literature was conceived as a developing species, subject to the laws of supply and demand, of survival of the fittest, existing on an evolutionary scale that led progressively to the present. There were, however, at least two flaws in the application of this model. One was the implicit assumption of a progressivist view of literature, that the species in its later evolutionary stage was somehow an improved, "fitter" version of earlier evolutionary stages. But the course of literary history flies in the face of this assumption, since Homer and the Greek tragedians, not to mention the Bible—both Old and New Testaments—have, in the eyes of many, never been surpassed. Nor would anyone maintain that the later periods of literature were always improvements over earlier stages. Surely, no drama since the seventeenth century has surpassed the Elizabethans in general, and Shakespeare in particular.

Ferdinand Brunetière's *L'evolution des genres dans l'histoire de la littérature* (1890) was perhaps the greatest example of a literary study that followed the evolutionary model, and it isn't much read today. The problem with the notion of applying evolution to literature is that it is at once too simple and too complex. Evolution is too simple a model because it assumes a species-wide collective phenomenon subject to demographic and statistical probability, whereas literature and its survival are often the result of individual rather than communal acts. Literature does not always depend on survival of the fittest: many authors popular in past eras are no longer read today, and other authors, like Stendhal and Emily Dickinson, who were scarcely read in their day or became nearly extinct, are part of the canon now. On the other hand, evolution is too complex a model because its chronological scale and its synchronic scope are too vast—its variables too numerous and too elusive—to serve as models for literature.

A third model that was popular, particularly during the era in which New Criticism held sway, was the organic model: that a work of literature was somehow a discrete, organic entity with a life and death, an adolescence, and a senility. But this metaphor, even while it romanticizes the ontology of literature and sees it as an inevitable part of Nature, misconstrues the arbitrary nature of literature as a human construct, with elements that are abstract in a way that organisms never are.

All three models prevailed for a time because they appeared to identify parallel structures between what Richards would call the "tenor," a theory of science, and the "vehicle," the development of literature, with the "ground" being the notion of knowledge as either empirical, evolutionary, or organic. They also responded suasively to the intellectual audience of the time, which was inured to a notion of knowledge that was scientific and positivistic rather than literary and aesthetic. And they generated a species of research in the application of these models to the texts of literature. Yet the results in each case were disappointing.

In the epistemology of research, logic, insight, inference, vision, and—if truth be known—serendipity play key roles. Yet, all—or almost all—of these mental operations involve metaphor, the transference of meaning from the known to the unknown, or the assumption of a parallel between the structure of something known to the structure of something unknown. While the ability to recognize and to make metaphor has traditionally been, since Aristotle, regarded as a trait of intelligence, the validity of metaphor as an infallible conduit to absolute truth has not often been challenged. Indeed, some metaphors are so embedded in our cognitive processes that the question of their validity is never raised.

To cite as an example, there has been, since Aristotle, a model of knowledge, based on Aristotle, that true knowledge is (1) systematic and (2) comprehensive. The systematic nature of certain theories as well as of certain sciences assures the researcher that there is a comprehensible and a consistent character to its activity: it is what gives a science its disciplinary character. But faith in system is based on two assumptions, neither of which—in the absence of omniscience—can be proven: that the nature of the world and of what is to be discovered is amenable to consistent laws and rules, and that comprehensiveness is possible despite the limitations of time, space, and human experience. But "systematicity" is a warrant not of validity but of consistency, which may or may not be an attribute of truth. We cannot deny that "systematicity" is effective in discovering truths that are structured, nor can we overlook the usefulness of system in engendering research that proceeds in an orderly, organized fashion. And we have to admit that "systematicity" is intellectually impressive, especially when it is both broad and profound, as in the case of Kant or Aristotle. But these assertions fall short of a proof of absolute validity for what is systematic. There are truths that are inconsistent, as in paradox, as well as contradictory, as in Plato's view of the poet in *The Republic* and in the *Ion*. On the other hand, there are also intellectual constructs like astrology that, for all their systematic rigor, fail to validate themselves as true. Not all systems are true, nor are all truths systematic. Bureaucracy is, after all, a system, and most paradoxes are true.

The epistemology of logical positivism, despite its putative neutrality and objectivity, is also built on a metaphor, the validity of which has not yet been proven. It assumes there is a correspondence between the laws that govern physical Nature, and the laws that govern all phenomena. It assumes validity as equivalent to measurability, confuses truth with experience, and conflates quantifiability with significance. To the extent that what is being explored involves truths that are measurable and quantifiable, the empiricist methodology will yield results; but logical positivism is distinctly illogical when it posits the irrelevance or meaninglessness of propositions that cannot be measured, or, more precisely, that cannot be measured with instruments presently available. If we acknowledge that progress has provided ever more precise measuring instruments, ever larger telescopes, ever more powerful electron microscopes, then we would have to come to the logical conclusion that the logical positivists of the past were chronological provincials: they assumed that what they knew was all that there was worth knowing. The validity of positivistic insights is in proportion to, and a reflection of, the crudeness or sophistication of the instruments used to measure experimental results. Since no instrument is precise to the nth degree, the conclusions one draws from one's instruments are only as reliable as they come close to being precise to the nth degree.

If the validity of logical positivism is, therefore, limited, one might ask why it prevailed as the paradigm of research for so long. The answer is that its methodology has the brilliant characteristic of not requiring overly profound intellects for success: what it does require are meticulous quantifiers. As the distinguished zoologist Peter Medawar has written: "Quite ordinary people can be good at science. To say this is not to depreciate science but to appreciate ordinary people" (Medawar, 9). If populousness is an index of the ordinary, then we would have to agree with Medawar, since there are probably more scientists living today than there have been in the entire course of human civilization. Medawar has suggested that there may be a symbiosis between the development of science and the growth of an egalitarian society: "Because a scientific career does not," he writes, "call for rare, high or unusual capabilities, it is accessible to almost all, and a career in science stands out as one of the great opportunities of a liberal and democratic society" (10). Meticulousness is neither always necessary nor always sufficient to do science. Imagination is, however, another matter. One can define imagination as the instinct to learn what one does not know in order to understand the unknown. James Watson, one of the discoverers of DNA, confesses in his *Double Helix* that he knew very little biology and that he was entirely ignorant of crystallography, which turned out to be the key to the discovery of the helical structure of the DNA molecule.

All theory, from Galileo to Einstein, has turned out to be, in significant ways, wrong. Ernest Rutherford won the Nobel Prize in 1908 for the theory that the configuration of electrons, neutrons, and protons resembled the structure of the solar system, a model that no self-respecting scientist takes seriously today. Even Rutherford's contemporary, Heisenberg, remarked on the contingent nature of Bohr's hypothetical construct. "The Bohr atom can be described as a small-scale planetary system, having a central atomic nucleus about which the central electrons revolve. For other experiments, however, it might be more convenient to imagine that the atomic nucleus is surrounded by a system of stationary waves whose frequency is characteristic of the radiation emanating from the atom" (Peterfreund, 97). Newton's construction of the universe in terms of billiard-ball causality has long been abandoned by scientists. Yet neither Newton nor Bohr is considered a defective or inadequate scientist. Why were these imaginative constructs valued, even if they turned out to be, ultimately, invalid? If science is undeterred by the ultimate invalidity of theory, what distinguishes good science from bad science? If being wrong ultimately does not appear to tarnish the reputation of a scientific genius or to diminish his or her importance for later generations, how does science add to the sum total of knowledge, which would also appear not altogether different from the sum total of error?

To be fair, one should remember that great scientists have been more often right than wrong. It is not the infallibility of scientists that distinguishes them but the galvanizing, fructifying, or inspirational nature of their error. Important theories conform to the sum total of known facts yet empower researchers with the means to disprove the theory. The greater and more complex the theory, the more difficult the disproof. Theory is what Stanley Fish might call a "self-consuming artifact."

The value of theory is in direct proportion to the complexity of the analysis required to disprove the theory. When asked in 1965 why Einstein's papers had still not been published ten years after his death, J. Robert Oppenheimer remarked: "It's because Einstein made errors, but *what errors !*" Or, as Niels Bohr put it, reminiscing about his father, "One of the favorite maxims of my father was the distinction between the two sorts of truths, profound truths recognized by the fact that the opposite is also a profound truth, in contrast to trivialities where the opposites are obviously absurd" (Rozental, 328).

If metaphors that derive from science have prevailed for a time but are now in disrepute, the same cannot be said for metaphors from literature that are influencing other fields. In physics, for example, the subnuclear structure of matter has taken an inevitable Joycean character through the intercession of Murray Gellman, who adopted the word "quark" from *Finnegans Wake* (383: "Three quarks for Muster Mark!") as the label for any one of the six elementary particles that make up matter. We have now discovered the "up," "down," "charm," "strange," "bottom," and most recently "top" quark. It is no longer axiomatic to differentiate science as a discipline that discovers from literature as a discourse that invents. Even mathematics, the so-called "queen of the sciences," perhaps the most universal of all the sciences, is no longer unequivocally considered a discovery. The nineteenth-century mathematician Leopold Kronecker declared, "God made the integers; all else is the work of man" (*The New York Times*, 20 July 1994, sec. 4, p. 6). Einstein went further and deprived God of credit for integers: he maintained that even integers are "obviously an invention of the human mind, a self-created tool which simplifies the ordering of certain sensory experiences" (ibid.).

Fiction, one is perhaps surprised to discover, has been a revelatory metaphor for research for fields outside the study of literature. The historian Hayden White views history primarily as narrative. For White, "far from being one code among many that a culture may utilize for endowing experience with meaning, narrative is a meta-code, a human universal on the basis of which transcultural messages about the nature of shared reality can be transmitted" (*Content,* 1). In two key articles, "The Historical Text as Literary Artifact" and "The Fictions of Factual Representation" (*Tropics*, 81–100; 121–34), White propounded a virtual "poetics" of history.

Anthropology has likewise discovered the notion of authorship and its importance to analyzing reality. Clifford Geertz, in his *Works and Lives* (the title declares its narrative concern by alluding to both Hesiod's *Works and Days*, and Proust's *Pleasures and Days*, his imitation of Hesiod), recommends literary criticism as a methodological metaphor for evaluating anthropological research:

> As the criticism of fiction and poetry grows best out of an imaginative engagement with fiction and poetry themselves, not out of imported notions about what they should be, the criticism of anthropological writing . . . ought to grow out of a similar engagement with *it*, not out of preconceptions of what it must look like to qualify as science. (6)

"It may be that in other realms of discourse," Geertz speculates, "the author . . . is in the process of dying; but he . . . she . . . is still very much alive among anthropologists" (6–7).[2] Geertz sees anthropology "pretty much on the side of 'literary' discourses rather than 'scientific' ones" (8). Anthropology is a personalized study, a science with a point of view. Anthropologists are no longer apologists for the use of the first person.[3] And, like literature, it boasts its major authors as well. Just as literary scholars talk about a Dickensian or Shandean world, or a Dostoyevskian vision, so anthropologists speak of anthropology as Boasian or Levi-Straussian. It even allows Geertz, following Talcott Parsons, to invoke Ruth Benedict with almost monkish glee by referring to her school as "Benedictine anthropology."

Even sociology—that most jargon-ridden, quantitative, least readable of the social sciences—has turned to literature for inspiration and guidance. Sara Lawrence-Lightfoot, the Harvard sociologist, has coined the term "human archaeology," which, presumably, merges the aesthetic with the empirical. According to one account, "Dr. Lawrence-Lightfoot is sociologist as storyteller," and her latest work, *I've Known Rivers: Lives of Loss and Liberation* (1994) provides "sociological portraits that are a marriage of arts and science, literature and empirical description" (*New York Times*, 31 August 1994).

Cosmologists and chaos theorists are talking more and more like humanists these days. Ilya Prigogine and Isabelle Stengers write that "the irreducible plurality of perspectives on the same reality expresses the impossibility of a divine point of view from which the whole of reality is visible" (Peterfreund, 97). One recalls Joyce's claim for the artist in *The Portrait of the Artist as a Young Man*, which "like the God of the creation, remains within or behind or beyond or above his handiwork, invisible, refined out of existence, indifferent, paring his fingernails." In this postmodernist age, that characterization seems outmoded now not only for the artist but for the scientist.

Even animal behaviorists have overcome their suspicion of a humanist perspective and adopted certain forms of anthropomorphism in their studies, ascribing human emotions to nonhuman forms of life. One animal behaviorist (Dr. Marc Bekoff of the University of Colorado) proclaims: "I'm an advocate for anthropomorphism these days because I really believe it helps me do my science. It helps me formulate testable hypotheses" (*New York Times*, 9 August 1994, B5). Here, a humanist perspective should not be restricted merely to the West but must be comparative. Even today, there are arrant claims to universality that do not bother to survey all available empirical evidence. In research being conducted at Yale University, Sally Shaywitz, in her comparative studies of the male and female brains, used the ability to recognize rhyme as an index of reading ability; no less an eminence than Dr. Norman Krasnegor, who directs the human learning and behavior department at the National Institute of Child Health and Human Development, claims that "rhyming may also be a window on the mind"; "Everyone likes rhymes," says Steven Pinker, author of *The Language Instinct* and director of the Center for Cognitive Neuroscience at M. I. T. (*New York Times*, 19

February 1995, E3). But none of these researchers seems disconcerted by the fact that in Japanese—with but five vowel sounds and no final consonants at the end of syllables—rhyme occurs too often to please the ear. Dr. Pinker's question, "Why is rhyme so pleasurable?" is a totally unwarranted pseudouniversal, which the Japanese would hardly subscribe to. Perhaps, if there were a comparative science, as there is a comparative literature, empirical errors like this one might be avoided.

If rhyme is not universal, metaphor is so pervasive as to be virtually universal not merely across cultures but across disciplines. As T. R. Wright puts it: "If narrative is the way we construct our sense of identity, metaphor is how we think, especially in areas in which we need to build our knowledge of the unknown by comparison with the known" (*Oxford Companion*, 654).

We may therefore conclude with a celebration of all three uses of metaphor. For the logical and descriptive use of metaphor is inevitably empirical and recognizes the old. The rhetorical or suasive use of metaphor is resolutely experimental and affective; it acknowledges the present. The heuristic use of metaphor is iconoclastic and provocative, on occasion even mystical; it discovers the new.

The examples that we've explored are instances of what might be called—without contradiction or paradox—"scientific humanism," a term that is by no means new. Indeed, we find it as early as 1942 in the writings of that great historian of Chinese science, Joseph Needham, who wrote, historically—and prophetically:

> Scientific humanism is at least as old as the pre-Socratic philosophers in Greece and the Chinese philosophers of the time of the Warring States in China. But its universal triumphs were reserved for the last few centuries, and its greatest are yet to come. (97)

Works Cited

Geertz, Clifford. *Works and Lives: The Anthropologist as Author*. Stanford: Stanford University Press, 1988.

Heisenberg, Werner. *The Physicist's Conception of Nature*. Translated by Arnold J. Pomerans. London: Hutchinson, 1958.

Joyce, James. *Finnegans Wake*. New York: Viking Press, 1982.

Medawar, Peter. *The Limits of Science*. Oxford: Oxford University Press, 1984.

Needham, Joseph. *Within the Four Seas: The Dialogue of East and West*. Toronto: University of Toronto Press, 1979.

Ortony, Andrew, ed. *Metaphor and Thought*. Cambridge: Cambridge University Press, 1979.

Oxford Companion to the English Language. Edited by Tom McArthur. Oxford: Oxford University Press, 1992.

Peterfreund, Stuart, ed. *Literature and Science: Theory and Practice*. Boston: Northeastern University Press, 1990.

Rozental, S., ed. *Niels Bohr: His Life and Work as Seen by His Friends and Colleagues*. Amsterdam: Elsevier Science Publishing Company, 1967.

White, Hayden. *The Content of the Form: Narrative Discourse and Historical Representation*. Baltimore: Johns Hopkins Press, 1987.

————. *Tropics of Discourse: Essays in Cultural Criticism*. Baltimore: Johns Hopkins Press, 1978.

Wright, T. R. *Theology and Literature*. Oxford: B. Blackwell, 1988.

Notes

Paper presented at the annual convention of the American Comparative Literature Association, 18 March 1995, at the University of Georgia, Athens, Georgia.

1. This sentiment has often been attributed to Swift, which is not entirely accurate, since he puts the expression in the voice of the King of Brobdingnag in chapter 6 of *Gulliver's Travels*. The king, in turn, is responding to Gulliver's description of England under Queen Anne.

2. Geertz is, of course, alluding to Michel Foucault's famous article "What is an Author?" an article with which he is in postmodernist accord. It is an article, he writes, "which in fact I agree with, save for its premises, its conclusions, and its cast of mind" (7).

3. See "Ruth Behar, "Dare We Say 'I'—Bring the Personal into Scholarship," *The Chronicle of Higher Education*, 29 June 1994, sec. 2, pp. 1–2.

Part 3
Genre

Feng Zhi and His Goethean Sonnet

MARIÁN GÁLIK

I hope that it will be considered appropriate for me to begin with two reminiscences of my meetings with Feng Zhi (1905–93), the eminent Chinese poet, literary scholar, and foremost expert on German literature.

We met for the first time on 14 April 1986 in the Institute of Foreign Literature of the Chinese Academy of Social Sciences in the presence of Ge Baoquan (1913–), the well-known Chinese Slavicist. We discussed, among others, the problems connected with Feng Zhi's writings, as evident from his relations with German Romanticism, Rainer Maria Rilke (1875–1926) (especially his *Die Sonette an Orpheus* [Sonnets to Orpheus]), Vincent van Gogh, and Feng Zhi's Venetian sonnet. I repeated an idea expressed in my book, just published at that time and entitled *Milestones in Sino-Western Literary Confrontation (1898–1979)*. According to my interpretation, Feng Zhi's poetic universe is different from that of his Chinese contemporaries and quite opposite from the "solar" poetic cosmos of Guo Moruo (1892–1978), for the former, especially in his youth, depicted in his poetry

> rather an astral myth and astral universe with myriads of apparently little things, unmarked, shining or bright, such as the heavenly bodies in the immense sky, but also pearls in our hearts, flower buds, a small brook, musical instrument, embroidery, steps in the night, dusk, a song of love in the moonshine during which "tens of thousands of space phenomena whirl about us, / and there is not one among them in which love would not be manifest."[1]

Feng Zhi did not agree with my arguments concerning, for example, Zhinu (Weaver girl) from the constellation of Vega and the Lyre, and Qianniu, or Niulang Herdsman, from Aquilla on either sides of the Tianhe (The river of heaven) from his poem *Kuangfeng zhong*

(Hurricane). Neither did he accept my references to *Creation of Milky Way*, from the same poem, written in imitation of the famous canvas by Jacopo Tintoretto (ca. 1518–94), now in the National Gallery, London. He simply did not admit that he was, in his best years, such a mythopoeic poet of the kind I tried to show to my readers.

He changed his mind later, however, probably after browsing through my essay on his Venetian sonnet and chapter 9 of the *Milestones* mentioned above.[2] In the second half of August 1987, during my visit to his flat, he admitted that I was right, gave me his newly published article entitled *"Wailaide yangfen"* (What I have learned from abroad) and informed me that he would distribute copies of my essay on his Venetian sonnet to his friends during his trip to Italy in September that year.

1

Rereading my earlier views now, when writing an *hommage* to my old friend and colleague Professor A. Owen Aldridge, I have to add that the "astral universe" of Feng Zhi is not only full of really or seemingly small things reminding us of the drops of milk from the breasts of divine Hera and the "small" people of his environment, but in its overall framework also alludes to the "stars" from the world of indigenous and foreign literature, art, philosophy, and religion.

At the time he wrote the Goethean sonnet and all the other twenty-six pieces from the thin collection entitled *Shisihang ji* (The sonnets), Feng Zhi was living near the town of Kunming, in Yunnan Province, between the "eucalypti and gunsmoke" of the Anti-Japanese War (1937–45). In 1941, while he was staying in the village hut, his obligation was to go twice a week to town to read his lectures to students at the *Xinan lianhe daxue* (Southwest associated university) and to buy some vegetables or other things to eat. He recalled those times and his "wanderings" in this way:

It was a trip of about fifteen miles (Chinese miles, M.G.), and walking back and forth was a pleasant exercise. A person alone on mountain paths and meadows cannot help but look around him and ruminate. At that particular point in my life, it seemed as if I saw a great deal more and thought more exuberantly than usual. . . .

Once, on a winter afternoon, when I was looking at a few silvery airplanes, blue like crystals, hovering in the azure sky, I was reminded of the "Peng bird dream" of the ancients. Following the rhythms of my footsteps, I casually composed a rhymed poem. When I got home, I wrote the poem down and found, quite incidentally, that it was a sonnet.[3]

"Peng bird dream" is an allusion to the first chapter of the book *Zhuangzi* (third century B.C.). There are different explanations of this dream: a "happy excursion,"[4] "free and easy wandering,"[5] "spiritual wandering,"[6] or "faraway wandering."[7] In Feng Zhi's case, this was an opportunity to recollect his readings and studies, meetings and encounters, whether in the present or in the past, at home or abroad, whether about domestic or foreign myths, the mystery of life and death, war and peace, dreams and realities, the vast universe full of loneliness and sorrow, usually with some hope, which dies last of all, and the possibilities or at least tendency of interhuman communication.

In his "spiritual wandering," Feng Zhi met and addressed sonnets to a few outstanding "stars" of cultural history, foreign and Chinese, including Du Fu (712–70), Cai Yuanpei (1868–1940), Lu Xun (1881–1936), Johann Wolfgang Goethe (1749–1832), and Vincent van Gogh (1853–90). One sonnet he devoted simply to stellar being.

The Goethean poem has been numbered in Feng Zhi's collection as Sonnet 13, and in *pinyin* transcription it reads as follows:

> Ni shengchan zai pingfangde shiminde chiating,
> ni wei guo xuduo pingfangde nuzi liu lei,
> zai yidai xiongzhude mianqian ni ye jingwei,
> ni bashi niande suiyue shi nayang pingjing
>
> haoxiang yuzhou zainaer jimode yunxing,
> danshi buhui you yifen yimiaode tingxi,
> suishi suichu du yanhuachu xinde shengji,
> buguan fengfeng yuyu, huoshi ri langtian jing.
>
> Cong shenzhongde bingzhong huanlai xinde jiankang
> Cong juewangde ai li huanlai xinde yinyang,
> ni zhidao fei o weishenmo tou xiang huoyan,
>
> she wei shenmo tuoqu jiu picai neng shengchang;
> wanwu du zai hengyong nide na ju mingyan,
> ta daopo yiqie yiyi: "Si he bian."[8]

Here is the translation into English by Dominic Cheung:

> You were born into a family of commoners,
> shed tears for many ordinary girls.
> You feared, revered the one who rules the realm
> and lived a life of eighty tranquil years.

Just as the globe turns silently
without a minute or a second's rest,
new signs evolve, all the time, everywhere,
in wind and rain, fair weather and foul,

comes new health from heavy sickness,
new strength out of desperate love;
you know why moths plunge into fire,

why snakes shed their skins in growth;
all things observe your creed
which reveals the meaning of life: Death and metamorphosis.[9]

In this and all five sonnets devoted to the great personalities, one becomes acquainted with major elements of their lives. All of them contain a strong "spiritual" accent. Nobody knows which of them was written first, although it is possible that Feng Zhi had put on paper the one on Cai Yuanpei earlier than others at the occasion of the first anniversary of the latter's death on 5 March 1941. The most important idea of this sonnet, as well of the whole volume, whether delineated directly or indirectly, was that of "spiritual renewal." In allusion to one of R. M. Rilke's letters, dated 19 November 1917, regretting the loss of Auguste Rodin (1840–1917) and Emile Verhaeren (1855–1916) to wartime and postwartime European literature and art, Feng Zhi manifested his deep sorrow at the death of one of the fathers of modern Chinese Renaissance and the popular chancellor of Peking University.[10]

During the fourth year of the Anti-Japanese War, Feng Zhi had enough time to muse over the "burden" of his past experiences and studies in China and in Germany. The recollection of the death of Cai Yuanpei brought him to Rilke, a poet who had already been his literary love for years. In the article presented to me, Feng Zhi analyzes in some detail his relation to Rilke from 1931 on. For his development during the year 1941, the Rilkean years between 1912 and 1922, the period of his work on *Duineser Elegien* (Duino elegies) and *Sonnets to Orpheus*, were important. Feng Zhi wrote these sentences about his experience from this study, which he found extremely attractive and exciting:

During the years before, during and after the World War I, [Rilke, M. G.] lived through ten years of sorrow and hesitation. . . . Here we do not find anymore his *meiyou ziwo* [non-ego spirit], but his personality fuses with *wanwu* [all things], and he on one side expresses his grievances, just like two lines from Tao Yuanming's (365–427) poem: *wanzu ge you tuo, / gu yun du wu yi* "all the myriads creatures have their refuge, / the lonely cloud alone has no support." On the other hand Rilke feels that in the world all is real, whether it has got its name or remained nameless, notwithstanding its value. All this should be admired.[11]

During the 1930s, especially in the first half, Feng Zhi read Rilke's novel *Die Aufzeichnungen des Malte Laurids Brigge* (Notebooks of Malte Laurids Brigge) and his letters. Very soon he realized that Rilke's poems were difficult to comprehend. "At that time," he wrote recently, "when I deliberated enough long, I was able to understand some of Rilke's poems. It meant for me a new discovery, I felt a moment of great joy surpassing the one I experienced after writing a satisfactory poem myself. When reading *Duino Elegies* or *Sonnets to Orpheus* (although I was not able to understand everything), from time to time I pondered over the last lines of *Faust, Part Two*, its *Chorus mysticus*. . . . I suppose that those who throughout their lives struggle for the cause of literature and art, would in the end sing this noble hymn."[12] Feng Zhi forgot his older colleague Guo Moruo, who put this quatrain at the beginning of his first poetic collection *Nushen* (The goddesses).[13]

2

Feng Zhi was enthralled, as were many young Chinese, with Guo Moruo's translation of Goethe's early novel *Die Leiden des jungen Werthers* (Sorrows of young Werther), which appeared in Shanghai in 1921, the same year as *The Goddesses*. The Sturm und Drang tendency in Goethe's work, however, kept his attention for only a few years.[14]

During the second half of the 1930s, and especially after the Marco Polo Bridge Incident, which started the long Anti-Japanese War (1937–45), a new situation arose not only in Chinese cultural and political life but also in Feng Zhi's literary and philosophical development. Maybe ten years later, also under the impact of Rilke and his example, Feng Zhi came to Goethe once again.[15] This time it was no longer to a young Goethe but to a poet at least sixty-five years old, author of the collection *West-östlicher Divan* (West-Eastern divan) (1819) and of the last and definite version of *Faust* (1832).

Goethe started to write the poems, later collected in his *Divan*, after reading the translation by Joseph von Hammer (1812–13) entitled *Der Diwan von Mohammed Schemsed-din Hafis*.[16] Europe at that time was approaching the end of the Napoleonic Wars, and Goethe said: "I thank God that I am not young in so thoroughly finished world."[17] At that time,

"Europe lay prostrate. Millions of strong men had perished; millions of acres of land had been neglected or laid waste; everywhere on the continent life had to begin again at the bottom, to recover painfully and slowly the civilizing economic surplus that had been swallowed up in war."[18] For Goethe, Mephistopheles did not triumph and Faust remained a man of deed and of hope. He himself did not follow this aspect of Faust in his old age, but as a sage he tried to achieve moral and aesthetic perfection. He strained after new renewal in that age of pessimism, chaos, and skepticism; he searched for new springs for his creative life. For the first time, these should be in great measure from the Orient. Hafiz (ca. 1326–90), one of the best lyric poets of Persian and world literature, was "the first and chief source of 'East-Western Divan', and also the immediate impulse that provoked the unusual productivity of Goethe's poetic work in the first diwan years."[19]

In 1814, when one of the poems that had a decisive impact on Feng Zhi's Goethean sonnet was written, Goethe was able in one day to finish several pieces![20] The poem I have in mind, entitled *Selige Sehnsucht* (Spiritual yearning), is dated 31 July 1814.

Before we undertake a comparative analysis of Feng Zhi's sonnet, we reproduce the original wording of Goethe's poem:

> Sagt es niemand, nur den Weisen,
> Weil die Menge gleich verhöhnet,
> Das Lebendige will ich preisen
> Das nach Flammentod sich sehnet.
>
> In der Liebesnächte Kühlung
> Die dich zeugte, wo du zeugtest,
> Überfällt dich fremde Fühlung
> Wenn die stille Kerze leuchtet.
>
> Nicht mehr bleibst du umfangen
> In der Finsterniß Beschattung,
> Und dich reißet neu Verlangen
> Auf zu höherer Begattung.
>
> Keine Ferne macht dich schwierig,
> Kommst geflogen und gebannt,
> Und zuletzt, des Lichts begierig,
> Bist du Schmetterling verbrannt.
>
> Und so lang du das nicht hast,
> Dieses: Stirb und werde!
> Bist du nur ein trüber Gast
> Auf der dunklen Erde.[21]

We do not know (and cannot know) what Feng Zhi felt or what he had in mind when he composed the Goethean sonnet, especially its last tercet. We dispose of his later ruminations written in September 1947, more than two years after the end of the Anti-Japanese War and World War II. The situation in the China of 1941 was incomparably worse than that in Europe of 1814. Feng Zhi did not even consider the possibility of material improvement. Nationalist and Communist rule to a great extent repeated the horrors of Japanese militarists. He put his faith in the concept of interhuman communication, a notion he had acquired from the lectures of one of his German teachers, Karl Jaspers (1883–1969) in Heidelberg,[22] and in spiritual renewal, which he encountered in the works of Goethe and Rilke. Already in 1927–29, he believed in "cosmic love," a kind of mystic love, that as a mythopoeic demiurge of the universe is its most important source of energy:

> I am with all my cells industriously trying
> to work for hope that should be forever busy.
> Myriads of space phenomena whirl about us,
> and there is not one among them in which love would not be manifest.
> "Omnipresent and great God,
> receive, please,
> my thanks."[23]

Feng Zhi's Goethean sonnet is certainly one of the shortest exposés of Goethe's life and of his philosophy in world literature. The first quatrain delineates his family background, love life, and political career. It is not always to the point. Certainly, Goethe did not shed many tears for "ordinary girls." Maybe the deep impact of the *Sorrows of Young Werther* left its imprint upon Feng Zhi's memory. The word "globe" for *yuzhou* is not the equivalent term in Cheung's translation; "universe," used by Wolfgang Kubin, is more appropriate.[24] In the second quatrain and in the first tercet, we see *in nuce* Goethe's philosophic morphology explained in his essays and poems concerned with natural sciences.

The important last stanza became the most problematic part of the message both in Feng Zhi's original and in Cheung's rendition. Goethe's maxim *Stirb und werde* means neither *si he bian* nor Death and metamorphosis. I have to acknowledge that it does not even stand for "Die and Be!"[25] as I understood it more than ten years ago. In 1982, Feng Zhi admitted his "fault" by translating the German imperative *werde* as *yan,* i.e., "metamorphose or change!" and revealed to his readers that in Goethe's case it should be read as *wancheng* (make something perfect), "achieve excellence!"[26] We may come to the same conclusion about his own sonnet.

Feng Zhi was right when, in the essay *Gedede "Xidong heji"*
(Goethe's East-Western divan), from the year 1947, he simply asserted
that *Spiritual Yearning* was the poet's "most deep apprehension of
life."[27] Otherwise, he misjudged Goethe's message when he tried to
explain it by alluding to Goethe's views on natural science. The image of
the moth (or butterfly) coming to Goethe's poem from Hafiz's *ghazel*[28]
and plunging itself into the fire has nothing to do with metamorphoses in
Nature. It is a parable of the eminent human beings, aristocrats of noble
minds, "rich in spirit,"[29] who are the "salt" or the "light of the earth,"[30]
transcending the niveau of the "motley rabble."[31] They are selflessly
prepared to offer their services to higher epistemologic, moral, and
aesthetic realms. Here, the question is about the overcoming-motif of the
human psyche aiming at perfection within this above-mentioned framework. *Spiritual Yearning* was not the most suitable title for this allegedly
"most difficult among Goethe's poems."[32] One of its previous names,
*Vollendung (*Perfection*)*, was much more appropriate for alluding to its
noble content.[33]

3

According to Exodus 4:10–11, Moses said, "Unto the Lord, O my
Lord, I *am* not eloquent, neither heretofore, nor since thou hast spoken
unto thy servant: but I *am* slow of speech, and of slow tongue. And the
Lord said unto him, Who has made man's mouth? or who makes the
dumb, or deaf, or the seeing, or the blind? have not I the Lord?" In spite
of God's reproaches and assurances, Moses followed with difficulty the
instructions leading to the liberation of Israel from the hands of
Egyptians.

In Surah 20:26–29 of the *Koran,* we read the message and Moses's
words changed: "*Moses* answered, Lord, enlarge my breast, and make
what thou commanded me easy unto me: and loose the knot of my
tongue, that they may understand my speech."[34]

We do not know whether Feng Zhi read the *Koran* or not, but he
certainly had in his hand at least a quotation from Goethe's letter
(presumably of 10 July 1872) to Johann Gottfried Herder (1744–1803),
in which Goethe reproduced the first part (verse 26) of Mohammed's
version in the translation by David Friedrich Megerlin: "O mein Herr
mache mir Raum in meiner eigen Brust."[35] Feng Zhi's translation of this
verse into Chinese is exact: "*Zhu a, gei wo xiazhaide xiong yi
kongjian.*"[36] When using these words from Mohammed's and Goethe's

prayer in another of his sonnets, number 22, Feng Zhi proceeded unlike Goethe and used Megerlin's rendition but, like Mohammed using Exodus, changed its message to some extent, and made out of it a supplication to the "omnipresent and great God":

> Dilate my narrow heart,
> that it may comprise the Great Universe.[37]

"Great Universe" (*dade yuzhou*) is nothing other than what I have called his astral universe, nurtured by "cosmic love" comprising all myriads of things in our world and outside of it, a kind of pantheistic *Deus sive Natura*.

There is some difference between the sites of the two prophets—Moses on the sacred Mount Sinai and Mohammed in the sacred valley Towa—and the thatched hut near eucalyptus-clad Kunming where Feng Zhi addressed his prayer to the same but differently apprehended God. Notwithstanding this fact, the mission of the then young Chinese poet axiologically did not fall behind the two prophets.

Feng Zhi's resolution was the same as that of one of the humblest, poorest but most eminent Chinese poets and thinkers—Tao Yuanming, probably the greatest Chinese poet between Qu Yuan (ca. 340–278 B.C.) and Li Bai (701–82 A.D.). Feng Zhi, in quoting the two lines from Tao Yuanming concerning the myriad of creatures taking refuge with him, alludes to his forerunner as a paradigm of great personality, a "high-minded recluse"[38] living in poor conditions, in cold and hunger, but never compromising his ethical and aesthetic ideals.

It is a pity that Feng Zhi's poetry, especially his volume of sonnets, has received only scant attention and therefore has not contributed much to the spiritual renewal of those who should become its addressees.[39] It is also a pity that Feng Zhi in his old age (at least during the ill-famed Cultural Revolution and its aftermath) put aside the ideals that in his youth and adult years connected him with Moses, Tao Yuanming, Hafiz, and Goethe.

Notes

1. Marián Gálik, *Milestones in Sino-Western Literary Confrontation, 1898–1979* (Bratislava, Wiesbaden: Veda-Otto Harrassowitz, 1986), 183.

2. Ibid. and Marián Gálik, "Feng Zhi e il suo sonetto veneziano," *Catai* 2–3 (1982–83): 23–31.

3. Cf. Feng Zhi, "Xu" (Preface), in *The Sonnets* (Hong Kong: Sinology Book Center, 1971), 1, and Dominic Cheung, *Feng Chih* (Boston: Twayne Publishers, 1979), 77. The Chinese edition I used is a reprint of the Wenhua shenghuo publication, Hong Kong, 1949. My translation here is taken from Professor Cheung with minor changes.

4. Fung Yu-lan, *Chuang Tzu* (Shanghai: Commercial Press, 1933), 27.

5. Burton Watson, trans., *The Complete Works of Chuang Tzu* (New York: Columbia University Press, 1968), 31.

6. Max Kaltenmark, *Lao Tzu and Taoism* (Stanford: Stanford University Press, 1969), 94.

7. Cf. David Hawkes, trans., *Ch'u Tz'u. The Songs of South* (Oxford: Clarendon Press, 1959), 81–87.

8. Feng Zhi, *The Sonnets*, 27–28. The rhyme scheme of the sonnet is as follows: abba, cddc, efg, efg. For sonnets in modern Chinese poetry, see Xu Ting and Lu Dejuan, "Shisihang ti zai Zhongguo" [22], *Zhongguo xiandai wenxue yanjiu congkan* (Series in modern Chinese literature) 3 (1986): 135–54, and "Zaitan shisihang ti zai Zhongguo," *Zhongguo xiandai wenxue yanjiu congkan* 2 (1992): 186–94.

9. Dominic Cheung, *Feng Chih*, 83.

10. Cf. ibid., i–ii and 82.

11. Cf. Feng Zhi, "What I Have Learned From Abroad," *Waiguo wenxue pinglun* (Revue of foreign literature) 2 (1987): 5–6, and Wang Yao (comment.), *Tao Yuanming ji* (Tao Yuanming's works) (Peking: Zuojia Publishers, 1956), 81. The translation of the two lines is taken from James Robert Hightower, trans., *The Poetry of T'ao Ch'ien* (Oxford: Clarendon Press, 1970), 203.

12. Feng Zhi, "What I Have Learned From Abroad," 6.

13. Marián Gálik, *Milestones*, 67.

14. Feng Zhi, "What I Have Learned From Abroad," 4.

15. Ibid., 6.

16. Said H. Abdel-Rahim, *Goethe und der Islam*, diss., Free University, Berlin, Augsburg, 1969, pp. 199 and 414.

17. Will Durant, *The Story of Philosophy* (New York: Garden City Publishing Co. Inc., 1933), 227.

18. Ibid.

19. Said H. Abdel-Rahim, *Goethe und der Islam,* 193.

20. Ibid.

21. *Goethes sämtliche Werke in sechsunddreißig Bänden,* band 3. (Stuttgart: Cotta'sche Buchhandlung, n.d.), n.p. Here follows the approximate, poetic translation into English: "Tell it no man but the sages, / Since to scorn mobs oft are turning: / Life I'll praise on all my pages, / That for death in flame is yearning. / / In the cool of nights of loving- / Getting thee as thou begettest- / Feelings strange o'er thee are moving, / Where the quiet light thou settest. / / Thou'rt no longer in the mazes / Of a darksome obscuration, / And a new desire upraises / Thee to higher procreation. / / Though hindered by no distance, / Comest flying, spellbound, turned / To the light without resistance- / In the flame thou, moth, art burned. / / Till this thought has thee possessed: /'Die and be born over!' / Thou art but a sorry guest, / On this earth a rover." See Karl Viëtor, *Goethe. The Poet* (Cambridge, Mass.: Harvard University Press), 223.

22. Feng Zhi, "Zizhuan" (Autobiography), in *Zhongguo xiandai zuojia zhuanlue* (Short biographies of modern Chinese writers) (Chongqing: Sichuan People's Publishing House, 1981), 1:143.

23. Feng Zhi, "Yuexia huange" (Lovesong under the moon), in *Beiyou ji qita* (Northern journey and other poems) (Peking: Chenzhongshe Publishers, 1929), 93. This stanza is extracted from *Feng Zhi xuanji* (Selected works of Feng Zhi) (Chengdu: Sichuan wenyi Publishers, 1985), 1:109–11.

24. Cf. Dominic Cheung, *Feng Chih*, 83, and Wolfgang Kubin, *Die Sonette des Feng Zhi* (Bonn: Inter Nationes, 1987), 48.

25. Cf. Dominic Cheung, *Feng Chih,* 83, and Marián Gálik, *Milestones*, 199. Cf. also Goat Koei Lang-Tan, "Der Geist der deutschen Romantik in der Dichtung Feng Zhis," in Adrian Hsia und Sigfrid Hoefert (hrsg.), *Fernöstliche Brückenschläge* (Bern: Peter Lang, 1992), 108.

26. Feng Zhi, "Qianshi Gede shi shisan shou" (An experiment with explaining thirteen poems by Goethe), in *Lun Gede* (On Goethe) (Shanghai: Wenyi Publishers, 1982), 142.

27. Ibid., 64.

28. Said H. Abdel-Rahim, *Goethe und der Islam,* 249.

29. Ibid.

30. Matt. 5:13_14.

31. *Faust*, part 1, trans. by Philip Wayne (Harmondsworth: Penguin Books, 1986), 31. "Motley rabble" in Goethe's original sounds as *bunte Menge*.

32. Konrad Burdach (hrsg.), *Goethes sämtliche Werke. Jubiläums-Ausgabe in 40 Bänden. Band 5* (Stuttgart-Berlin, n.d.), 322. This very good review of different opinions concerning the *Spiritual Yearning* presents the study "'Selige Sehnsucht' and Goethean Enlightenment" by Robert Ellis Dye, Publications of the Modern Language Association of America, 104 (January 1989), pp. 190–200, where the arguments by Emil Staiger, Dorothea Hölscher-Lohmeyer, Ewald Rösch, Wilhelm Emrich, Ronald Gray, and others are critically evaluated. If the poem under analysis is not the "most difficult" in Goethe's poetry, then due to the "disagreement over its meaning, the insufficiency of all attempts at translation, and the paucity of comprehensive interpretations indicate that it is in fact difficult" (ibid., 190). According to Dye, Goethe's writing "is paratactic, dialectical, and self-referentially productive of a scintillating, many-colored intertextual web, articulating personal continuance through continuous metamorphosis in one context" where even the same text "may generate readings at opposite ends of several axes" (ibid., 197). After my own experience with Goethe's text and context, I regard my own explanation chiefly as a personal conviction.

33. Said H. Abdel-Rahim, *Goethe und der Islam,* 249.

34. The citation is taken from *The Koran Commonly Called The Alkoran of Mohammed. Translated into English from the Original Arabic by George Sale* (London: Frederic Warne and Co., n.d.), 234. It is possible that Goethe knew and read this translation, which appeared first in 1734. Cf. Said H. Abdel-Rahim, *Goethe und der Islam,* 43.

35. Said H. Abdel-Rahim, *Goethe und der Islam,* 48.

36. Feng Zhi, "What I Have Learned From Abroad," 7.

37. Feng Zhi, *The Sonnets*, 46.

38. James Robert Hightower, *The Poetry of T'ao Ch'ien*, 204.

39. The best piece of criticism among Feng Zhi's compatriots was undoubtedly a long essay by Li Guangtian (1906–68) entitled "Shenside shi. Lun Feng Zhide 'Shisihang ji'" (Poetry of spiritual thought) On Feng Zhi's 'The Sonnets'," (Hong Kong: Huiwenge shu dian Publishers, 1972), 71–100, originally published in *Shide yishu* (Art of poetry) (Kaiming shudian Publishers, 1943). Li Guangtian's article ends with a tercet from Goethe's sonnet from his drama *Was wir bringen* (What we bring): "Who wants to

achieve something great, / he should pluck up his courage. / A man who restrains himself becomes a champion, / and the order only gains him freedom" (*Goethes sämtliche Werke in sechsunddreißig Bänden,* band 8, 242).

Dystopia as an Alternative Historical Hypothesis of Eutopia:

The Life Histories of Eutopia in *Animal Farm* and *A Utopian Dream*

KOON-KI TOMMY HO

By definition, all eutopias are products of imagination and cannot be located on the spatial or temporal dimensions of human history. As products of human imagination, however, eutopias are inevitably closely related to human history. According to Darko Suvin, eutopia represents an alternative history and can be defined as a

> verbal construction [of society] whose necessary and sufficient conditions are the presence of a particular quasi-human community where sociopolitical institutions, norms and individual relationships are organized on a more perfect principle than in the author's community, this construction being based on estrangement arising out of an alternative historical hypothesis. (Suvin, "Defining the Literary Genre," 132; "The River-side Trees," 110; "The Alternate Islands," 242)

Suvin's definition immediately connects the eutopian imaginary world with the real world. Although eutopia is imaginary and therefore ahistorical, it is yet "historical" in the sense that it unfolds an alternative history that could be made possible by implementing a eutopian plan. It follows that a eutopia stands for what its eeutopist optimistically imagines human history should have worked out under a eutopian plan.

If a eutopia describes an imaginary and better alternative history of mankind, a dystopia depicts the other side of this better alternative history. That is to say, a dystopia provides a pessimistic but perhaps more realistic version of a eutopian alternative history. In the dystopist's depiction, this alternative history is not necessarily feasible; and even if a eutopia is realizable at first, the final product may not necessarily be desirable. In other words, the dystopist questions the feasibility and desirability of eutopia by providing an alternative historical hypothesis of eutopia itself. George Orwell and Mo Yingfeng are, in this sense, dystopian "historians."

Many eutopian stories begin in the middle of the history of a eutopia. That is to say, the authors do not show us how their particular eutopian societies have come into being. The history of the eutopia in such stories is therefore incomplete. *Animal Farm* (1945) by Orwell and *A Utopian Dream* (*Taoyuan meng*, literally, The dream of Peach Blossom Spring, 1987) by Mo, however, give a complete life history of a eu/dystopia, including its rise and fall. It is my aim in this article to compare the two versions of the eutopian alternative history in *Animal Farm* and *A Utopian Dream*, which incidentally can be seen as ramifications of the dystopian hypotheses of eutopia.

There is no question that *Animal Farm* contains historical elements. As Orwell himself confessed in the Preface to the Ukrainian edition of the novel, "Various episodes are taken from the actual history of the Russian Revolution" (Orwell, *CEJL*, 3:406). Matthew Hodgart even asserted that the story has a "point-to-point correspondence with the events of Russian history from 1917–1943" (138).

The story of *Animal Farm* is perhaps too well known to deserve a plot summary here. We may easily sum up the story in Orwell's own words, that it dramatizes a "history [of a swindle], in which the [animals] are first lured into revolt by the promise of Utopia, and then when they have done their job, enslaved over again by new masters" (*CEJL*, 4:177). In a nutshell, *Animal Farm* is a history of a eutopian revolution gone sour, so that everything in the end goes back to its historical origin. Thus, Manor Farm in the beginning becomes Manor Farm again at the end of the story. The only difference is that the human masters are replaced by the pigs. In such a way, Orwell seemed to suggest a cyclical concept of history, that history simply revolves round and round without any real progress, despite changes that can be made from time to time.

A Utopian Dream can be read as a dystopian parody of the two sacred Chinese eutopian prototypes, namely, the World of Grand Union and Peach Blossom Spring. The novel contains a complete history of the rise and fall of a eutopian community known as the Community of Benevolence. In the novel, Mo simply put a community embodying the eutopian ideals of the World of Grand Union and residing in an environment similar to that of the Peach Blossom Spring into a thought experiment.[1] The novel shows that such a eutopian experiment is neither feasible nor desirable in reality. While the story is about a history of gradual betrayal of a system of eutopian ideals, it is not the same process of "revolution gone sour" as in *Animal Farm*. Since the community finally destroys itself in an internal conflict, the story clearly indicates a linear concept of history in action.

Animal Farm is a "satirical beast fable" (Greenblatt, 62). The mode of narration of the novel has nothing to suggest that Orwell intended to write a historical allegory of the Russian Revolution. *A Utopian Dream*, however, looks like history because of its structure and mode of narration. If eutopian literature has something to do with history, *A Utopian Dream* comes closer to the genre of history than many other similar works. The narrator tells us in the Introduction to the novel that the story is based upon an authentic, oral report about the rise and fall of a eutopian community residing in a mysterious mountain area called Heaven beyond Heaven. Even though the reporter is insane, this oral report is believed to be a true record of the history of the eutopian community.

As if he wants to highlight the historical nature of the report, the narrator deliberately employs the generic style and form of classical Chinese official historical writings in recording the report. For this purpose, the narrator divides the novel into three parts: part 1, the beginning of the century (*shiji zhichu*); part 2, the biographies of the extraordinary men (*qiren liezhuan*); and part 3, requiem for the isolated land (*jueyu beige*).

It is impossible to go into a detailed account of classical Chinese historiography here. But, without some reference to classical Chinese historiography, a reader unfamiliar with its characteristics will miss the whole point of the narrative design of the novel.[2] It is generally agreed that the *Shiji,* or *Records of the Grand Historian,* by Sima Qian (145 B.C.-ca. 90 B.C.), laid down the generic paradigm of classical Chinese historiography, namely, *jizhuanti* or the Form of the (Imperial) Records and Biographies.[3]

Ji refers to *benji*, meaning the emperors' own biographies, whereas *zhuan* refers to *liezhuan*, meaning biographies of certain prominent figures in society. The seminal characteristic of this generic form is that the sequence of time is not the most important factor for the narration of history. Instead, history is unfolded through different biographies of individual important personae, ranging from members of the Royal Family to prominent figures in society. Readers acquire a whole or congruent picture of the history of a particular segment of time only when they integrate the relevant biographies.

The original Chinese titles of the three parts connote a connection between the mode of narration of *A Utopian Dream* and classical Chinese historiography. Both the words *ji* (in *shiji zhichu*) and (*lie*)*zhuan* (in *qiren liezhuan*) are found in the titles. The connection is further enhanced by the facts that the first part of the novel is actually the history of the foundation of the eutopian community as seen in the biography of the leader of the community and that this founder is also enshrined with the mythological elements that are commonly ascribed to founders of a dynasty. As such, this part highly resembles a *benji*. Moreover, as the title of the second part indicates, this part contains a series of biographies of some important members of the community and is actually called *liezhuan*. It is submitted that the narrator intends to adopt the generic form of official Chinese history, with a view to inducing readers to com-pare the history of the eutopian community with the history of the People's Republic of China (to be elaborated).

Both Orwell and Mo described the birth of their eutopias as sponta-neous and impulsive instead of carefully planned. In *Animal Farm*, although the eutopian blueprint has been vaguely outlined by Old Major and then developed by the three leading pigs into a system of thought known as Animalism, the revolution itself springs not from theory but from natural need and impulse (Lee, 562; Smyer, 58) and "the revolution [was] successfully carried through" "almost before [the animals] knew what was happening" (*Animal Farm*, 19).

Likewise, the eutopian community in *A Utopian Dream* is not a direct product of ideological formulation but a result of a contingent move of the eutopians. They retreat to Heaven beyond Heaven not because they wish to build a eutopia there but becaue they wish to escape from a gang of bandits who have constantly persecuted them. Although the leader of the community, Dragon[4] (*Lung Juzheng*, literally a dragon living at the center of the universe), does all along have a primitive eutopian vision in mind, he has never thought about turning it into reality.

His eutopian vision was inspired by a primer entitled *Trimetrical Classic* (*Sanziji*, literally, Three-character book), formerly the first text-book given to children for the purposes of teaching them basic Chinese characters in the traditional Chinese education system. The first two lines of the classic read like this: "In the beginning of human history man was born with a benevolent nature." Dragon's eutopian theory is based on an interpretation of these two lines and its elaboration. When he was eigh-teen years old, he "made a prophecy that the principle of benevolence would one day prevail in the world. Then, society would return to the beginning of human history when men were all of benevolent nature" (*A Utopian Dream*, 4). The eutopian world that Dragon prophesies is a rem-iniscence of the classical Chinese eutopian prototype, namely, the World of Grand Union.

It is interesting to note that, while Old Major's eutopian vision comes from a dream, Dragon's eutopian vision is inspired by a preschool primer. Such origins suggest that they do not deserve to be taken seriously. It seems that Orwell and Mo wanted to make the point that all eutopias are ultimately untested, historical hypotheses of their authors.

While Animal Farm is born after a blood-shedding revolution, the eutopian community at Heaven beyond Heaven also goes through a baptism of fire and blood. The eutopians, consisting of four families and twenty-one members, retreat to Heaven beyond Heaven in order to avoid the persecution of a gang of bandits, but in so doing they are forced to fight and to kill for the purpose of self-defense. After they decide to settle down at Heaven beyond Heaven, the families start to fight among themselves for the best land available for farming. The internal hostilities cease only when Dragon loses his arm in trying to stop one member from attacking another with an ax. The bloody scenes that precede the birth of these two eutopias suggest that the eutopian stage must inevitably be achieved by means that are contrary to the ideals that the eutopias themselves uphold. In *A Utopian Dream*, the transition is more of a dramatic irony because the eventual eutopian community calls itself the Community of Benevolence and upholds a principle of benevolence that is extended even to the level of animals so that they all become vegetarians in order not to kill any life.

A eutopian revolution may be led by impulse and accomplished by a temporary period of violence, whereas maintaining a eutopia relies upon long-term planning and efficient solutions to practical problems. It is through the maintenance of the eutopias that the two societies gradually turn into dystopias.

At the inception of Animal Farm, in the allocation of duties, the pigs have already assumed the roles of leader and supervisor, those who manage and direct but do not actually participate in the work. An aristocratic class arises immediately and spontaneously from the originally classless animal society. In order to defend Animal Farm, Snowball has to learn the tricks and vices of his human enemies so as to counteract them. After the expulsion of Snowball, the animals find that they need materials that cannot be produced on the farm, leading Napoleon to order trade relations with their former enemies. In the process of maintaining their eutopia, the pigs betray the ideals of Old Major, at first surrendering their principles to the practical needs of their society and then to their own selfish ends.

A similar gradual betrayal of eutopian ideals takes place in the history of the Community of Benevolence. As time passes and the population grows, the principle of benevolence that Dragon preaches is soon proven to be inadequate for regulating the social order. Benevolence without discrimination is also found to be not always desirable. Gardenia (*Zhimei*), the benevolent woman, shows benevolence to a baby cow that has survived its parents by breast-feeding the calf. The result, however, is that her own baby dies of starvation because the calf consumes all the milk Gardenia is able to produce. Gardenia is, nevertheless, rewarded by Dragon, who confers upon her the honorific title of "Benevolent Woman."

Further problems arise when Gardenia's benevolent action and the reward she receives inspire Hempstalk (*Magan*) to mate with the cow. Born deformed but determined to become prominent in society, Hempstalk decides to carry out this notion of a benevolent action in the hope that he will also be given some favorable recognition. Hempstalk's choice shows the absurd and possibly tragic result of encouraging "benevolent" actions without discrimination.

Dragon, in his principle of benevolence, has not allowed for any contingencies. He is found to be totally useless when disciplinary action is required to regulate the social order. Problems multiply when a dissenting figure, Cucumber (*Guoqing*), comes onstage. Cucumber is not a really bad person, but he enjoys a carnivorous diet, contrary to the community's vegetarian lifestyle, and he does not readily accept Dragon's authority.

As in Animal Farm, reforms must be introduced in the Community of Benevolence to deal with the problems inherent in its philosophy such as those brought on by Hempstalk and Cucumber. The reforms are initiated by First-born (*Tousheng*), who represents the leader of the second generation, corresponding to Napoleon in Animal Farm. Under the principle of benevolence, if Gardenia gets a reward after she stands in loco parentis to the calf, Hempstalk should also be given some kind of recognition after he serves as the "husband" of the cow. But, if the man-cow mating is rewarded, humanity will be degraded. First-born grasps the horns of the dilemma by conferring upon Hempstalk the title "Ox-man." In a way, the title seems to reward Hempstalk for his "benevolent" action. At the same time, the title reminds others that such action is against Nature. By his nomenclature, First-born twists the meaning of "benevolence" as the pigs alter the Seven Commandments of Animalism.

The Rite of Benevolence (*quanshanli*, literally, a rite to persuade someone to do good), introduced to cure the problems brought about by Cucumber, marks another twist in the meaning of benevolence. There is actually no benevolent element at all in the rite. It consists in locking Cucumber in a stone house and subjecting him without any food or rest to mechanical admonition by some performers. No matter how much

Cucumber protests, the performers simply repeat the lines of admonition. As a result, Cucumber dies in three days. It is true that the rite does not involve any violence or physical punishment, but its effect is even worse than ordinary corporal chastisement. It is also true that the rite cannot accurately be described as punishment in its usual meaning. By this device, First-born manages to circumvent the prohibitions against punishment that existed under the principle of benevolence. Although stability of the community is temporarily restored with the death of Cucumber, no one will really agree that the result of the rite is consistent with Dragon's vision for the Community of Benevolence.

Conferring the title of Ox-man on Hempstalk and introducing the Rite of Benevolence to Cucumber can be understood as reforms that are necessarily brought into play in the process of maintaining the community. These reforms can be compared with the reforms by the pigs in Animal Farm. No matter whether the motives behind such reforms are benevolent or malevolent, a common implication is that the eutopian ideals have to be amended sooner or later in response to needs and changes in society.

The need for change or reform in any society actually poses a fundamental challenge to all eutopian planning where change has not been envisaged in advance. It may be correct to say that a static society will ensure the preservation of its original eutopian ideals. The difficulty is that no eutopist is able to anticipate all possible contingencies and therefore provide all possible solutions beforehand. Any changes or reforms introduced to cope with unforeseen problems necessarily kill the original eutopia. The eutopian projects in *Animal Farm* and *A Utopian Dream* are consequently violated by the reforms introduced well before the endings of the stories. The latter parts of the novels simply initiate the final phases of the process by which the two once-eutopian societies are converted into real dystopias.

In *Animal Farm*, the revolution eventually comes full circle. Animal Farm becomes Manor Farm again, with the animals leading a life even more deplorable than that before the revolution. History goes back to its very beginning. For the Community of Benevolence, a civil war breaks out, and the result is that all but one member, the reporter of this story, are killed. Here, history appears as a river of no return.

Ironically, the ending of *Animal Farm,* also the (anti)climax of the story, takes place when the pigs walk on their hind legs and hold whips in their trotters. This is the first time in history when animals (although only one kind of them) and men are on an equal footing and no longer distinguishable. It also proves that animals can manage a farm as well as, or even better than, human beings, which is an ideal that underpins Animalism. In this sense, Old Major's eutopian ideals are not totally a castle in the sky, and the animals' efforts are not totally futile. Some achievements have at least been made toward the eutopian end.

In *A Utopian Dream*, on the other hand, the ending, or (anti) climax, is a dramatic irony: the only member left alive has an identical eutopian dream every night in which the slaughtered members of the community revive and live at ease in a Cockaigne-like harmony. While the efforts toward realizing a eutopia in the real world have totally failed, this member manages to build a replacement in his imagination. It may be that, while the author rationally rejected the feasibility of eutopia, he yet retained a nostalgia for the myth of eutopia, suggesting that the eutopian dream is part of human nature itself. Or, the ending may imply instead that the proper place for a eutopia to exist is in the imagination.

We may now return to the relationships between the two novels and real history. Orwell confessed that his intention in writing *Animal Farm* was to employ a historical allegory so as to expose "the Soviet myth in a story that could be easily understood by almost anyone" (*CEJL*, 3:405). Orwell should be happy to learn that the Soviet Union fell apart a few decades after publication of his novel and that communism has become a faded eutopian glory in Europe.

Since Mo Yingfeng imitated the generic style of classical Chinese history, it is at least arguable that he intended that his readers should read the novel as a historical allegory. If that is the case, it is legitimate to draw comparisons between the story and the history of the People's Republic of China. The principle of benevolence stands in stark contrast with Marxist-Leninist-Maoist tenets, particularly in Dragon's eutopian theory that "man is born with a benevolent nature," and with the theory of class determinism prevailing during the Cultural Revolution, as exemplified by the slogan "Dragons give birth to dragons, phoenixes give birth to phoenixes, and mice give birth to offsprings which can burrow." Both societies reveal the absurdity of the "virtues" of self-denial which are encouraged for the sake of collective goals in the two societies. Certain leaders of the People's Republic resemble such absurd heroes as Gardenia, the Benevolent Woman, Hempstalk, the deformed Ox-man, and the famous Chinese eutopian hero Lei Feng.[5]

Although the two authors drew their materials largely from history, they seem to have had a broader view than merely to demythologize communist myths and to expose the potential dangers inherent in all eutopian endeavors. Each work dramatized the actual transformation of a eutopia in real life. Their dramatizations reveal that eutopias may not provide a better future for mankind but perhaps even an alternative worse than past history. As such, they express the true spirit of anti-eutopianism in the twentieth century.

Works Cited

Greenblatt, Stephan Jay. *Three Modern Satirists: Waugh, Orwell, and Huxley.* New Haven & London: Yale University Press, 1965.

Han, Yu-shan. *Elements of Chinese Historiography.* Hollywood: W. H. Harvey, 1955.

Ho, Koon-ki T. "Several Thousand Years in Search of Happiness: The Utopian Tradition in China." *Oriens Extremus* 30 (1983–86): 19–35.

Hodgart, Matthew. "From *Animal Farm* to *Nineteen Eighty-four.*" Edited by Miriam Gross. In *The World of George Orwell,* 136–421. London: Weindenfeld and Nicolson, 1971.

Lee, Robert. "The Uses of Form: A Reading of *Animal Farm.*" *Studies in Short Fiction* 6 (1969): 557–73.

Mo, Yingfeng. *Taoyuan Meng* (A utopian dream). Beijing: Renmin chubanshe, 1987. Cited within the text as *A Utopian Dream.*

Orwell, George. *Animal Farm.* Harmondsworth: Penguin Books in association with Martin Secker & Warburg, 1977.

———. *The Collected Essays, Journalism and Letters of George Orwell.* Edited by Sonia Orwell and Ian Angus. 4 Vols. New York: Harcourt, 1968. Cited within the text as *CEJL.*

Smyer, Richard I. "*Animal Farm:* The Burden of Consciousness." *English Language Notes* 9 (1971): 55–59.

Suvin, Darko. "The Alternate Islands: A Chapter in the History of SF, with a Select Bibliography on the SF of Antiquity, the Middle Ages, and the Renaissance." *Science-Fiction Studies* 3 (1976): 239–48.

———. "Defining the Literary Genre of Utopia: Some Historical Semantics, Some Gemology, A Proposal and A Plea." *Studies in the Literary Imagination* 6.2 (fall 1973): 123–45.

———. "The River-side Trees, or SF and Utopia: Degrees of Kinship." *Minnesota Review* 2 & 3 (1974): 108–15.

Notes

1. For a brief account of the World of Grand Union and Peach Blossom Spring as utopias, see my article "Several Thousand Years in Search of Happiness: The Utopian Tradition in China."

2. For a brief account of Chinese historiography, see Han Yu-shan, *Elements of Chinese Historiography.*

3. The twenty-four Dynastic Histories, which are the official historical records compiled to cover the entire history of China from the time of Sima Qian to the Qing Dynasty, were also written in this generic form.

4. Since most of the names of the characters in the novel have certain meanings, I prefer to translate the names according to their meanings instead of simply romanizing them. In this case, *"Lung"* is translated as "dragon."

5. Lei Feng is a well-known hero idealized by Mao Zedong and the Communist Party since 1963. He represents, inter alia, a totally unselfish and altruistic figure. He has been made a model for emulation in a number of political movements in the nearly thirty years' history of the PRC.

High Finance in Emile Zola and Mao Tun

YIU-NAM LEUNG

Opinion is divided on whether a genuine naturalist movement ever existed in China. The author whose novels come closest to conforming with the work of his Western predecessors is Shen Yen-ping, who wrote in the second quarter of the twentieth century under the pen name Mao Tun. Mao Tun's portrayal of the breakdown in Chinese society leading to the rise of communism comprises the background of his novel *Midnight*, which in this aspect parallels the exposition, in Emile Zola's *L'Argent,* of the final years of the Second Empire in France and the origins of the Third Republic. Another major resemblance consists in the depiction of the financial worlds of Paris and Shanghai, respectively. Less obvious in both novels is an underlying sympathy for workers and poorly paid clerks, a feature of much naturalist fiction.

Midnight was originally published in Shanghai in 1933,[1] and a later edition was brought out by the People's Literature Publishing House in 1955, from which an English translation was made and published in 1957 and a reprint in 1979.[2] Since I shall be dealing with *Midnight* in its English version, I shall likewise quote from the English translation of Zola's *L'Argent*.[3]

Mao Tun has denied that he wrote *Midnight* under Zola's influence, and most critics have accepted his demurral. When queried on the subject, he replied emphatically that there was no direct connection between his work and Zola's.[4] On another occasion, he remarked that, although he was very fond of Zola, he had not read all of *Les Rougon-Macquart,* the chain novel or collection of separate novels of which *Money* is one link. Of its twenty volumes, Mao Tun claims to have read only five or six, not including *Money*.[5] Obviously, however, he was subject to many of the same literary and ideological trends that enter into Zola's works.

Shortly after publication of his first novel, *Eclipse*, Mao Tun compared Zola with Tolstoy, indicating that the former "explored human conditions because he wanted to be a novelist," while the latter "started to write novels only after he experienced the vicissitudes of life." He summarized Zola's attitude toward life as "cool detachment" and Tolstoy's as "warm embrace," and characterized the works of both men as "criticisms of and reflections on reality." Mao Tun indicated that at one time he "enthusiastically propagandized for naturalism," but when he tried his own hand at writing, it was Tolstoy who comprised the major source.[6] In these remarks, Mao Tun overlooks the strong currents of humanitarianism in Zola and fails to take into account the many divergences from strict scientific analysis in the latter's works. A prominent example is the highly romantic attachment between the youthful lovers Silvere and Miette in the first volume of Zola's *Rougon-Macquart* saga.

Two major differences separate Mao Tun from Zola. The French author wrote most of *Les Rougon-Macquart* before attempting a definition of naturalism in his treatises *Le roman sentimental* (1880) and *Les romanciers naturalistes* (1881). His theory, therefore, was based squarely on his own practical experience in the creative process. Mao Tun, however, wrote his theoretical articles on naturalism before he had written a single line of his novels, and his concepts were derived at second or third hand from Western critics, chiefly German and American. His critical work "Naturalism and Contemporary Chinese Fiction" (1922) was published eleven years before *Midnight*.[7]

The second difference is structural. Zola's *Money* is the seventh in the series of novels comprising *Les Rougon-Macquart*, and it utilizes some of the same characters as those in the previous and later ones in the series. Although *Money* can be read as an entity, complete in itself, it is essentially an episode in a massive historical framework. Mao Tun's *Midnight*, to the contrary, is a self-contained narrative of conventional length with no links in plot or character to forerunners or followers.

A number of articles in Chinese and English have been written on Mao's naturalism, but they deal entirely with his theory and almost completely ignore his practice.[8] They tell us what Mao Tun said about naturalism before he became a novelist in his own right, but they do not analyze his fiction in order to reveal his practice. They give no hint as to whether Mao Tun followed the techniques of Zola or developed his own special methods of portraying human nature. The best of these critical articles is the first and most extensive, "Naturalism: A Changing Concept," an early study by the Czechoslovakian sinologue Marián Gálik.[9] Although his title does not so indicate, Gálik's purpose is to study the sources of Chinese naturalism as a literary phenomenon originating in the

West with Mao Tun as its principal exponent. Gálik traces naturalism from Zola to Mao Tun with German, Japanese and American critics as intermediaries. [10]

Gálik reveals that Mao Tun's knowledge of naturalism in 1922, when he wrote his critical articles on the subject, was not based on a reading of Zola but on theoretical statements by other critics: a German, Arno Holz; a Japanese, Shimamura Hogetsu; and an American, F. W. Chandler. In an article on the German naturalist Gerhardt Hauptmann, Mao Tun included a definition of naturalism, based on philosophical materialism, that has been widely quoted:

> First, there is the teaching about the struggle for life and the survival of the fittest; second, the teaching of the biological equality of the sexes; third, the conception of environment and heredity as boundless forces. . . . The life of the people who are defeated in the struggle for life is the commonest form of life in our time, hence this is the form that must be described. . . . [A]nd since men are situated in one environment under the burden of one great heredity, the naturalist believes in mechanistic determinism. [11]

Gálik reveals that this definition is almost identical to a passage in a book by F. W. Chandler, *Aspects of Modern Drama* (1919). The rest of Gálik's article indicates that Mao Tun's knowledge of naturalism in 1922 came to him primarily from this and other secondary sources. The closest direct link between Zola and Mao Tun from the perspective of theory exists in another 1922 article by Mao Tun, "The Danger of Zolaism," with a mark of interrogation following the title, in which he expresses faith in Zola's narrative technique. [12] Here, Mao Tun affirms: "The essential trait of Zolaism is a scientific descriptive method. Write what you see, don't attempt to cover up ugly things with a beautiful cloak! This is what they [the naturalists (Gálik's comment)] have in common. I believe there is nothing wrong in this fact, it has a long-term value."[13] Immediately after quoting this passage, Gálik concludes, "It appears very probable that Mao Tun's literary criticism of 1922 was influenced mostly by Chandler."

The basic plots of *Money* and *Midnight* are quite similar. *Money* concerns the manipulations of a stockbroker, Saccard, who succeeds in erecting a worldwide financial empire based on a number of companies that are sound in themselves, but the financial empire falls apart as Saccard allows its paper securities to exceed its solid assets. The reader's interest is sustained through the skillful delineation of the personality of the protagonist and of the minor characters who come under his sway. *Midnight* deals with the financial battles of an entrepreneur, Wu Sun-fu, in two directions: on a small scale, in connection with attempts to destroy the independence of the workers in a small factory he owns and controls; and on a large scale, in connection with attempts to influence the stock market in a consortium with two other speculators. He wins the battle against the workers in his factory but is cleaned out through his market transactions. Great human interest is aroused in accounts of the women workers in their valiant, but unsuccessful, efforts to organize and oppose Wu's wage-slashing policies.

The theme of both novels, the struggle for power through wealth, is one that developed in the nineteenth century as a consequence of the rise of industrial capitalism. By itself, this theme can hardly be considered typical of naturalism. The elements of naturalism enter when the theme is intertwined with social and historical developments such as Darwinism, Marxism, and various scientific discoveries.

A further element of naturalism is the concentration on the lower classes of mankind, the proletariat of the city rather than the peasantry of the country. Although most naturalist authors sought an attitude of objectivity, they highlighted poverty, oppression, and disease in their portrayal of social conditions and described workers' efforts toward reform, resistance, and revolution.

Theoretically, it would be possible for a novel with none of the characteristics of naturalism to be written on the theme of the rise of capitalism, but it is unlikely that any naturalist novel could be written without some influence of Zola. Although Mao Tun did not specifically rank himself as a disciple of Zola, he not only proclaimed himself a naturalist but led the movement to promote the concept in China. Since he devoted ten years to literary criticism, mainly of authors associated with naturalism, before writing a novel of his own, it is logical to separate his theoretical opinions from his practice. He was closer to Zola in theory than in practice. According to David Der-wei Wang, Mao Tun favored contemporary naturalistic writing over traditional Chinese fiction because of its exposing of social reality from a moral perspective.[14] It vindicated individual dignity and social justice in contrast to the vulgar and inhumane standards upheld by Chinese tradition.

The English edition of *Midnight* contains as a preface an excerpt from a lecture about this novel given by Mao Tun to a group of students in 1929. Here he says that the idea for the work had come to him nine years previously in Shanghai as a result of his dissatisfaction with the articles then being written about the characteristics of Chinese society. He felt that he could give new information by combining his previous knowledge of industrialists, civil servants, businessmen, and bankers with his later observations of the fierce struggles then being waged on behalf of the full-scale revolutionary movement. He planned his novel to portray three groups: industrialists, the working class, and imperialists. The industrialists threatened by the international capitalists were forced brutally to exploit the workers; the workers were obliged to resist fiercely; and the national capitalists were forced to surrender to the imperialists.

The novel does not openly favor the working classes or the rising Communist party. This may have been part of Mao Tun's acceptance of the theory of scientific objectivity required by the naturalists. In his lecture, however, he gives a different explanation: the extremely severe censorship of the reactionary government of the time. "If I had given a full, frank account of the activities of the revolutionaries I would never have got the book published" (iv). In some passages of the novel, Mao Tun even seems to combat revolutionary ideology. After one of the characters gives a tirade loaded with Marxist vocabulary, Mao Tun remarks that this "'formula' sounded simple, clear and 'reasonable,' and along with a lot of other jargon, had been firmly memorized" to be instilled into workers "whose simple minds and warm hearts were just the right sort of fertile soil for 'formulas' of this kind" (356).

Although very few positive examples have been discovered of any direct influence of Zola upon Mao Tun either before or after 1922, many general and theoretical relationships between the two authors may, nevertheless, be discerned. The most important, of course, concerns the essence of literary naturalism. In the preface to *Les Rougon-Macquart*, Zola wrote,

> I hope to explain how a family, a small group of beings, reacts on a society in spreading out by giving birth to ten or twenty individuals who appear at first sight to be profoundly unlike but when analyzed are shown to be intimately linked, one to the others. Heredity like weight has its own laws. I shall try to discover and to follow, in resolving the dual question of temperaments and milieux, the thread that leads from one man to another. And when I shall hold all the threads, when I shall have an entire social organization within my hands, I shall reveal the group as comparable to an actor in a historical period. I shall show it struggling in the complexity of its efforts; I shall at the same time analyze the sum of the wills of each one of its members and the general thought of the whole. (1:3)

These lines encompass a famous theoretical scheme of the great French critic of the nineteenth century Hippolyte Taine, who argued that literary creation was the result of three main causes: race, moment, and milieu— equivalent to heredity, historical period, and milieux in Zola's preface. Zola adds to these a fourth element, the struggle for survival.

As I have already indicated, Mao Tun in 1922 described naturalism in

similar terms as arising from philosophical materialism. "We can speak
of three sources: first, the teaching about struggle for life and the survival
of the fittest; second, the teaching of the biological equality of the sexes;
third, the conception of environment and heredity as boundless forces."[15]
Even though, as Gálik has shown, these ideas came to Mao Tun in an
indirect manner, they are, nevertheless, generally associated with Zola.
Gálik has also shown that, of these three elements, Mao Tun considered
milieu as the most important.[16] Zola, in keeping with the philosophical
principles outlined in his preface, gave his chain novel *Les Rougon-
Macquart* the subtitle "Histoire naturelle et sociale d'une famille sous le
Second Empire" (Natural and social history of a family under the Second
Empire), but it could also be described as a naturalistic history of a
family during a period of significant social change.

Zola himself made no attempt to distinguish naturalism from its
predecessor, realism, although the elements of heredity and struggle for
survival, mentioned in his preface, are sufficient to distinguish them. He
considered naturalism as the application to literature of positivism, a
philosophical method originated by Auguste Comte. The essence of
positivism consists in regarding all phenomena as subject to invariable
natural laws and seeking to discover and schematize these laws. In one of
the early novels in *Les Rougon-Macquart*, Zola speaks of the positivism
of art as "modern art, completely experimental and completely material-
ist" (1:776). This emphasis on science led Zola and most other naturalists
to embrace philosophical determinism and Darwinian evolution. Some
critics have affirmed that naturalism can be separated from realism in the
novel only when the environment is considered more important than the
characters, that is, when the environment displaces the protagonist as the
central feature. This is merely another way of describing Taine's element
of milieu. Although Mao Tun agrees that milieu is the most important of
the three elements, it plays a greater role in Zola's novels than in his
own.

In his essay "Naturalism and Contemporary Chinese Fiction," Mao
Tun maintains that the novels of Chinese naturalists do not necessarily
introduce sordid aspects of life. "Western naturalist novels expose only
the animal side of humanity in terms of determinism and are full of despair and pathos. But this is due to the fact that life in nineteenth century
Europe is ugly, subordinated to the fate of mechanical materialism."[17]
Mao Tun's supposition that the ugliness of life in Europe was responsible
for the portrayal of the "animal side of humanity" is wide of the mark.
This feature of naturalism derives directly from Zola's conception of the
experimental novel as a kindred phenomenon to experimental science—
that the study of man in the abstract, the metaphysical man, "gives way

to the study of *natural man*, man submitted to the laws of physics, chemistry, and physiology." Because of the latter factor, naturalism has been associated with the portrayal of sex, particularly aspects hidden from common gaze. Authors and critics with a puritanical bias have reacted against this feature, objecting, with Henry James, that "the real has not a single shade more affinity with an unclean vessel than with a clean one."[18] As I shall show later, Mao Tun, when he came to write his own novel, was just as willing as Zola to introduce sexual interludes, whether for titillation or for illustrating man's animal nature.

Joseph S. M. Lau has expressed the opinion that "*Midnight*'s only legitimate claim to naturalistic realism rests in its rigorous research and impeccable documentation on the stock market and industrial management."[19] Mao Tun himself had a great deal to say about this subject of documenting and collecting material, devoting an entire chapter to the subject in his manual for writers *Preparation to Creation* (1936). Here, he resolutely opposed those critics who affirmed that a writer must choose only those subjects about which he had personal experience. Admitting that such a relationship is the ideal one, he argued that, in China especially, it is not possible for a writer to have personal experience in every social sphere; the writer must, therefore, look beyond his own environment and collect material about other areas. He noted two methods for doing so, that of Zola and that of Chekhov.[20] Zola's method consisted of observing people in the target environment and conversing with them while at the same time consulting printed sources, both newspaper reports and books. According to Gálik, Mao Tun found this method "opportunistic" and indicative of an insufficiently sincere attitude toward life and art (136). Zola, moreover, "collected material for certain themes only and always at the time when he needed it," whereas Chekhov collected "continuously and strove to get closer to people and things which were outside the bonds of his own life's sphere" (137). Mao Tun criticized Chekhov on only one point: his recommending writers to take notes when undertaking a topic and using these notes when they became relevant. He "wanted the writer to return to his notes continually, to study them, compare them with reality and thus bring corrections to his original observation which need not have been correct" (137). Evidence shows that Zola's practice in the writing of *Money* produced impressive results. A single one of his notebooks, entitled "The Personnel of the Exchange," is filled with information supplied by one of his business acquaintances. "He explains the function of the exchange agents and their commissions, their customary phrases and gestures in conveying bids and offers; he explains precisely how prices are established, how transactions take place, the role of the price quoters, the functioning of the balance of activity between the floor and behind the scenes" and a host of other details (*Les Rougon-Macquart*, 5:1256). Zola read and made notes, which have survived, on the standard treatise on the exchange (5:1254–55), analyzed the records of a famous lawsuit over a stock-broking scheme, and interviewed two of the main financial minds of Paris who had personally followed the trial (5:1258). Mao Tun, on the other hand, seems to have derived his knowledge of the Shanghai exchange exclusively from personal experience. In the preface to *Midnight*, he indicates that in 1930, during the period of the Chinese civil war and labor demonstrations in Shanghai, he suffered from eye trouble and neurasthenia and so decided on a complete rest.

> Among my friends in Shanghai at that time were active revolutionaries and liberals, while old acquaintances from my home town included industrialists, civil servants, businessmen and bankers. Having little else to do then, I passed much of my time among them and learned from them much that had been unknown to me before and began to understand a little of what went on "behind the scenes." It struck me that all this new information might be put into a novel. (i)

This procedure has nothing in common with Chekhov's method, which Mao Tun recommends in his *Preparation to Creation*. Some critics have, nevertheless, considered Mao Tun's documentation in *Midnight* to be excessive. C. T. Hsia depicts the novel as "a work of tremendous research, impeccable in documentation, larded with allusions to topical figures, and crammed with political and economic facts," but concludes that "all this adds up to a work that is quite often irritating and boring."[21] Joseph S. M. Lau similarly charges that Mao Tun "squeezes into his book one technical detail after another whenever a chance for displaying his knowledge of the stock market offers itself. . . . We get page after page of unrelieved boredom . . . when Mao Tun the novelist is carried away by Mao Tun the amateur stock broker."[22] These commentators greatly exaggerate the amount of documentation in *Midnight*, which is meager compared to Zola's copiousness. Most of the transactions in *Midnight* take place over the telephone, and almost no information is given about the daily routine of the market and its personnel. In *Money*, however, every step in the buying and selling of stocks and the establishing of their prices both on the floor and behind the scenes is fully explained. *Midnight* has nothing to match the tenth chapter of *Money*, which provides a detailed and fascinating portrayal of the machinations of rival financial interests.

In addition to documentation, both authors write preliminary sketches for their respective novels. Zola's, which is titled merely *Ebauche*

(Sketch), consists of 100 manuscript pages, now conserved at the Biblio-thèque Nationale in Paris. Large extracts are published in notes to the Pléiade edition of the novel (*Les Rougon-Macquart,* 5:1243–54). Mao Tun also wrote an outline for *Midnight,* less detailed and circumstantial, which has never been reproduced in a Western language. Some notion of the differences between his outline and the actual text of the novel may be gleaned from the following extract. The complete text of the outline together with Mao Tun's own comment on these differences, covers twelve pages.

> A comparison between the outline and *Midnight* indicates that there are a lot of differences between them. For example, in addition to emphasizing the opportunistic mania of the stock exchange and labor strikes in my outline, I plan to spend some space in describing the relationship between the several transactions in the stock exchange and the war and the resulting change in situation. The struggle, whether open or secret, between the two major capi-talist groups is more fierce as it is stated in my outline. They even attempt to take such measures as kidnapping, assassination, and tracking down. How-ever, they befriend each other finally when they confront the Communists. Three labor strikes are scheduled in the outline, the third of which is evoked by Chao Po-tao. It is completely different from *Midnight.* In the outline, I also plan to describe in detail the labor strike headed by Li-san and the underground advisors for the workers in the labor strike. [23]

Opinion is divided over Mao Tun's treatment of social classes. Since naturalist writers customarily deal with the lower segments of society and since Mao Tun was a committed Communist, it has been assumed that he is more comfortable and more successful in portraying the proletariat than the bourgeoisie. C. T. Hsia affirms that Mao Tun reveals a "supercilious attitude toward the bourgeoisie" that "lacks the accent of passion or conviction."[24] "He tries merely to be aloof and superior, with the disastrous result that most of his bourgeois characters are only pup-pets, now and again occupying the stage with their expected patter and love-making" (158). Whether or not Mao Tun intended his portrayal to be realistic, satirical, or supercilious, he wrote consciously and purposely for a bourgeois audience. According to David Der-wai Wang, Mao Tun, in opposition "to Zola's concerns with the lower class people who are victimized by heredity and environment, . . . likes to treat the urban youth's spiritual crisis and eventual salvation through Marxism, and for this reason he was bitterly attacked by his fellow leftist writers as indulging in middle class sentimentalism."[25] Citing Mao Tun's article "From Kuling to Tokyo" (1928), Wang argues that Mao Tun assumed that educated youth would "become the key figure arousing a 'proletarian revolution'" and that he should, therefore, "write about *and* for young bourgeois intellectuals, since they have more potential to change their consciousness and act than do the common people in the given historical context" (191). In practice, Zola treated all levels of society in *Les Rougon-Macquart*, and *Money* in particular deals almost entirely with the bourgeois. *Midnight* is divided into two almost equal sections, one that treats the bourgeoisie, the other, the proletariat. Neither novel favors one class over the other. Zola wrote in his preliminary sketch, "To oppose the upper class and the poor class. Then the irresistible force of money, a lever that lifts the world. There is nothing but love and money" (*Les Rougon-Macquart*, 5:1244). In keeping with his naturalist thinking, Zola suggests that the bourgeois characters, like all the others, are the product of their heredity and environment, but Mao Tun does practically nothing in this direction. Actually, Zola reveals in *Money* more sympathy with the lower classes and much more support of Marxist theory than Mao Tun does in *Midnight*. By means of one of his characters, a disciple of Marx, whom the character is said to have known personally, Zola gives a persuasive portrayal of collectivism (41). Elsewhere, he introduces a discussion of *Das Kapital* (296).

On the question of whether money as a component of the capitalist system is good or evil, Zola is ambivalent. Mao includes a passionate defense of speculation along with a tirade against it delivered by one of his characters, condemning it as "the great evil one, the go-between in all human cruelties and filthiness" (226). Subsequently, the same character apostrophizes, "Money, horrible money, that dirties and devours" (229). One scholar has argued that *Money* was intended as "both an anatomy of the Bourse and a study of the role of money in society," the Bourse functioning as a "paradigmatic representation of the capitalistic system itself."[26] "The creative potential of money is magnified by its association with the magical qualities of science, figured in the grandiose engineering projects" of one of the characters (171). The general attitude toward money in the novel is best summed up by Huysmans—it is like a compost pile, necessary for the production of great things (*Les Rougon-Macquart*, 5:1277). In Mao Tun, there is neither vilification nor glorification of money. In *Midnight,* he depicts both revolutionaries and capitalists but presents both classes in a highly objective manner. He reproduces Communist slogans but does so in a way to suggest that they reflect superficial thought and mechanical expression. His preface suggests, however, that this objectivity was in large measure due to the strict censorship in China during the last days before the Communist takeover.

In addition to the preceding mainly theoretical issues, several resemblances in structure and narrative technique may be noted in *Money* and

Midnight. Both novels have the same basic plot: the efforts of the protagonist to control the market for his own ends. The fundamental elements
of the schemes in the two works, however, have as many differences as
ramifications. Wu Sun-fu, the protagonist of *Midnight*, engages in a
relatively simple venture: persuading several of his associates to join him
in an attempt to force down the price of government bonds. He hopes to
gain the concurrence of a financier backed by foreign capital (a comprador, in the language of the time). However, the latter, instead of join-
ing Wu, secretly places his resources with the opposite side. Despite this
setback, Wu's scheme would have succeeded, had it not been for one of
the other partners, who follows the comprador, and Wu is wiped out. The
financial scheme in *Money* is far more complex and sophisticated,
involving the formation of a giant holding company, the floating of stock
in this company, and the development of subsidiaries, mainly in the Near
East, including railroads, an international shipping line, a silver mine, oil
wells, several banks, and a publishing house. Rather than mere speculation, this scheme entails manipulation by means of stock issues of a
company called the Universal Bank. The venture in *Money* is based on an
actual historical episode at the Paris Bourse; that in *Midnight* is purely
fictitious. The protagonist, Saccard, succeeds in pushing the price of
Universal Bank stock to a highly inflated level, but it tumbles when a
rival, Gundermann, a character based on the historical financier Rothschild, begins selling off large blocks to deflate the price. Saccard is not
only forced into bankruptcy but sent to prison. The protagonists of the
two novels share an ambiguity in character. On the surface, each is a
materialistic egoist driven by a compulsion for gain and sensual satisfaction. But each has a certain grandeur, even nobility, in his ambitions.
Saccard at the outset of the novel dreams of being the conqueror of all
Paris; at the height of his success, he conceives of extending French
prosperity, civilization, and culture throughout the empire and the Near
East. The reader wonders, with one of the characters, Is he a hero or is he
a knave? (411). Wu's range is far less extensive—limited to gaining
control of a few factories and profiting from government bonds—but
even his relatively modest operations have a social vision: to keep
capitalism in China in the hands of national entrepreneurs rather than
under the control of comprador capitalists funded by foreign interests. As
Joseph Lau has pointed out, Mao Tun has visions of an industrialized
China, a "forest of tall chimneys belching black smoke, a fleet of
merchantmen breasting the waves and a column of buses speeding
through the countryside."[27] Neither *Money* nor *Midnight* touches directly
on the theme of the biological equality of the sexes, an aspect that Mao
Tun considered one of the essential ingredients of naturalism. Zola, how-

ever, in his preliminary sketch for *Money,* stressed the importance of a
woman to balance the plot, conceiving of her variously as superb, beautiful, and a mistress (*Les Rougon-Macquart*, 5:1247). This conception was
translated into the character of Caroline in the novel, a woman whose
virtues represent almost the contrary of Saccard's defects. No such
female paragon exists in *Midnight*. Its female characters are all wispy and
superficial, with the possible exception of one of the factory hands, who
displays evidence of independence and humanity in a brief appearance.
The novel as a whole has nothing to attract modern feminists.

One of Zola's contemporary journalistic critics accused him of painting his characters "less as individuals than as types" (*Les Rougon-
Macquart*, 5:1280). According to this critic, Saccard and Gundermann,
Saccard's chief opponent, "are not merely two rival financiers; they are
two commanding generals, two paladins, two heroes of the *Iliad* or the
Nibelungenlied." This is a gross exaggeration in regard to Saccard, who
is skillfully and minutely portrayed as a manifold, even ambivalent,
personality, but it has some relevance to Gundermann, who is somewhat
a wooden figure, even though based on the historical Baron Rothschild.
The basic difference between the two men is that Rothschild did not
gamble; he dominated the exchange and profited on the investments of
others. Zola wittily observed that he could make the market go up or
down the way God controls thunder (14). Wu's nemesis in *Midnight*, the
comprador capitalist Cha, plays a role similar to Gundermann's, but he is
not a historical figure and is not portrayed in any depth.

A widely held view is that Zola intended his portrayal of the shattering
downfall of Saccard's Universal Bank enterprise as an allegory for the no
less sensational demise of the empire of Napoleon III. A long passage in
Money similarly affirms a parallel between autocratic governments,
uncontrolled financial speculation, and sexual orgies. The portrayal of
sordid sex is not only a structural device for bringing together passion
and power in this particular novel but a recognized generic ingredient of
naturalism. Caroline remains Saccard's mistress even while realizing that
he is unfaithful, and she subconsciously associates his duplicity in love
with his stock market banditry (236). One of Saccard's many sexual
partners, also a player on the market, is a baroness. On one occasion, her
maid arranges for the man who is her keeper to watch secretly while she
performs fellatio on Saccard (*Les Rougon-Macquart*, 5:209), a scene that
is omitted in the English translation. Even though Zola uses an ultrar-
efined narrative style, the passage exceeds in daring anything in Mao
Tun. Although the episode may seem to violate verisimilitude, the
circumstances of the encounter are based upon an actual event in Parisian

society (*Les Rougon-Macquart*, 5:1326–27). Saccard subsequently allows his second wife to romp sexually with his son from a previous marriage, and he himself pays a fortune to gain the distinction of sleeping with a woman who has granted the same favor to the emperor. Finally, Saccard's illegitimate son, a social monster, rapes a virgin of noble blood. Mao Tun also associates sexual lust with economic greed, but he falls far short of Zola in providing lurid examples. In the closest parallel, Wu forcibly violates his maidservant in order to ease his fury over his financial setbacks, but the maid seems to be willing and offers no resistance. Mao Tun narrates the scene by suggestion rather than explicit detail. He similarly portrays mild lesbian encounters, which one of the characters in both the original and the translation describes as nymphomaniac! (425) In other passages, the wastrel son of a country landlord attempts to rape a peasant woman and in the process fires a pistol at her at close range (105). A concubine commits incest with her master's son (98); the master, however, contrary to Saccard, is furious over the relationship. Directly related to the theme of sex and finance, one of the men in Wu's stock market scheme sends his virgin to the bed of another financier in order to root out the latter's investment plans (198–302). In his descriptive passages, Mao Tun frequently dwells on the anatomy of his female characters, not a characteristic of Zola. He mentions breasts (10, 134, 214), nipples (395), thighs (283), and buttocks (289).

Previous criticism has had little to say about Mao Tun's treatment in *Midnight* of historical background, a major ingredient of the naturalist method. Actually, as he says in his preface, his novel is not literally historical, dealing as it does with "the current situation" or conditions in China at the moment of composition. The background is primarily economic, consisting of the depiction of the three primary groups, "comprador-capitalists, reactionary industrial capitalists, and the revolutionaries and the working masses" (iii). The political chaos of the time is reflected in the rise and fall of the price of government bonds, but Mao Tun does very little in the way of revealing the impact of current political and military events on the activities and attitudes of his characters. Zola, by contrast, was writing about events that had taken place twenty-five years previously. Since he was a generation removed from the historical period of his novel, he needed to explain it to his readers and engage in historical research in order to do so. In addition to his prevailing theme that money is the compost heap necessary for the realization of great projects, he attempted to portray a major historical epoch. In a private letter early in the period of composition, he outlined his aspirations: "I have not only wished to study the actual role of money but I have desired to indicate what had been its destiny in the past and what it will perhaps be tomorrow; hence I have included a little historical section and a little socialist section" (*Les Rougon-Macquart*, 5:1274).

To conclude, there is no evidence whatsoever of a direct influence of *Money* upon *Midnight*, and Mao Tun should be taken at his word when he denied reading Zola's novel. Many similarities in plot, character, and theme, however, may be discerned in the two works. With regard to the literary genre of naturalism, *Midnight* conforms to the main characteristics of the genre, those characteristics that critical consensus has associated with Zola.

Works Cited

Gálik, Marián. "Naturalism: A Changing Concept." *East and West* 16.3–4 (1966): 310–28.

Lau, Joseph S. M. "Naturalism in Modern Chinese Fiction." *Literature East and West* (1968): 49–56.

Mao, Tun. *Midnight*. 2nd ed. Peking: Foreign Language Press, 1979.

———. "Tzu-jan-ch-i yu Chung-kuo hsien-tai hsiao-shuo" (Naturalism and contemporary Chinese fiction). *Fiction Monthly* 13.7 (1913): 1–12.

———. "Ts'ung Ku-ling tao Tung-ching" (From Kuling to Tokyo). In *Mao Tunp'ing-chuan*, edited by Fu Chih-ying. Hong Kong: Nan-tao Books, 1968.

Miller, J. E, ed. *Theory of Fiction: Henry James*. Lincoln: University of Nebraska Press, 1972.

Nelson, Brian. "*L'Argent*: Energy and Order." In *Zola and the Bourgeoisie: A Study of Themes and Techniques in Les Rougon-Macquart*, 158–89. London: The Macmillan Press Ltd., 1983.

Shen, Gloria. "The Theoretical Approach to Naturalism and the Modern Chinese Novel: MaoTun as Critic And Novelist." *Tamkang Review* 25.3 (1993): 37–65.

Wang, David Der-Wei. "Mao Tun and Naturalism: A Case of 'Misreading' in Modern Chinese Literary Criticism." *Monumenta Serica* 37 (1986–87): 169–95.

Zola, Emile. *Les Rougon-Macquart*. Vol. 5. Gallimard: Bibliothèque de la Pléiade, 1967.

———. *Money*. Translated by Ernest A. Vizetelly. London: Alan Sutton Publishing Ltd., 1991.

Notes

1. Mao Tun, *Midnight* (Hong Kong: Nan-kuo chu-pan-she, 1933).
2. Mao Tun, *Midnight*, trans. Hsu Meng-hsiung, 2nd ed. (Peking: Foreign Language Press, 1979). Further references to the novel are taken from this translation and will be incorporated parenthetically in the text.
3. Emile Zola, *L'Argent*, in *Les Rougon-Macquart*, vol. 5 (Gallimard: Bibliothèque de la Pléiade, 1967), and *Money*, trans. Ernest A. Vizetelly (Britain: Alan Sutton Publishing Ltd., 1991). Further references to the novel are taken from these editions unless otherwise noted.
4. Mao Tun, "Mao Tun tung-chi ta-wen" (Mao Tun's response to the queries by his comrades), in *Wen-chiao Chih-liao Chieh-pao* (Newsletter for teaching materials in literature) 7–8 (1981), quoted in Shao Po-chau, "Liang-pu cheng-chiu-pu-tung ti hsieh-tai-chu-i hsiao-shuo" (Different achievements of two realistic novels: a comparative study on *Midnight* and *Money*), in *Special Issues on Mao Tun* (*Mao Tun Chuan-Chi*), ed. Tang Chin-hai and Kung Hai-chu, 2 vols. (Fuchow: Fuchien Jen-min chu-pan-she, 1985), 2:1149. *Special Issues on Mao Tun* will hereafter be abbreviated as *SIMT*.
5. "*Tzu Yeh* hsieh-tso-ti-chin-chin-hou-hou" (The pre- and postwriting condition of *Midnight*—a reminiscence [#Thirteen]), *Shin-wen-hsueh-shih-liao* (Materials of new literary history) 4 (1981): 717.
6. Mao Tun, "Ts'ung Ku-ling tao Tung-ching" (From Kuling to Tokyo), in *Mao Tun p'ing-chuan* (Critical biography of Mao Tun), ed. Fu Chih-ying (Hong Kong: Nan-tao Books, 1968), 341. The translation is quoted from David Der-wei Wang, "Mao Tun and Naturalism: A Case of 'Misreading' in Modern Chinese Literary Criticism," *Monumenta Serica* 37 (1986–87): 173.
7. Shen Yen-ping, "Tzu-jan-chu-i yu Chung-kuo hsien-tai hsiao-shuo" (Naturalism and contemporary Chinese fiction), *Hsiao-shuo Yueh-pao* (Fiction monthly) 13.7 (1913): 1–12.
8. See, for example, Wong Chi-ch'ih, "Kuan-yu Mao Tun yu tzu-jan-chu-i ti wen-ti" (Questions related to Mao Tun and Naturalism), in *SIMT* 1:526–47; Lu Hau-ping and Sun Shen-chi, "Mao Tun yu tzu-jan-chu-i" (Mao Tun and naturalism), in *SIMT* 1:583–605; Chu Te-fa et al., "Mao Tun yu wen-hsueh-shen ti tzu-jan-chu-i" (Mao Tun and naturalism in literature), in *Mao Tun ch'ien-chi-wen-hsueh-shih-hsiang san-lun* (Study of the preliterary thoughts of Mao Tun) (Chi-nan: Shan-tung jen-min-chu-pan-she, 1985), 73–111; Bonnie S. McDougall, "Realism and Naturalism," in *Introduction of Western Literary Theories into Modern China 1919–1925* (Tokyo: The Center for East Asian Cutlural Studies, 1971), 147–89; Marián Gálik, "Naturalism: A Changing Concept," *East and West* 16.3–4 (1966): 310–28; David Wang Der-wei, "Mao Tun and Naturalism," 169–95; Gloria Shen, "A Theoretical Approach to Naturalism and the Modern Chinese Novel: Mao Tun as Critic and Novelist," *Tamkang Review* 25 (1993) 37–65. The last attempts to decide whether Gálik was correct in stressing realism over naturalism in Mao Tun, which from my perspective is nothing but an inconsequential logomachy.
9. Gálik, "Naturalism," 310–28.
10. Gálik has also written an extensive monograph on all aspects of Mao's literary theory: *Mao Tun and Modern Chinese Literary Criticism* (Wiesbaden: Franz Steiner, 1969). This comprehensive study outlines Mao's general attitude toward Zola (77–79) but does not subject *Midnight* and *Money* to comparison and contrast.
11. Gálik, "Naturalism," 319.

12. Lang Sun (Mao Tun's pseudonym), "Tsao-la-chu-i-ti wei-hsieh-hsing" (The danger of Zolaism), *Wen-hsueh hsun-k'an* (Literary decade) 50 (21 September 1933): 2.

13. Gálik, *Mao Tun*, 82.

14. Wang, "Mao Tun and Naturalism," 176.

15. Ibid., 147.

16. Gálik, *Mao Tun*, 66–67.

17. Shen Yen-ping, "Naturalism and contemporary Chinese fiction," 12; quoted in Wang, "Mao Tun and Naturalism," 178.

18. J. E. Miller, ed. *Theory of Fiction: Henry James* (Lincoln: University of Nebraska Press, 1972), 134.

19. "Naturalism in Modern Chinese Fiction," *Literature East and West* (1968): 55.

20. Gálik, *Mao Tun*, 136–37.

21. C. T. Hsia, *A History of Modern Chinese Fiction*, 2nd ed. (New Haven: Yale University Press, 1974), 155.

22. "Naturalism in Modern Chinese Fiction," 55.

23. *"Tzu Yeh* hsieh-tso-ti-chin-chin-hou-hou" (The pre- and postwriting condition of *Midnight*—a reminiscence [#Thirteen]), *Materials of New Literary History* 4 (1981): 709–10. The English translation is mine.

24. C. T. Hsia, *A History of Modern Chinese Fiction*, 157.

25. Wang, "Mao Tun and Naturalism," 172.

26. Brian Nelson,"*L'Argent*: Energy and Order," in *Zola and the Bourgeoisie: A Study of Themes and Techniques in Les Rougon-Macquart* (London: The Macmillan Press Ltd., 1983), 170.

27. Joseph S. M. Lau, "Naturalism in Modern Chinese Fiction," *Literature East and West* (1968): 154; *Midnight* 119.

Part 4
Themes and Influences

A Woman's Search for Identity
in *A Certain Woman* and *The Portrait of a Lady*

MASAYUKI AKIYAMA

Within the range of modern Japanese and American literature, Yoko in Takeo Arishima's *A Certain Woman* (*Aru Onna*, 1919) and Isabel Archer in Henry James's *The Portrait of a Lady* (1881) are skillful and evocative portraits of women who transcend their cultural identity as women. In *A Certain Woman*, Yoko has obtained a divorce from an unsatisfactory husband in order to have independence and freedom of action. She is, therefore, easily persuaded to become engaged to Kimura, a young Christian living in the United States. But she begins an affair with Kuraji, a purser on the ship taking her to that country. After she returns to Japan with Kuraji, she continues to live apart from society. She wants to live in opposition to the existing social system in order to lead a free life as Kuraji's mistress. Yoko tries to find her own identity in a society that was still bound by feudalistic customs and traditions. Arishima proposes freedom and independence from all authority in his description of Yoko's relationship with Kuraji. There is no doubt that Arishima was strongly influenced by Walt Whitman's ideas of liberalism and personal independence as expressed in *Leaves of Grass*, a book that had a tremendous impact on Japanese writers and thinkers of his day.

If we say that Arishima's Yoko embodies the dilemma felt by modern Japanese women of her time, just exactly what does this mean with respect to her position as a woman in society? Well, try as she might, Yoko, during her marriage and her later affair, could not walk along the traditional road prescribed for women of her class and time. Her efforts to conform to correct social decorum took her down a different road from the one that was presented by Japanese custom, and she fell down, losing

her footing. It seemed to her that those who saw it happen gave a sneer-
ing laugh at her folly. Arishima describes Yoko's response as follows:

> The experience, repeated time and time again, had made her into a wayward
> crossgrained woman for whom no one was to be trusted, for whom there was
> nothing left but to follow boldly where "instinct" led. (95)

Yoko was attracted to Kimura because he lived in the United States,
and she thought that by living in America she could break with her
narrow, distressful past, as exemplified by the old customs prevailing in
Japan. She thought that she could win recognition in the United States
through personal talent and ability. In order to realize her potential as an
individual, Yoko first had to leave her tedious, threadbare husband Kibe
and then rather cold-bloodedly get engaged to Kimura. Arishima again:

> To go with Kimura, any way, had been her decision. A new start in America,
> a rebirth, would give her another chance to search for the self she had
> despaired of ever finding in Japan. She wanted to try out what it meant to be a
> woman in America, where women were thought of differently. (130)

However, before she could realize her goal, Yoko met Kuraji, a purser
on the Ejima Maru, the ship taking her to the United States. Yoko fell in
love with him, and this love ignited her life with a passion she could not
control. She now felt it inconceivable to link herself with Kimura, whom
she did not love, so she returned to Japan with Kuraji. She cohabited with
Kuraji against the advice of Kimura's friend, Koto, and many others.

By creating such a plot and characters, it seems that Arishima wants to
explore new possibilities of life through the destruction of preconceived
ideas. He does this by exposing the naked features of human nature.
Yoko's love for Kuraji stood in opposition to the good sense and moral
consciousness of Japanese society. Her behavior was antisocial and
treasonous to her class, however resolutely and courageously she faced it.
It is possible to understand Yoko's love for Kuraji as a desire for revenge
against a society in which women are not free and independent. Ironically, however, Yoko's love for Kuraji did not render her a free woman.
Instead, it made her a slave to her passion, and as long as she was under
the control of this passion, she would never find personal fulfillment as
an independent human being. In the end, Yoko betrayed Kuraji, just as
she had betrayed Kimura and cheated him out of his money, the man who
exists in the novel as a kind of "mari complaisant." Yoko and Kuraji
found pleasure at the expense of personal disgrace and moral corruption,
though Yoko herself was not unaware of the cost. Arishima sympathetically describes Yoko's inner conflict as follows:

Amid all the seeming emptiness, Kuraji lived on in her heart as the one truly alive man she had ever known. They had dragged each other down by the way they had loved, but that love too was a sweet memory now. (371)

However, as a realist, Arishima knew that it would be difficult for Yoko to live outside of society, and, by the end of the novel, he has Yoko showing unmistakable signs of repentance in her acts of self-examination. She confides to an older man whom she had known before marriage.

Uchida . . . of course, she would ask Uchida. A strange affection accompanied her memory of him. For the first time she seemed to see hidden in the recesses of that stubborn bigoted heart, a small bright flame, a spirit of crystal beauty. (382)

Keeping in mind that Uchida is a Christian, Arishima, through the person of Yoko, is now suggesting that Christian social structures, in their opposition to traditional Japanese feudalistic society, offer her an escape within her own country, a chance for her to reestablish herself as a free and independent woman in Meiji era Japan.

Similarly, Isabel Archer in Henry James's *The Portrait of a Lady* expresses a romantic longing for the spirit of freedom and independence. She seeks to express her identity as a woman in Europe because she feels stifled by the oppressive atmosphere of puritanical New England society. While Isabel is staying at Gardencourt, her uncle Daniel Touchett's house in the suburbs of London, her cousin Ralph decides to give her a large sum of money so that she may live a life of independence and freedom, money being the usual means by which such liberty is to be achieved. James depicts Ralph's intentions as follows:

I take a great interest in my cousin, but not the sort of interest you desire. I shall not live many years; but I hope I shall live long enough to see what she does with herself. She's entirely independent of me; I can exercise very little influence upon her life. But I should like to do something for her. . . . I should like to put it into her power to do some of the things she wants. She wants to see the world, for instance. I should like to put money in her purse. (1:126)

Ironically enough, though, it is through Ralph's bequest that Isabel loses her liberty and independence: when she meets and decides to marry Gilbert Osmond, a man who values her only for her property. Ralph's bequest, which had been meant to free her, resulted in a far greater oppression in Europe than the one she left behind her in America. The following quotations concerning Isabel's character will be helpful in our understanding of her vulnerability to Osmond.

> It may be affirmed without delay that Isabel was probably very liable to the sin of self-esteem; she often surveyed with complacency the field of her own nature; she was in the habit of taking for granted, on scanty evidence, that she was right; she treated herself to occasions of homage. (1:67)

James specifies "her meagre knowledge, her inflated ideals, her confidence at once innocent and dogmatic, her temper at once exacting and indulgent, her mixture of curiosity and fastidiousness, of vivacity and indifference, her desire to look very well, to be if possible even better, her determination to see, to try, to know, her combination of the delicate, desultory, flame-like spirit and the eager and personal creature of conditions" (1:69). Knowing this about her character, we can understand her blindness to Osmond's artifice. In her struggle to assert her own identity, to act alone, she is heedless of Ralph's expressions of concern.

Let us examine Isabel's character: First, she has an indomitable spirit of freedom and independence as well as invincible courage and vitality. Second, she has a strong thirst for knowledge and a violent passion for novelty. Third, she has a longing for artistic and refined things, and she admires those who are highly gifted and talented. James describes Osmond as a fellow spirit: "He was fond of originals, of rarities, of the superior and the exquisite" (2:9).

Osmond clearly conforms to Isabel's expectations. She is greatly charmed by him because he has something in common with her inner self. These are the reasons why she accepts his proposal of marriage over those of Lord Warburton and Casper Goodwood, with both of whom she would have been more evenly matched. Being guileless herself, she is unable to recognize egoism and affectation in others. Ralph, discovering Osmond's true character, says,

> He rather looks like one, by the way—like a prince who has abdicated in a fit of fastidiousness and has been in a state of disgust ever since. (1:358)

Isabel chooses to disregard his words, just as she disregards Osmond's own words of revelation when he says of himself:

> There were two or three people in the world I envied—the Emperor of Russia, for instance, and the Sultan of Turkey! There were even moments when I envied the Pope of Rome for the consideration he enjoys. (1:328)

Having heard the above-mentioned statements, Isabel should have realized to some degree that Osmond held opinions contrary to her American frontier-forged feelings for democracy and independence, feelings by which she defined herself as a woman.

* * *

Both Yoko in *A Certain Woman* and Isabel in *The Portrait of a Lady* manifest a dangerous romantic inclination to realize a dream of personal independence that sets them in opposition to long-established social traditions within their respective societies. In both novels, such a danger-ous romantic quest leads our protagonists to personal disaster far more distressing than the situations they had wanted to cast aside. Yoko wres-tles free of social convention only to turn herself into a slave to passion, while Isabel lands herself in a loveless marriage to a cad. In his book, Arishima is interested in exploring the idea of individual freedom set against that of social duty, and he comes to the conclusion that it is impossible for any one person, a woman in late nineteenth-century Japanese society in particular, to live outside of society. Escape through Christianity, a lifestyle and belief system opposed to Japanese feudalistic practices, which Yoko appears to be toying with from time to time in the novel, is equally illusory, considering Christianity's traditional intoler-ance of independent, practical women. The only escape for a woman such as Yoko, who is unwilling to compromise, is through madness and ultimately death. While, unlike Tolstoy's Anna, a woman of similarly wayward temperament, death comes not by suicide but through sickness, the end result is the same.

It is interesting to note how Arishima first introduces the idea of the United States as an escape for a woman such as Yoko, then just as pre-cipitously dismisses it, as though he were all too aware of the conflict between American ideals and the sordid reality of not just the situation of women in that country but the placement of "Asian women" within the American social structure. James, on the other hand, has no compunction about removing his heroine from her social setting and dropping her down in another. It is as though he had concluded that Isabel's world, though wider and more "international" than the one available to her Japanese sisters, was ultimately just as narrow and confining. As noted earlier in this essay, it is through the acquisition of great personal wealth that Isabel loses her personal freedom. *The Portrait of a Lady*, although it predates in publication Arishima's *A Certain Woman* by almost forty years, is distinctly more "modern" in the sense that James easily disposed of such nineteenth-century romantic clichés as madness inflicted upon female transgressors of social order. But then again, it is worth consider-ing that Isabel is hardly what we would call a social transgressor, the point being that she submits to her fate, as did most women who found themselves in a similar position. There was no need to kill her off, as she

had violated no hallowed social law. This, I submit, is the major difference between James's novel and that of Arishima, which begins with
Yoko having run away from her fiancé and thus already having put
herself in a state of transgression. Yoko's daring act is ultimately not so
much a bid for personal freedom as it is a step into anarchy and chaos,
hardly the norm in any society. In contrast, James's story of Isabel
Archer is more than just a portrait of a single "lady"; it is by extension of
its carefully wrought theme a portrait of the condition of the typical
woman of her time, while Arishima's dramatic rendering (no disrespect
intended) is nothing more than what it calls itself, that of a "certain"
woman.

Works Cited

Arishima, Takeo. *A Certain Woman*. Translated by Kenneth Strong.
    Tokyo: University of Tokyo Press, 1978.
James, Henry. *The Portrait of a Lady*. 2 vols. New York: Charles Scribn-
    er's Sons, 1936.

Notes

This essay was presented at the XIVth Congress of the International Comparative
Literature Association.

Koyo Ozaki's *The Golden Demon*
in the Light of Western Fiction

YOKO MATSUI

Konjiki Yasha (The Golden Demon) (1897–1903) by Koyo Ozaki (1867–1903), which appeared originally in newspapers, is generally considered as one of the masterpieces of writing during the period between the Sino-Japanese War (1894–95) and the Russo-Japanese War (1904–5). During that period, Japan adopted a capitalist economy, established gold as its monetary standard and developed trade with foreign countries. Japan also borrowed much from the West in literary theory and practice. In 1885, at the height of the enthusiasm for foreign models and techniques, a group of opposition intellectuals known as the *Kenyusha*, or Friends of the Ink-stone Society, reaffirmed classical Japanese standards, styles, and genres. Koyo Ozaki was the moving spirit of this society. The members of the group followed his lead in considering interesting plots and appropriate vocabulary the major elements of fiction. Intellectuals who did not agree with *Kenyusha*'s ideas adopted modern Western thought and assimilated foreign literature into Japanese writing. These experimental writers used naturalism in particular as a rallying point against *Kenyusha*. In their opinion content or background was more important than style.

In 1882, when Ozaki was sixteen years old, he studied English as a preliminary to taking the entrance examination for the preparatory course at the Imperial University. He entered at the age of seventeen and a year later transferred to the general culture course. In 1888, he enrolled at the College of Law but transferred to the College of Japanese classics in order to study literature. During this academic year, he published several short stories instead of concentrating on his studies, and as a result he failed in his courses. Although spending three years at the university, he left without a degree.

After Ozaki and his group became intensely involved with traditional Japanese fiction, he turned away from the study of English. Somewhat later, he returned to prenaturalist Western fiction for intellectual nourishment and strength to oppose the rise of naturalism in his own country. He translated Tolstoi's *Anna Karenina* and *Kreutzer Sonata* and adapted several older and more traditional Western works into Japanese. Overcoming writer's block, he drew up a plan for his new novel, one of his most famous, *The Golden Demon*.

An investigation of the inspiration for this novel offers a challenge for the study of comparative literature in Japan. Essential background may be obtained from the works of Suiin Emi, a writer affiliated with *Kenyusha*, who learned at first hand some of the details concerning the evolution of *The Golden Demon*.[1] In May 1896, Ozaki outlined to the group the plot of an American novel he had recently read, and he admitted that he had instantly derived from it inspiration for a new novel of his own. According to Ozaki's recollection, the title of the American work was *White Lily*. Its plot involves a heroine tempted by a large fortune who decides to marry a wealthy man even though she is engaged to another, the male protagonist. Ozaki remembered in particular one scene in which the latter runs away from his community in order to escape from hearing the bells pealing for the wedding of the heroine to another man. Ozaki indicated that he would immediately set to work on his own novel based on the American model.

In January of the next year, *The Golden Demon* appeared in serial form in Japanese newspapers. The plot of the work reveals the direct influence of its presumed American forerunner. In it, the hero, a college student, Kwanichi, becomes engaged to Miya, the daughter of the family in which Kwanichi is living as an adopted son. Miya nevertheless decides to marry Tomiyama, who, in contrast to Kwanichi, is wealthy, mature, and established. Kwanichi, bitterly disappointed, abandons his academic career and becomes a loan shark. When Miya finds no satisfaction in her mercenary marriage and tries to reestablish contact with her former lover, he refuses. The title, *The Golden Demon*, refers to both the heroine's marriage for money and her rejected lover's occupation as usurer.

It seems plausible that Ozaki adopted from some American source the plot of a heroine abandoning her lover in order to consummate a marriage with a wealthy man. According to his recollection, he created the heroine first and then filled in the details of the plot as he proceeded. The problem for scholars is to discover Ozaki's alleged American source.

One possible candidate for the American novel in question is *Dora Thorne* (1883) by Bertha M. Clay. In 1961, this possibility was suggested by Ki Kimura, a scholar previously known for a his study of Japanese literature in the Meiji era.[2] Kimura, however, could not find the precise title of *White Lily* in any of Clay's works, which he indicates amount to the incredible figure of more than one hundred titles. He nevertheless provided two reasons for assuming that *Dora Thorne* is the inspiration for *White Lily*.

First of all, the plots of the two works have similar elements. In the Clay narrative, Ronald Earle falls in love with a farm girl, Dora, but Ronald's parents oppose their engagement because of the unequal social standing of the two lovers. Ronald is disinherited by his parents but nevertheless marries Dora and goes with her to Italy, where he barely earns a living as a painter. As each year passes, the two expatriots discover major differences in their personalities, and they decide to separate. Dora returns to England, where she rears her two daughters on a farm. When one of these daughters, Beatrice, reaches adulthood, she meets a world traveler named Hugh Fernely and falls in love with him. Despite their mutual attraction, he leaves for another destination overseas. A few years later, Ronald assumes charge of the daughters, who have in the meantime transcended their rural milieu to become beautiful and accomplished ladies in the world of fashionable society. Beatrice, whose charms have only increased, becomes engaged to a young nobleman. Fernely, however, suddenly reappears after an absence of several years and expects her to recognize their earlier liaison. She has a secret rendezvous with him on the shores of a lake, during which she accidentally falls into the water and drowns. After her death, Ronald realizes that her relationship with Fernely had been built on sorrow. This thought makes him regret his own separation from Dora, and when he sees her again at Beatrice's funeral, they become reconciled. The other daughter, Lilian, is so shocked at the death of her sister that she becomes ill but gradually recovers from her illness and has a happy marriage.

The latter part of the plot is similar to that of *The Golden Demon*. Beatrice accepts the nobleman's proposal despite her previous engagement to Fernely. Like Miya of *The Golden Demon*, she places wealth and station above romantic feelings. A further resemblance and reason for assuming that *Dora Thorne* was Ozaki's inspiration is that Bertha Clay's work made its way into Japan. In 1887, it was translated into Japanese by Kensho Suematsu under the translated title *Lilies of the Valley*. This title presumably derives from the description of the white lilies that serve as a symbol or recurring theme of the novel.

"There are so many of them (flowers)," said Valentine, "and they are all so beautiful. I am always at a loss which to choose."

"I should never hesitate a moment," said Ronald laughingly.

"You will accuse me perhaps of being sentimental, but I must give the prefer-ence to the white lily-bells. Lilies of the valley are the fairest flowers that grow."

Valentine entered the ballroom to see white lilies in her fair hair.[3]

Moreover, one of Dora's daughters, Lilian, was called Lily as a nick-name. Suematasu indicates that Ozaki may have read both the Japanese translation and the original novel in English, but have become confused over whether the original title was *White Lily* or *Lily of the Valley*. Kimura insists on the conjecture that *White Lily* remained strongest in Ozaki's memory.

* * *

In 1980, Peter Kornicki, a well-known Ozaki scholar, furnished another hypothesis.[4] He suggested that Ozaki's inspiration was another American novel *White Lilies* published by Alice K. Hamilton in 1895. The plot is even more closely linked to *The Golden Demon* than is *Dora Thorne*. While visiting her aunt, the heroine, Lilian, meets a fellow college student named Hancock at a social ball. They fall in love, but the aunt does not approve of their relationship. She introduces Lilian to a young and wealthy man, Thontorn, as a replacement for Hancock. Lilian. rejecting her aunt's scheme, reveals to her mother her attachment to Han-cock. Unfortunately, the young lovers have a misunderstanding, which leads eventually to Lilian's decision to marry Thontorn. After six years of marriage, he dies. Four years later, while Lilian is sailing on a boat bound for West Point, she happens to meet a cousin who, surprisingly, is engaged to Hancock's brother. The latter, knowing the sad love story of Lilian and Hancock, decides to arrange a meeting for the two ex-lovers.

The word "lilies" is again the key word. In the last part of *White Lilies*, the cousin says:

"Oh, see, Cousin Lilian, my lilies that had faded, how bright and beautiful they are again!"

"Have flowers prophetic souls?"[5]

"Lilies" symbolically describes the heroine's future, in which she will be reunited with Hancock.

For the reasons stated above, Peter Kornicki's argument is far more convincing than Kimura's. The title of the book is *White Lilies*, the author is an American, and the plot has the similarity indicated by Ozaki. It must be noted, however, that there is no evidence that Alice Hamilton's story ever penetrated into Japan, for no Japanese copy is anywhere recorded. The problem seems unfathomable. The scene that allegedly impressed Ozaki cannot be found in either *Dora Thorne* or *White Lilies*. The possibility still remains that some other American popular novel may have been his inspiration. Ozaki's pupil Shusei Tokuda once said that he saw many collections of American short stories in Ozaki's bookcase, and the possibility exists, therefore, that *White Lilies* may have been one of these stories.

                              * * *

A third comparative study of *The Golden Demon* and Western literature suggests that Emily Brontë's *Wuthering Heights* (1847) may have been the source of *The Golden Demon*. This hypothesis was presented by Kenkichi Yamamoto in 1962.[6] Although he could find no direct evidence that Koyo Ozaki had ever read *Wuthering Heights* in English or in Japanese translation, he based his conjecture on the similarity of plots.

The heroine of *Wuthering Heights*, Catherine, marries a wealthy man, Edgar Linton, even though she loves the hero, Heathcliff, who had been taken in by her father when he was a child and had grown up with her. In *The Golden Demon*, Miya marries Tomiyama, although she loves Kwanichi, who had been cared for by Miya's family. The male protagonists in both novels disappear when they hear of the heroine's marriage but eventually return with thoughts of revenge. Catherine dies mad, and Miya in the end loses her mind. Yamamoto focusses on the act of confession by each female protagonist as a theme linking the two novels. In the ninth chapter of *Wuthering Heights*, Catherine confesses to her maid, Nelly, her ardent love for Heathcliff along with her decision to marry Edgar. Like the narrator of the events in a story, Nelly attempts to interpret Catherine's words as a window into her soul. During the conversation, Heathcliff is concealed somewhere in the room.

"Why do you love him, Miss Cathy?"

"Nonsense, I do—that's sufficient."

"By no means; you must say why."

"Well, because he is handsome, and pleasant to be with."

"Bad," was my commentary.

"And because he is young and cheerful."

"Bad, still."

"And because he loves me."

"Indifferent, coming there."

"And he will be rich, and I shall like to be the greatest woman of the neighbourhood, and I shall be proud of having such a husband."

"Worst of all! And, now, you say how you love him.[7]

"I've no more business to marry Edgar Linton than I have to be in heaven; and if the wicked man in there had not brought Heathcliff, now; so he shall never know how I love him; and that, not because he's handsome, Nelly, but because he's more myself than I am. Whatever our souls are made of, his and mine are the same, and Linton's is as different as a moonbeam from lightning, or frost from fire." (9:121)

After this conversation, Heathcliff disappears from the room without hearing Catherine's motive for accepting Edgar.

"As soon as you become Mrs. Linton, he loses friend, and love and all! Have you considered how you'll bear the separation, and how he'll bear to be quite deserted in the world? Because, Miss Catherine—"

"He quite deserted! we separated!" she exclaimed, with an accent of indignation. "Who is to separate us, pray? They'll meet the fate of Milo! Not as long as I live, Ellen—for no mortal creature. Every Linton on the face of the earth might melt into nothing, before I could consent to forsake Heathcliff! . . . If Heathcliff and I married, we should be beggars? whereas, I marry Linton, I can aid Heathcliff to rise, and place him out of my brother's power?" (9:121–22)

Critics admire this chapter especially because in it human feelings and actions are portrayed as contradictory and the depth of the characters' consciousness is fathomed. Heathcliff and Catherine break the rules of mundane common sense and create a world of absurdity. Throughout the narration of Nelly, the confidante of both characters, readers are brought to understand in a natural manner the existence of passion and evil hidden in the minds of the hero and heroine. Nelly reveals both the emotional and rational sides of Catherine's heart, creating a threedimensional effect. According to Yamamoto, this chapter is one of the most important and impressive in the novel.

A similar dialogue takes place in *The Golden Demon* when Miya announces to Kwanichi her decision to marry Tomiiyana.

> Miya clung to him with hysterical sobs.
>
> "Don't give way like this, Kwanichi, please don't. I can't tell you everything now, but please have patience with me, and forbear. I can assure you that, come what may, I shall never forget you."
>
> "But, if you are not going to forget me, why give me up? I don't want to hear your assurances. "
>
> "But I have not given you up."
>
> "Not given me up, when you are going to marry another? Are you intending to have two husbands?"
>
> "I have a plan in my head. Please have patience with me. You will then have proof positive that I have not forgotten you."[8]

When the novel was dramatized in 1902, the scriptwriter asked Ozaki how Miya felt about Kwanichi while breaking up with him in this scene.[9] Ozaki told him that Miya had an audacious plan that would give her a luxurious life by marrying Tomiyama and later by divorcing him and acquiring a fortune. Then she would marry Kwanichi, when he had completed college and become financially independent.

Miya's motive for marriage is similar to Catherine's. Miya's feelings in the depth of her heart are not revealed in detail, however, because there is no narrator in the novel. Her confession in the conversation with Kwanichi is so plain and matter-of-fact that readers consider it to be forced or unnatural. Yamamoto insists that a new understanding of the theme of *The Golden Demon* emerges from subjecting it to comparative study. He is correct in maintaining that the aspects of plot and character in *Wuthering Heights* may be of significant value in interpreting similar elements in Ozaki's novel, but the British work cannot be considered as Ozaki's source because he himself attributed this function to an American one.

The parallels in plot and theme between *The Golden Demon* and
Clay's *Dora Thorne*, Hamilton's *White Lilies,* and Brontë's *Wuthering
Heights* represent merely circumstantial rather than conclusive evidence.
In short, one cannot prove that any one of the Western stories is the work
named *White Lily* in Koyo Ozaki's reminiscences communicated to Suiin
Emi. I am obliged, therefore, to reject Ki Kimura's opinion that the
source of *The Golden Demon* is limited to a single story that Koyo Ozaki
read before writing the novel. It is said that he used to visit the Maruzen
Book Store, noted for selling foreign books, where he bought various
kinds of foreign books, from serious literature to popular fiction. For this
reason, it is logical to conclude that he adopted various elements from the
books he read as materials for the theme and organization of *The Golden
Demon*.

It is generally recognized that the aim of *The Golden Demon* was to
create a new woman or heroine for the Meiji period. In his early works,
Ozaki did not have a progressive or positive attitude toward women. He
agreed with general opinion that men were dominant over women. At the
time, most female protagonists were portrayed as working in a bar, a
cabaret, or a red-light district. and to love someone of the lower class was
immoral and impossible. Other female characters were separated from
their lovers because they had to follow their fate, which was decided by
their family or by custom. Readers, therefore, sympathized with the
heroines who were to suffer a cruel fate or who were in helpless circumstances, living with their despair.

When *The Golden Demon*, representative of Ozaki's final period,
appeared in print, readers paid attention to its modern plot, and the novel
became very popular entirely apart from its literary value. Readers were
so involved with the fate of Miya and Kwanichi that they did not realize
that Ozaki was challenging the old ways of thinking by creating a new
heroine.

It should be emphasized that Miya decided to marry Tomiyama of her
own free will. She had to take responsibility for her fate and unhappiness
because of her own choice. There is a scene regarding her decision in a
conversation with her mother.

"Mother dear, what shall I do?" said Miya.

Her mother, who had been gazing at the flowers, turned her eyes on her
daughter. "What shall you do? That depends entirely on yourself, it was you
that caused these difficulties by saying you would like to marry into the
Tomiyama family." "I know all that." returned Miya. [10]

In the feudal age, Japanese women exploited their beauty in order to compensate for the disadvantages that society had placed in their way, and they frequently succeeded in life by using that beauty. In this sense, Miya had the same opinion as had other women. She was of two minds about her marriage to Tomiyama.

> She concluded that she had better be prudent and wait a little before she allowed herself to be irrevocably tied to the man whom her parents had chosen and, as it were, thrust upon her. She thought that if she played her cards well she might still be married "in a carriage of gems" to a wealthy husband, who could afford to keep her in wealth and luxury. (6:36)

Moreover, Tomiyama was also a new-type Japanese man in the Meiji period. It was unusual for Japanese men to wear rings and smoke cigars.

> They (the groups of card players) caught a glimpse of something brilliant on his ring-finger which dazzled them for a moment and attracted their curiosity. It was a large diamond set in a handsome gold ring, the biggest diamond they had ever seen. (3:15)

> The fortunate gentleman seeing himself the cynosure of all eyes smoked his cigar with a nonchalant air. (3:17)

Tomiyama was a child of capitalism in the Meiji period.

> He was the son of a nouveau riche who lived in Shitaya, who had founded the Tomiyama Bank with his own capital. (3:17)

He refused to join a Japanese card game because, for him, it was an old-fashioned social activity.

> The fact was the gentleman had been so savagely torn and trampled upon by his adversaries that he had come to the conclusion that the game was scarcely a civilized one. (4:20)

He was looking for a wife himself and wanted a love marriage.

> He had returned from England a little more than twelve months since, and had been looking for a wife. But he had as yet failed in spite of all his trying. Nothing but a tiptop beauty would satisfy him, and he had rejected a score of suggested brides already. (4:25)

These are examples proving that Tomiyama was a very Westernized man.

Miya's meeting with Tomiyama was equal to her first meeting with Western culture. Her reaction to him was stony.

> Miya showed no sign of emotion. Her eyes were cool, and shone with a cautious brightness which seemed to vie with the lustre of the diamond though apparently unconscious of its presence. (3:18)

Her cool attitude toward Tomiyama reflected her strong will to accomplish her purpose. She believed that only love for Kwanichi would bring her happiness.

The Golden Demon appeared serially from April to June in 1897, almost contemporaneously with an adapted novel also by Koyo Ozaki, *The Disposition of Western Women.* [11] In the novel, he says that a woman who wished to be a viscountess and proposed to a viscount had a different set of values from those of a Japanese women. He was interested, therefore, in describing a new type of Japanese woman who would act with her own will, like a Western woman in a Western novel. In the same vein, he portrayed Miya's concealed purpose of marrying Tomiyama to fulfill her love for Kwanichi. Readers considered her a traitor because of the incident involving her marriage, but in her mind the act of apparent treachery was transferred into an action of love for Kwanichi. The conversion of her values was complete.

The Golden Demon was truly epoch making in conception. Ozaki was forced by public opinion to change the circumstances of the story because Miya's plan of balancing one suitor against another went contrary to Japanese traditional concepts. As the story actually appeared in the newspapers, she did not divorce Tomiyama and marry Kwanichi. All she did was to regret her misjudgment. The original conception of the novel had to be abandoned because Koyo Ozaki and *Kenyusha* had already exceeded the limits of their literary activity by introducing into their love stories elements taken from Western popular novels.

Works Cited

Brontë, Emily. *Wuthering Heights*. Middlesex: Penguin Books Ltd., 1965.

Clay, Bertha M. *Dora Thorne*. New York: Hurst and Company, 1883.

Hamilton, Alice K. *White Lilies*. In *Captain Dream and Other Stories*. New York: Grosset and Dunlap, 1895.

Ozaki, Koyo. *The Golden Demon*. Translated by A. M. Lloyd. Tokyo: Seibundo, 1919.

Notes

1. Ryohei Shiota, "Konjikiyasha-kaidai" (The explanatory notes of *The Golden Demon*), in Ozaki Koyo Zensh (Tokyo: Chuoukoron, 1941), 6:569–94. Suiin Emi, *Jikochusin-Meijibundanshi* (Self-centered literary circles in the Meiji era) (Tokyo: Hakubunkan, 1927), 237–39.

2. Ki Kimura, "Bertha Clay to Meijibungaku" (Bertha Clay and literature in the Meiji era), in *Shimada Kinji kyoju-kanreki-kinenronbunshu: hikakubungaku hikakubunka* (Comparative literature and comparative culture) (Tokyo: Kobundo, 1961), 387–406.

3. Kensho Suematsu, *Tanima-no-himeyuri* (Lilies of the valley) (Tokyo: Kinkodo, 1887), 7:33.

4. Peter Kornickie, "Konjikiyasha-shiron" (The literary essay of *The Golden Demon*) (Tokyo: Nihonbungaku, 1980), 60–63.

5. Alice K. Hamilton, *White Lilies*. In *Captain Dream and Other Stories* (New York: Grosset and Dunlap, 1895), 111.

6. Kenkichi Yamamoto, "*Arashigaoka-to-Konjikiyasha*" (*Wuthering Heights* and *The Golden Demon*) (Tokyo: Bungakukai, 1962), 119–23.

7. Emily Brontë, *Wuthering Heights* (Middlesex: Penguin Books Ltd., 1965), 9:118.

8. Koyo Ozaki, *The Golden Demon,* trans. A. M. Lloyd (Tokyo: Seibundo, 1919), 14:83–84.

9. Ukai Hanabusa, "Koyosanjin-to-engekito" (Koyo and drama) (Tokyo: Shinshosetsu, 1904), 220–22.

10. Ozaki, *The Golden Demon*, 11:66.

11. Koyo Ozaki, *Seiyo-musume-kishitsu* (*The Disposition of Western Women*) (Tokyo: Yomiurishimbun, 1897).

The Role of Ogai Mori's Translation of Hans Christian Andersen's *Improvisatoren* in the Poetical Works of Takuboku Ishikawa

MATOSHI FUJISAWA

I

Hans Christian Andersen (1805–75), one of the greatest writers in Denmark in the nineteenth century, has acquired even in Japan many readers, from children to adults. He wrote excellent fairy tales and romantic novels. Although their arrival in Japan was later than in Europe, they were translated and introduced to Japan only thirteen years after his death.

At that time, modern realistic techniques of the novel had already reached Japan, where some authors had begun using them; for example, Shimei Futabatei's novel *Ukigumo* (Floating cloud) was written in 1887. Fairy tales (German folk tales) by the brothers Jacob Ludwig Grimm (1785–1863) and Wilhelm Karl Grimm (1786–1859) were also introduced to Japan at this time. The influence of foreign literature accordingly became much more extensive, and Masakichi Kono, Zenji Iwamoto, Kimiko Koganei, Sazanami Iwaya, and Takuboku Ishikawa became involved in the translation process.

Among Andersen's novels, his early representative work *Improvisatoren* (1835) became extremely popular. Ogai Mori devoted himself to translating Andersen's writings, and, during his residence as a student in Germany for almost five years, he encountered *Improvisatoren*, which had a strong impression upon him, for he knew that the work was read extensively by the German people. So, on 10 September 1892, he started his translation, based on a German version that he had brought back from Germany, and continued intermittently until 15 January 1901, when he finally finished his task. The translation, which required more than eight years and four months of hard work, was serialized in journals such as *Shigarami Zoshi* and the subsequent *Mesamashi Zoshi.* At the end of seven months of serialization it was published in two volumes by Shunyodo. Thanks to the publisher's kind consideration, the translation of *Improvisatoren* was printed in large letters, which attracted many readers, including old people. By April 1915, it had been printed twelve times. After that, there was a pocket edition and, by February 1918, nine more editions had been printed. It became the first best-selling Japanese translation of any book.

Ogai's great popularity rests in large measure upon his theories of translation. His version is far more successful than the later one by Ohata Suekichi (*Iwanami Bunko*, 1960). The latter is known as a meticulous translator whose work is quite faithful to the original, in contrast to Ogai's creative rendering of the Danish author, which even sacrifices literal fidelity according to the translator's interest.[1] Despite the fact that Ogai's translation has many parts that stray from the original, his translation has not destroyed the original narrative quality and imagery. On the contrary, "it is often said that it is better than the original," as was pointed out by Shizuka Yamamuro, who wrote an article on Andersen and modern Japanese literature in *Kindai nihon bungaku daijiten.*[2] Standing out as a brilliant work among Ogai's corpus, this translation of Andersen's *Improvisatoren* has been highly praised, although at the same time considered very old fashioned.

The history of literary translation in Japan cannot possibly be written without considering Ogai's contribution. Especially among the young people of the Meiji period, several authors tried to connect their own creative activities with this long novel from the Scandinavian country. One of the earliest of these was Ichiyo Higuchi. After eight of her contributions to the magazine *Shigarami zoshi,* including *My First Boundary* and *Water Buffalo,* she was motivated to write, under Andersen's influence, *Koto no oto* (The sound of the Koto, 1983). Subsequently, Kyoka Izumi, after reading all of the installments in *Shigarami zoshi,* wrote a novella called *Teriha kyogen* (1896), based on his impressions of that work. After the series became a book, authors such as Kyukin Susukida, Bin Ueda, and Toson Shimazaki were also noticeably influenced, so that their creative activities also showed the influence of *Improvisatoren.* There is no doubt that many more young authors were also influenced by it.

II

The genius poet Takuboku Ishikawa (1886–1912), who died at an early age at the beginning of the twentieth century, was one of the authors who came under Andersen's influence. As a precocious, individualistic child he left school when he was sixteen and a half and went to Tokyo with the hope of becoming a writer. He started reading foreign authors while wanting to learn the foreign languages themselves, and at the same time he showed an unusual interest in the techniques of translation. This is the early history of Takuboku, before his birth as a poet.

His first diary, *Shuraku tekigo,* describes his initial encounter with Ogai's translation of *Improvisatoren* during his preparation period. He records his experiences twice as introductions to his translations.

> In the afternoon I read *Improvisatoren* in the library. Something fresh assailed my heart. Oh, what exquisite writing this is! (18 November 1902)

> In the afternoon I went to the library and suddenly felt a high fever, but continued reading. . . . In *Improvisatoren* people compare the world to a beautiful maiden and try to examine the detailed parts and yet the poet should observe and sing the whole of beauty. This must be the criticism of poets and artists in general. (21 November 1902)

The library mentioned in the diary is the Ohashi Library,[3] which was within walking distance of Takuboku's lodging house. The very first day that he visited this library was thirteen days after he had moved to Tokyo. That means that very soon after that day he must have found in the library Ogai's translation of *Improvisatoren*. He must have read it very carefully, as the second paragraph quoted above shows.

The part of *Improvisatoren* that is referred to is in the second volume, called *Night Attack*, in which the description seems to have been done instinctively. This section of Andersen's novel is crucial from the point of view of reception, and so I shall quote it here:

> Gennaro came over to ask me [Antonio] to take a walk. He said, "What an *Improvisatoren* poet you are! Let's go down there and see whether the scenery is the same over there. There is no doubt that women's beauty is superior in the lower parts of the body because, if you look at the pale, cold-blooded faces of women from our neighboring country England, it is clear. I cannot stand such women's faces. You don't dislike looking at women, do you? Pardon me for asking such a question."[4]

The essence of the description of *Improvisatoren* in Takuboku's diary is in the above quotation. Let us now consider its context. Antonio, who got on the stage of the theater in Naples as an improvisational poet, was chosen by Borghese, who was among the audience, and because of the strong invitation all of them went on a trip. They went down south to Paestum, famous for its ruins, and took a walk. The quotation derives from this scene. Here, Gennaro is, characteristically, incessantly talking in a one-sided way to Antonio, the narrator of the story. Beside them is an inelegant-looking Englishwoman, used as an object of sarcasm leading to the remark about women's beauty being in the lower part of the body, which in turn fosters expectations of natural beauty in the coral rock area of the Caribbean Sea, where they will go next. This arouses the reader's anticipation and leads to the development of complications later. The previously cited passage in the diary is actually a deep contemplation of the semantic structure of sentences. In other words, common people consider only the phenomena of the world, but the poet looks at the wholeness of the world. Therefore, the diary functions as an interpretation of cautionary aphorisms for poets and artists.

At this early stage, Takuboko had already stepped into the poetic community, where his entry as a poet had been foretold. In fact, Takuboku soon began creating symbolist poetry with amazing fervor. He published his first collection of poetry, entitled *Akogare* (Longing), when he was only nineteen years old.[5] Around 1905, the world of poetry considered him a genius, but a few intellectuals raised the suspicion that Takuboko's work was actually an amalgam of originality and imitation. At that time, the Japanese literary world was going through a transition from romanticism to naturalism, and because of that the time of symbolist poetry had almost come to an end. Consequently, not only *Longing* but also the poet himself seem to have lost their appeal. This circumstance triggered Takuboku's change from poetry to prose, which was confirmed by the fact that the author later rejected *Longing*. This was a crucial point in his life.

III

The process described above of Takuboku's reception of Ogai's translation of *Improvisatoren* demonstrates, as earlier suspected, that Takuboku's work is largely imitative. It is truly so. But when it comes to concrete proof of the influence, there has been no previous research, nor even a perspective for research. So I should like to examine the actual details.

What I want to discuss is the poem called "A Blind Girl," which was written on 18 March 1905 and given to the publisher Odajima Shobo along with other manuscripts. This is why it was attached to the end of *Longing*.

A Blind Girl

"Is the sun shining?" said the voice in the blue sky.
A white crane is calling far away—
Thus asked a blind girl
leaning against the white marble pillar
next to the tall building's beautiful staircase
which overlooks the eastern sea.
A brave soldier, kneeling down
taking off his beautiful helmet
made out of white silver, responded,
"That's right, the sun is now leaving the horizon, becoming fresh waves of
    light
flowing over the hills,
flowing beyond the summer hills.
Oh, now it is shining, my dear,
it is shining on your streaming hair, yellow gold
on the upper half of the column of white marble
where you are leaning.
Soon your beautiful face will be lighted.
Oh, summer kisses!
Soon it will shine around your hips
resembling the sculptor's figure
in the rose garden
and extra golden light will light my own face
with lingering emotions."

The above section constitutes the first twenty-three lines of the poem. The entire poem consists of eighty lines with a pattern of 5/7 syllables. Therefore, sixty-seven lines remain. Let me offer a summary of the entire poem from the first to the last line.

On a summer morning in a Western-style palace, a blind girl asks a young brave soldier next to her, "Is the sun shining?" He removes his white silver helmet and, kneeling down, says, "Of course it is. The sun is now shining on the upper half of the round pillar of marble. Pretty soon it will also shine on your face, your hips, and also my face." The girl, listening to him carefully and extending her hand to the pillar, says, "Oh, the sun is beating here, and is warm. Do you see any sailboat or cloud?" The brave soldier stands up and says emphatically, "Oh, a couple of sail-boats are floating in the ocean just like the remote relationship between you and me. They will deliver to foreign countries letters from people who care for each other. Oh, one boat has just raised a crimson sail. Since there is not a single cloud it could be the blissful sunshine which will enable us to hug each other and be intoxicated in the scent of the rose bushes." Then the girl says, "My heart, inside, my heart is burning like the sun itself. If you have eyes that can see the truth you could definitely see these hot intense emotions in it." Then the brave soldier approaches her and says, "You also would be able to see the richly burning passionate luster of my two pupils." Whispering this, he holds the girl tightly and presses their lips together. The sunlight wraps the two people in bliss and the sense of love's victory fills the entire area.

So far I have traced the development of the whole poem. A reader, reaching this point in *Longing,* would be extremely surprised because, instead of Takuboku's usual technique of expressing emotions in a straightforward way, through the author's point of view as the narrator, this poem uses the narrator from a third-person point of view to present a kind of short story revolving around the blind girl heroine and the hero, a young brave soldier. This is a very fresh attempt in the use of Takuboku's imaginative power, creating a Western, non-Japanese, medieval, chivalric style of love drama.

Takuboku's idea of depriving the heroine of eyesight and of providing her partner a white-silver helmet as techniques to aid in the creation of unrealistic poetic emotions is a part of creativity that really intrigues readers. They wonder where in the world this combination of imagery and emotion comes from. Critical evaluation of this episode of the blind girl has been very uneven because of suspicion about its originality. This suspicion is only too well warranted since I have discovered that this poem has a definite source. This work derives directly from the dramatic climax of the chapter of the second volume of Ogai's translation of *Improvisatoren* that I have treated above.

Let me summarize the development of this chapter. Duke Borghese and his group, who had started on a trip to visit historical sites, came to the village of Paestum, which has two thousand years of history, and were enjoying Nature in a most relaxed way. They were improvising poetry in front of the stone pillars of the temple. At that time, Antonio, who was one of the members of the group, read his poems, upon the duke's request. He had noticed that a beautiful blind girl had been stand-ing a little further away, leaning over, behind a stone pillar, listening carefully. Noticing her and feeling pity for this pure, refined attitude, he

had spontaneously kissed her forehead, then had been surprised that the
girl ran away. Her name was Lara. This encounter and separation were
going to become a heartbreaking memory later.

Of course, this is a very simple summary, but the similarities between
the two works become very clear if we make a chart of comparisons.

Works: Categories:	*Improvisatoren*	*A Blind Girl*
Time:	Premodern times?	Premodern times?
Place:	Sea shore, Paestum, Italy	Non-Japanese (Western) seashore
Buildings:	Columns, Temple of Poseidon Pillars, stone staircases	Tall Building of Love, jeweled staircase
Scenery:	Pink fog (in ancient times this village was called Roses)	Crimson sail
Characters (female):	A girl is blind A blind girl A girl with such eyes	A blind girl
	Her hair is bound flat The girl's face If it is a statue of stone sculpture Her only two eyes The girl called Angelo	Streaming hair Jeweled face Resembling the figure of the stone sculpture My two eyes "Is the sun shining," asked thusly
Characters (male):	Antonio (a young improvisational poet) He squats down and peeks in He squats down again He kissed the girl's forehead	The young brave soldier The young brave soldier coming closer Holding the girl . . . kiss of love

This is a rough comparison, but it is adequate to demonstrate resemblances between the two works. This fact seems quite sufficient, but just
to be sure, let me examine the structures of the two works. Of course, the
forms of expression differ from novel to poetry, but when it comes to the

characters, the blind girl that Takuboku describes seems to have been based upon the blind girl that Andersen created. Her partner, the young brave soldier, seems to be a variation of the improvisational poet Antonio. Also, the plot in which the young brave soldier approaches the blind girl, and the latter utters the first words, and the former responds to them and kisses her, surely resembles the relation between Antonio and Lara. The palace that is situated in a non-Japanese (Western) area corresponds to the old temple in Paestum in South Italy. And the roses, which are blooming in the neighborhood, seem to correspond to the place that used to be the rose garden. This is obviously more than coincidence. Another thing in common is that the season and time are the early morning in summertime. In terms of human psychology, a powerful emotional explosion takes place between both pairs of young man and woman.

I said earlier that the source of the poem *A Blind Girl* is Ogai's translation of *Improvisatoren* because I recognized these correspondences. Rightfully, Takuboku should have added some kind of acknowledgment of his source for this poem, just as Ariake Kambara included detailed notes to his long poem called *Hime ga kyoku* in his *Shunchoshu* (The spring bird collection).[6] His literary secret has been finally elucidated.

IV

A further poem by Takuboku has resemblances to *A Blind Girl*. Although this poem, *A Dish of Fire for Heaven*, written 18 November 1904, has no narrative line, it also concerns an emotionally charged love experience between a young man and a blind girl.

A Dish of Fire for Heaven

Love, just like the sun shining from the sky,
is just like wax made from coagulated tears, burning.
That wax, made of tears, enters the chasm of dreams
of the closed cold door of the heart-mind
of the blind child on earth, and turns on the light.

The dream is illusory earth with wild grass.
One piece of fire fell and burnt
from the chasm of heaven pointed by the leaf of grass.
The wind danced with the flames all over the field
spreading as the fire of life on the plain.

Sunflowers receiving the sunlight
burning golden yellow, the flowers just like small caps
my own heart burns with vehement fire.
If the sun is a dish of fire for heaven
this burning sensation reflects the sublimation of your soul.

This poem, as you can see in the original, consists of three stanzas of five lines each, with patterns of alternating 5/7 syllables. As the title, *A Dish of Fire for Heaven* indicates, the burning light is the sun, considered as a dish of fire for heaven. The poet tries to absolutize this fire as the reflection of love between himself and the blind girl in the dreamy illusion—the distinctive feature of the plot. The sense of the victory of love seems to have become a motif of another poem called *The Young Author*. In any case, the "I" in *A Dish of Fire for Heaven*, appears as the person who pours out emotions in the loving relationship with the blind girl—a relationship that has become the archetype of love between male and female. In other words, "the brave young soldier" has become the "I," and the "blind girl" (Lara) has become the "blind child."

V

In addition to these two poems, there seem to be other works deriving from Andersen. The poem called *Omoide* (Remembrance*)* (December 1904) and also the poem called *Ogongenkyo* (The illusory state of gold*)* (6 May 1904) have phrases drawn from *Improvisatoren*. In the third stanza of the poem called *Shizuneru kane* (The sunken bell*)* (19 March 1904), there is a line about a vehicle decorated with a treasure of seven jewels (gold, silver, lapis lazuli, squilla shells, coral, agate, and amber) that goes through the purple clouds of eternity. This seems to be taken from a reference in *Improvisatoren* to a vehicle of victory running on a path in ancient Rome.

For Takuboku, the influence of Andersen's literature seems to have been limited to only one work, Ogai's translation of *Improvisatoren*, but its impact seems to have been considerable. His young sensibility functioned in a straight line and enabled his poetic structure to be very flexible. On the other hand, it was too artificial, stripping him of his real life. Unfortunately, he left poetry soon after this. If he had continued writing poetry, utilizing the techniques he had learned in this period, he would have succeeded as a great poet.

Takuboku, who went through his period of youth at a much faster speed than ordinary people, never publicized or even mentioned the fact that he had ever learned from *Improvisatoren*, but it must have served as a memento of his youth.

Notes

1. See Kinji Shimada's "The Study of *Improvisatoren* translated by Ogai Mori," *Japanese Literature Liberal Arts Lectures*, vol. 13 (*On Translated Literature*).

2. *Modern Japanese Literature Museum*, edited, vol. 4, Tokyo: Kodansha, 1947.

3. After going to Europe, the publisher, Sahei Ohashi, founded this library in 1902, the first library in Japan established by a foundation. Unfortunately, it was closed after being burned in the Great Kanto Earthquake on 1 September 1923.

4. C. Andersen, *Improvisatoren*, ed. Ogai Mori (Tokyo: Shunyodo, 1902), 421–22.

5. Including seventy-seven symbolist poems, *Akogare* was published by Odajima Shobo on 3 May 1905.

6. When Ariake Kambara wrote the long poem *Hime ga kyoku,* he got his materials from *Myths and Songs from the South Pacific,* ed. W. W. Gill, in which there is a chapter called "The Fairy of the Fountain." When Kambara published his first collection of poems, *Shunchoshu* (1905), he mentioned the previously cited source in detail.

Part 5
Gender

Class Conflict and the Politics of Gender in *Arden of Faversham* and *Kan Tou Chin*

I-CHUN WANG

Ordinarily, class and gender are considered independent, although inter-locking systems of social order. Class divisions seem to take precedence over those of gender in the sense that both sexes of any specified class are by definition opposed to both sexes of one or more other classes. I propose to show, however, that in two representative dramas, one English and the other Chinese, class distinctions exacerbate gender con-flicts. In both plays, an adulterous couple is responsible for the murder of the woman's husband. In the English play, the couple hires two ruffians to carry out the deed, but the plot is discovered and the guilty are executed. In the Chinese play, the lover carries out the homicide but attempts to place the blame for it on a beggar who had previously had an altercation with the victim and had publicly threatened revenge. In the end, the beggar is exonerated and the guilty ones punished.

It has long been recognized that the realism of the English stage of the sixteenth and seventeenth centuries grew out of both human moral frailty and the tension created by the interaction of social and economic classes. The play *Arden of Faversham* (1592) successfully presents a shocking murder complicated by the social ranks of the three main protagonists. Arden, a representative of avarice and social mobility, is also a victim of his wife's adulterous passion. His wife, Alice, a woman whose social status is circumscribed by her marital subjection, defies the marriage bond, while her lover, Mosby, enters the world of economic individual-ism by challenging the social system in which he occupies a subordinate position as a tailor.

Class conflict and the politics of gender are also recurrent themes in
Chinese drama. In the Yuan dynasty especially, known as the Golden
Age of the Chinese theater, many *Kung-An* plays (those associated with
the court) underlined economic and societal pressures in one way or
another. *Kan Tou Chin* (Detecting the hood), like *Arden of Faversham*,
deals with the involvement of social order and individual passions in the
murder of a husband. A wife and her lover carefully plot the crime in
such a way that a beggar's dispute with a landlord leads to the former
being unjustly charged with murdering the latter. The wife employs class
divisions as a cover for her violation of matrimonial conventions, her
adultery leading to the murder of her husband and the false accusation
leveled against the beggar.

Both plays illustrate a twofold challenge: the first to the hierarchy of
social classes and the second to the institution of marriage. They reflect
in the first category the instability of the prevailing social order and in
the second the politics of gender.

This essay aims to explore the two-faceted conflicts in these two
plays, their combining of a revolt against the social institution of marriage with a struggle for economic power. The combination reveals how
the politics of gender contributes to the instability of the social order.

According to Richard Terdiman, the word "class" stems from the
Latin "classic," designated as a category in Roman law concerning property and taxation. The *classici* in Rome, as the most prosperous citizens,
paid the most taxes (226). Certainly class always implies the distribution
of power, which is ordinarily accompanied by symbolic violence. Almost
every society is imbued with rank, hierarchy, and degree, and usually the
rank or class reflects the contexts of a person's private, social, economic,
and even cultural relationships. In early modern society, social class
always implied birth, wealth, occupation, and lifestyle, and class distinctions were assumed to provide ideal harmony as contributing to the orga-
nizing of society as an organic whole, envisioned as a chain extending
from high to low. [1] The household was considered a small kingdom in
which each man and woman occupied an assigned role in the family and
in the commonwealth. In an age when economic growth and social
mobility are rapid, however, the assumed reciprocity of the social hierarchy no longer exists, and it is almost inevitable that economic changes
make shifts in the social hierarchy. Theoretically, social position suggests
fixed status, which nearly always depends upon the amount of wealth
possessed. Ironically, however, wealth motivates social mobility and
aspirations for greater power and more wealth. Some people attempt to
climb the ladder of status by marriage and even homicide, although these

actions are actually transgressive ones that break the boundaries of the "social self."

Interpersonal boundaries mirror and are mirrored in the social body (Rubenstein, 6–7). Individual autonomy traditionally represents a notion of responsibility; to reach individual autonomy without considering the consequences certainly implies the subversion of natural law. However, in the premodern society, class assigns boundaries; in the politics of gender, boundaries for females are defined by men. The breaking of the boundary often involves class struggle and subversion of the consolidation of a civil society. Obviously, Alice Arden and her Chinese counterpart trespass the boundaries set for them.

The murder of Arden was recorded within the "public arena of history" (Belsey, 130). The account of it was collected in Holinshed's *Chronicles* and in Stow's *Annals of England.* To modern critics like Catherine Belsey and M. L. Wine, the story of Arden is something more, however, than a dramatized sociological tract or renarrativization of events.[2] The murdered victim, Arden, was a bureaucrat, a customs officer, and a landowner, "having given good service to the court of Augmentations which controlled the disposal of monastic property" (Attwell, 333). Beyond this, he was an emblem of avarice. According to Holinshed, in 1551 he even insisted that the St. Valentine's fair be held on his realm so that he could reap "all the gaines to himselfe, and bereaved the towne of that portion which woont to come to the inhabitants" (157). After Arden's death, the field where the conspirators had placed his corpse miraculously showed the imprint of his body for two years afterwards (Belsey, 133). The exposure of Arden's body and the supernatural overtone support the theory that his death revealed the class conflicts and value contradictions separating the different social groups involved. Historical records document the fact that lower or marginalized groups were heavily criminalized in Tudor and Stuart England (Travitsky, 171). The people who carried out the actual killing belonged to the lower social class. One of the statutes at that time defined the punishment to be inflicted "when a servant slayeth his master, or a wife her husband, or when a man secular or religious slayeth his prelate to whom he oweth obedience" (*Statute* 2:51–52).[3] Although the statute suggests terrible punishment to those who break up boundaries, historical records show that the punishment itself did not abhor petty traitors who hate suppression and are in need of money at the same time. Arden's murder involved both money and sex. Even Mosby, a person representing economic individualism, was motivated less by love of Alice than by desire to acquire Arden's money (Belsey, 134). Belsey's comment on Alice's crime is

illuminating when she says that it concerned social and economic problems rather than providential ones and that the event itself was primarily
an instance of the breakdown of order that is caused by the subversion of
old loyalties, obligations, and hierarchies in the changing process of the
market economy (ibid.). Under the hierarchy of the Renaissance, the
potential avenues for escape from one's social status were few and
narrow, the dissolubility of the conjugal bond almost impossible. Wives
were required to be subordinate to husbands, as servants are to masters;
husband-murderers as well as master-murderers were subject to serious
punishment. Since the upholding of the marriage bond was considered a
major social duty, extramarital sexual activity was a threat to the well-
being of the commonwealth. Marriage in England at this time, similar to
the traditions of the East, required proof of parental consent. At the upper
social levels, marriages were normally arranged by parents, rather than
by the bride and groom, and dynastic financial and other practical con-
siderations largely dictated the choice. Since parental decision dominated
matchmaking, romantic love was regarded with disapproval by the
restricted patriarchal nuclear family. When Alice tells Mosby, "You
know who's master of my heart: He well may be the master of the house"
(*Arden* 1, 640), Alice reveals the problem of an unhappy and indissoluble
marriage. To Alice, Arden is a person hindering Mosby's love and hers.
She persuades a certain Greene, together with the other man, to carry out
the murder by offering a payment of only ten pounds, with twenty more
and possession of his lands after his death. The conflicts represented in
Arden involve the development of individual autonomy—in Raymond
Williams's term, "the conflict between a dying feudalism and the new
individualism" (15). In the Renaissance, man is believed to be rational,
and the essence of man is regarded as freedom. The claim of autonomy,
however, undercuts the ordinary association between fundamental human
values and the acknowledged social system. The claim of Alice's actual
love contradicts her duty within the family; Greene's awakened consciousness of a right to subvert the oppressor contradicts his originally
assigned social role of servitor. As Williams has affirmed, "In the transition from a feudal to a liberal world, such contradictions are common and
are lived out as tragedy" (67).

These underlying contradictions and disorders become apparent and
terrible only when they are embodied in action. In Arden's case, it is only
when the action of murder is carried out that the conflicts between genders and classes expose themselves in their respective tragic modes.

Tragic discourse between classes in *Kan Tou Chin* also derives from
the fundamental pattern of conflicts. A poor beggar intending to attract
the attention of a rich family throws a stone at one of the family's dogs.

The stone does not hit the dog but a water container. The dog immediately barks while the beggar tries to escape, since he has no money to pay for the container. When he is captured, his excuse that he has been bitten by the fierce dog is not accepted by the rich landlord, who accuses him of ingratitude. When the landlord at the same time praises the fierce dog for his fidelity, the beggar is enraged and threatens to kill the landlord if he should happen to meet him in a quiet lane (Sun, 273–74). Traditionally, society is composed of customs and conventions; conventions, however, often stand opposed to individual desires. In *Kan Tou Chin*, the threatening words of the Beggar Wang are employed by Mistress Liu, the wife of Landlord Liu and her secret lover, the Taoist Monk Wang, to get rid of her husband. Like Mosby, Monk Wang is motivated by greed for money, while Mistress Liu seeks power to control domestic affairs and satisfy her carnal desire. Her aspiration for individual autonomy is so strong that it becomes destructive.

According to Chang Yian-Ching, the early Yuan dynasty was not encumbered by strict disciplining systems. The Mongolians' sense of hierarchy and bonds of morality were not as strong as those of the Han tribe. The coming of the Mongolians became an inevitable impetus to the breaking up of the traditional Chinese value system (50–51). Within the amorphous society of the Chinese Yuan dynasty,[4] the attempt to improve the individual human condition was considered acceptable, but what we have seen in Kan Tou Chin is the private distress of Beggar Wang. Distress of this kind could initiate profound conflicts between different classes. Class distinction implies ideological separation between different groups of people. Beggar Wang's capture and his being accused of murdering the landlord are in large measure the result of class conflicts. As in *Arden of Faversham*, property and personal interest motivate individual behavior. The ill-fortuned Wang is accused of murder on the assumption that the behavior of the lower classes is determined by economic necessity. Even the judge of the court imprisons the beggar under the assumption that the landlord had attempted to preserve order and hierarchy by threatening Wang with court action and that the murder was the direct outcome of the beggar's challenge to this order.

It is apparent that irresistible sexual passion lies behind the behavior of Mistress Liu, although the dramatist's psychological exploration of her behavior is not successful. It is not clear how she would cultivate her autonomy and speak for her own subjectivity under the conventional notion of virtue while conspiring to have her husband murdered immediately after his quarrel with the beggar. As we know that her illicit relationship with her lover had begun several months before the action of the play, we can only assume that it is her foolish lust and the hidden instability of her marriage that cause her transgression. Within her careful plans, there is a request of a guarantee from the beggar that he should not touch or harm the landlord. She also claims that should there be any harm within 100 days, the beggar should be held responsible. In this way, she successfully imposes the title of murderer on the beggar. Mistress Liu's secret lover, the Taoist monk, surely does not belong to the common ranks of society. His religious profession seems to make his crime all the more heinous. His ability to make Beggar Wang appear guilty of a crime that he did not commit implies the instability of the social order and of religious doctrine. Mistress Liu might represent a woman suddenly unfettered, a being independent of others, while Monk Wang might be a symbol of religious crisis and inappropriate social mobility. The Chinese notion of conjugal relations presupposes the husband's authority over his wife; Mistress Liu's status as murderer indicates the ambiguity of the relationship. When asked about the details of the whole process of conspiracy, Mistress Liu, by revealing her secret partner, seems to stamp her own character as foolish and careless. These characteristics also suggest that her personal love for the monk is very shallow. She seems to consider him as merely a means for her to dispose of her husband. Humanity is by nature a mass of contradictions (Brain, 26). Impulses for conformity are always at war with those for individual development. Invisible tensions emerge and feelings of hate are aroused against closest kin, spouses, and acquaintances, even though such feelings are socially unacceptable. If patriarchal authority means perpetual control of women, the transgression of this authority inevitably leads to domestic tragedy. Women like Alice and Mistress Liu, who seek to attain their goals by manipulating the power they possess (that is, by becoming murderers), threaten the patriarchal society.

Both the Yuan dynasty and the Elizabethan period are famous for social mobility. But mobility without changing property ownership and without threatening the established hierarchy would not entail the conflicts of classes and genders. In other words, it is class struggle and attachment to property that cause conflicts by employing even witchcraft and secret conspiracy in the power struggle. In the satirical subplot of *Kan Tou Chin*, another landlord with a small piece of property is jailed only because the jailer does not have enough money to pay him back for some hay he had borrowed. The irony that the landlord, without committing any crime, is imprisoned suggests the conflict buried between different classes of people. Therefore, the subplot both parallels and underlines the breakdown of the maintenance of order. The person who prosecutes is not far removed from his neighbors, but by means of his professional status he disrupts the economic class order. Class and gender are related in hierarchical power. As found in literature and history, they provide a schematic structure within which to analyze challenges to order. It is obvious that the tensions caused by class and gender hierarchies often result in conflicts and tragedies.

The murders in *Arden of Faversham* and *Kan Tou Chin* represent symbols of disorder, challenging the received notions of appropriate relations between the rich and poor, husband and wife. It is understandable that punishment of the crime will eventually bring justice, but it can never relieve the tension. Punishment itself has become a symbol of the aspiration for order, but throughout world history the breaking out of civil war has repeatedly raised the problem of class tension. It is manifested on a small scale in the two dramas discussed above. They reveal that gender tensions become more complicated once they are joined with those related to class. These dramas also challenge the criteria for determining status and call into question assumptions of the inherent superiority of the wealthy and inferiority of the poor.

Works Cited

Amussen, Susan. *An Ordered Society*. New York: Columbia University Press, 1988.

Anonymous. *Arden of Faversham*. Edited by Martin White. London: Ernest Benn Limited, 1982.

Attwell, David. "Property, Status and the Subject in a Middle-Class Tragedy: *Arden of Faversham.*" *English Literary Renaissance* 21.3 (1991): 328–48.

Belsey, Catherine. *The Subject of Tragedy*. London: Routledge, 1990.

Brain, James. "An Anthropological Pespective on the Witchcraze." In *The Politics of Gender in Early Modern Europe,* edited by Jean R. Brink, Allison P. Coudert, and Maryanne C. Horowitz, 15–28. Kirksville: Sixteenth Century Journal Publishers, Inc., 1987.

Chang, Yien-Ching. *History of Chinese Drama*. Taipei: Wen-ching, 1990.

Coke, Sir Edward. *The Third Part of the Institutes of the Lawes of England: Concerning High Treason, and Other Pleas of the Crown, and Criminal Causes*. 1644. 6th ed. London: printed by W. Rawlins for Thomas Basset at the George near St. Dunstan Church, 1680.

Fletcher, A. J. and J. Stevenson. "Introduction" to *Order and Disorder in Early Modern England*. Cambridge: Cambridge University Press, 1985.

Harrison, William. *Description of England in Shakespeare's Youth*. London, 1877.

Holinshed, Ralph. *The Chronicles of England, Scotland, and Ireland*. 2nd ed. 1587.

Rubenstein, Roberta. *Boundaries of the Self*. Urbana: University of Illinois, 1987.

Sun, Chung-Chang. "*Kan Tou Chin*" (Detecting the hood). In *Yuan Drama*, edited by Hsin-Yi Hsu, 271–302. Taipei: Hwacheng 1992.

Terdiman, Richard. "Is There Class in this Class?" In *The New Historicism*, edited by H. Aram Veeser, 225–30. London: Routledge, 1989.

Travitsky, Betty. "Husband-murder and Petty Treason in English Renaissance Tragedy." In *Renaissance Drama*, 171–98. Evanston, Ill.: Northwestern University Press, 1981.

Williams, Raymond. *Modern Tragedy*. London: Chatto & Windus, 1966.

Notes

1. William Harrison has listed four degrees of people: gentlemen, the citizens and burgesses of the cities, yeomen in the countryside, and those who had "neither voice nor authority but are to be held and not to rule other." Thomas Wilson listed nobles, gentry, citizens, yeomen, artisans, and rural labourers. See William Harrison, *Description of England in Shakespeare's Youth,* 23, and Fletcher and Stevenson, "Introduction," 1.

2. The story of Arden under the description of the playwright is different from the historical records. The playwright apparently has elaborated on and clarified certain murder attempts by complicating the personalities of the characters. The play is significant also because of the social structure presented. The play therefore becomes a microcosm of rural Tudor society. See Attwell. See also Martin White's introduction to *Arden of Faversham*.

3. One manner of treason described by the statute is petty treason, which indicates a social hierarchy. If a servant kills his master or a wife kills her husband, the murderer has to be punished. This part refers to the 1352 statute of treasons. See Sir Edward Coke's *The Third Part of the Institutes of the Lawes of England*.

4. The Yuan dynasty, under economic development, has in a way promoted communication and cultural exchange. While a race problem still exists, many people intend to make money in different ways.

Female Rebellion: Old Style and New

KAI-CHONG CHEUNG

The major symbol in world literature of a strong woman walking out on a home and husband is probably Nora Helmer in Ibsen's drama *A Doll's House* (1881). Like much of his work, it deals with the emancipation of women and their rights and capabilities independent of husbands and fathers. Nora abandons her husband because he fails to defend her for committing a forgery that she does only to save him from succumbing to a near-fatal sickness. When this incident makes her realize that through-out her marriage she has been treated as a doll rather than a responsible human being, she leaves him and her children to build a life of her own. Although this dramatic action created a sensation in its time, it contains no hint of the violence and sexual harassment that has accompanied the theme of female liberation in its postmodern dress. But whether sparked in the late nineteenth century merely by domination and neglect or in the late twentieth century by violence and harassment, female revolt in litera-ture ordinarily leads to independence, if not to triumph. To illustrate this principle, I shall treat three works: a historically important short story of the American local color school, "The Revolt of Mother" (1887), by Mary Wilkins Freeman; a Taiwanese work of short fiction, *In Liu Vil-lage,* by Yu Li-hua (English translation 1976); and a popular American feminist novel, *The Color Purple* (1982), by Alice Walker.

Freeman's story has become a kind of showpiece for feminists. When originally published by Harpers in 1891 in *A New England Nun and Other Stories*, it was accorded no particular attention. In 1974, however, an edition of the Feminist Press gave it top billing in a collection of Freeman's work published under the title *The Revolt of Mother and Other Stories*. The plot is as clear as the author's style. The protagonist, Mrs. Penn, had been promised by her husband on her wedding day forty

201

years prior to the events in the story that before the end of that year he would build her a new house. Instead, he erected over the years a series of barns while requiring her to live in the makeshift structure they had occupied on the day of their wedding. One day, she notices digging taking place in an adjacent field and, confronting her husband about it, discovers that he intends to erect a new barn and purchase more cows to occupy it. Her chagrin is intensified by the circumstance that her daughter is engaged to be married and needs a conventional parlor as a setting for the wedding ceremony. When the new barn is almost ready for occupancy, the husband receives a letter concerning a horse available at a bargain price some distance away, and he leaves home to investigate. During his three days absence, Mrs. Penn takes possession of the barn, moving in all the family's furniture and belongings and adjusting the interior to resemble that of a house.

In the course of the narrative, Mrs. Penn explains to her daughter the gulf dividing "men-folks" from "women-folks." "One of these days you'll find it out, an' then you'll know that we know only what men-folks think we do, so far as any use of it goes, an' how we'd ought to reckon men-folks in with Providence, an' not complain of what they do any more than we do of the weather" (120). No matter how deeply she resents her husband's treatment, however, she is sedulously attentive to his wants. One day, while baking his favorite mince pies, she glances at the foundation of the new barn, a "sight that rankled in her patient and steadfast soul." Freeman considers her forbearance an example of the "nobility of character" that manifests itself "at loop-holes when it is not provided with large doors" (122). Freeman has her protagonist express a similar maxim by reasoning that "unsolicited opportunities are the guide-posts of the Lord to the new roads of life" (130).

The "unsolicited opportunity," or *deus ex machina* of the story, consists of the letter concerning the bargain horse, an element that could conceivably be used to argue that the heroine's apparent courage, self-reliance, and resistance were not due to "nobility of character" but to external circumstance. The qualities of moral strength could be more securely attributed to her had she on her own initiative arranged for the husband to be called away. Freeman allows Mrs. Penn herself to introduce the question of her strength of character. "S'posin' I *had* wrote to Hiram," she mutters to herself. "S'posin' I had wrote, an' asked him if he knew of any horse? But I didn't, an' father's goin' wa'n't none of my doin'. It looks like a providence" (130). Although she emphatically denies initiating the opportunity for her act of rebellion, she nevertheless suggests that her internal character is responsible for carrying it out. Whether or not she had planned the strategy, her daring was the same.

Freeman describes the transforming of the barn into a dwelling place as a feat equal in its way to one of the major military victories in the war on the American continent in the previous century between the French and the English, "Wolfe's storming of the Heights of Abraham. It took no more genius and bravery for Wolfe to cheer his wondering soldiers up those steep precipices . . . than for Sarah Penn, at the head of her children, to move all their little household goods into the new barn while her husband was away" (132). The awesome nature of the deed is debated by all of the neighbors, male and female. Opinion is divided. "Some held her to be insane; some, of a lawless spirit" (134). When the husband returns to face the *fait accompli*, the protagonist boldly stands her ground, declaring "I've done my duty by you forty year, an' I'm goin' to do it now; but I'm goin' to live here." In the face of this intransigence, the husband surrenders completely, "like a fortress whose walls had no active resistance" (139). He promises to install partitions in the building and to do everything else his wife wants. And she is "overcome with triumph."

Freeman ends the story on this note of triumph, which can be considered the theme of the work. Yet, thirty years later, she affirmed that her portrayal of the protagonist was not true to character.

> There never was in New England a woman like Mother [Mrs. Penn]. If there had been she certainly would not have moved into the palatial barn. . . . She simply would have lacked the nerve. She would also have lacked the imagination. New England women of the period coincided with their husbands in thinking that the source of wealth should be better housed than the consumers. (from a 1917 article in the *Saturday Evening Post*, quoted in Freeman, 191)

Tsui-O, the protagonist of Yu Li-hua's *In Liu Village*, has even less nerve and imagination than her American counterpart. As a typical female in the patriarchal society of early twentieth-century China, she was expected to conform to the Confucian requirement of submission to her father in youth, submission to her husband in marriage, and submission to her eldest son if she attained widowhood. She was also required to exemplify the four female virtues: purity of speech, modesty of attire, diligence in labor, and absolute chastity in every relationship. Although *In Liu Village* was originally published in the 1960s, the historical period it describes is that of the Japanese occupation of the Chinese mainland thirty years previously. In those days, the wife was ordinarily absorbed into the nuclear family of her husband's parents. Marriage for a woman, therefore, meant waiting on parents-in-law, taking care of children, toiling in the fields or in an urban workplace from morning until night, and satisfying a husband's sexual needs. Immediately after her marriage, Tsui-O is taken to live on a farm occupied by her husband's parents. After the passing of a single month, he goes back to his job in a dry goods store in Shanghai, returning home only three times each year, on national holidays. Tsui-O looks forward to these visits, each lasting only ten days, for she is happy with every moment that they spend together. After the birth of a son and a daughter, her husband promises that, once the children are married and his parents have passed away, he will take her to Shanghai to live permanently, a parallel to the promise Mrs. Penn receives about an eventual new house. Both promises are remote and insincere.

Tsui-O's trials and hardships, however, come from her husband's parents. On her wedding day, in a further parallel to Freeman's story, her mother warns her that the rules of her future husband's family are strict. "You have to be extremely careful. . . . Rise early and retire late; when wronged, no matter how badly you feel, don't show it on your face" (103). Tsui-O's mother-in-law turns out to be extremely cruel, possessed by both jealousy and avarice. On the three occasions in the year when her son comes for a visit, she racks her brain, "searching for extra work" for Tsui-O in order to keep her away from her son as much as possible. The father-in-law on the wedding day adopts an air of indifference that he retains thereafter, hardly ever speaking to her and never looking at her on the few occasions when he does. For the first twenty years of her marriage, Tsui-O's life pattern is very much like Mrs. Penn's, except that, in accordance with Chinese custom, she is a slave to both her husband and her mother-in-law. Yet her triannual conjugal visitations give her a degree of contentment, if not complete satisfaction.

At this point, postmodern variations on the submissive female theme, sexual abuse and violence, are introduced in the story. During the Japanese invasion, a vicious n'er do-well, Ch'ang-ch'ing, collaborates with the enemy to become head of the village. Taking a fancy to Tsui-O, he forcefully confronts her one afternoon when the other occupants of the house are either absent or sleeping. He forces her into an abandoned room on the upper floor and brutally possesses her. The resilient mattress gives Tsui-O the illusion of being in a boat, and the afternoon heat makes both bodies so slippery that she is forced to hold tightly to her assailant's body. As a result, he gloats, "You wanted me too, am I right?" When it is all over, she begs him to take her with him, but he retorts cynically, "Are you asking me to abduct a decent married woman? How would I dare commit such a crime?" (113) The author describes these events without exteriorizing Tsui-O's thoughts. The reader must decide independently whether she derived any degree of pleasure from the sexual experience and whether she actually felt that leaving with the rapist would improve her way of life or, on the other hand, whether she merely recognized realistically that her condition had deteriorated so radically that she could never regain the respect of her husband.

In practically no time, the mother-in-law learns of the rape. She calls Tsui-O a harlot, maintains that she should have killed herself, and demands that she leave the house at once. Other members of the family point out, however, that such a move might bring retaliation from Ch'ang-ch'ing; they decide to allow Tsui-O to remain in the home until the following month, when her husband is scheduled to return for their daughter's wedding. She is not permitted, however, to serve tea or any of the meals and is confined to the kitchen like a lower servant. All of this punishment and humiliation "she endured without a murmur." When the husband returns, he immediately possesses her sexually and then falls asleep before she is able to tell him of her being violated. On subsequent nights, when she has finished her duties and retires to their room, he is already snoring. On the eve of the wedding, she makes several efforts to unburden herself, but each time he assumes that she is about to complain of some mistreatment from her mother-in-law, and Tsui-O does not dare to persist. He keeps repeating his promise to take her back to Shanghai.

The wedding itself goes off so smoothly that Tsui-O believes that because of the assurances of the previous night the time is finally auspicious for her to unburden herself. Unfortunately, the mother-in-law gives her son an inflammatory account during the wedding banquet, and he reacts in a rage. When he encounters Tsui-O in their room, he roars, "Why didn't you kill yourself when he was forcing you? Why didn't you knock your head against the leg of the bed and kill yourself?" (137) He kicks her, strikes her across the face so hard that blood oozes from her mouth, and orders her to get out of the house. Then he abruptly leaves the room. She remains, however, hoping to persuade him to change his mind. After tearful entreaties, he agrees to allow her to stay in the house, but adds "There is nothing between you and me anymore" (141). This is the conclusive blow for Tsui-O. She pleads no more, but for the first time in their married life calls him by his first name instead of the household term of respect. "Don't say anymore. I only hope you won't regret it." And she leaves. The next morning, the husband tells his mother that he is going to look for Tsui-O to take her back to Shanghai, and he strides out of the door. Here the narrative ends. The reader is not told whether he finds her and works out a reconciliation or whether they remain separated forever. The author does not use the word "triumph," and the reader is left to decide whether or not it is applicable.

From one point of view, that of conservative family values in China of the time, Tsui-O had been indelibly disgraced. Not only was the family justified in driving her away, but she should have taken her own life. Both her husband and her mother-in-law had taunted her for not doing so. From their perspective, she was violating their culture by staying alive. Only by means of suicide could she convert herself into a triumphant heroine. Lucrece of Roman times and Clarissa of eighteenth-century England, both of whom committed suicide, the first actually and the second psychologically, belong to the comparable Western tradition of chastity at any price. The postmodern reader, however, feminist or not, will take Tsui-O's part, even though the author fails to do so overtly. Her quiet decision to leave can be construed as brave and dignified. She has finally realized that in her husband's eyes she is merely a sexmate, a servant for his parents, and a nursemaid for his children, but not a wife to be protected and cared for. It is hard for her to leave, for she has loved him for twenty years and has believed in his promise to be taken to Shanghai in the future. But she realizes that henceforth she must rely on herself. Life will not be easier, but she will be independent and free. But even this interpretation does not place her in the same category with Ibsen's Nora, who had consciously sought and obtained liberty. Even though Tsui-O's departure may have ruined her husband's life, what compensation is this to her if she still loves him and does not resent his maltreatment, which she had for twenty years accepted as inevitable. *In Liu Village* is not a work of protest or of feminine triumph, nor is it the portrayal of a victim. It is merely a record of the way things were in one part of China during the previous generation.

The Color Purple, as a novel, has a number of major themes, including racism, sexuality, and international politics. Although feminine revolt is interwoven into these themes, it may be analyzed as an independent segment of the plot. As the novel opens, the protagonist, Celie, a black girl of fourteen, has been raped by her father. Since her mother is on her deathbed, she is required not only to fulfill her mother's function in the bedroom but to take care of the other children and do all the work of the household. She eventually gives birth to two children sired by her father, who disposes of them secretly. Eventually, she becomes sterile, and her father forces her to marry one of his acquaintances. The latter wants her only as a domestic servant, to look after his children, to cook, clean the house, and work like an animal in the field. Although he regards her as ugly, he still uses her for his sexual needs when he can find no alternative. Her lack of education keeps her in a state of slavery even though she rigorously studies the schoolbooks of her younger sister, who is allowed to attend school because of her immaturity. Salvation comes to Celia in the person of a black female entertainer named Shug (short for Sugar), who enters her life as the mistress of her tyrant husband but eventually engages in an amorous relationship with Celia herself. Experiencing love for the first time, Celia gradually learns to value her body, her mind, and her talents. With this self-realization comes the strength to leave her husband and live with Shug. Eventually she becomes self-supporting and an agent for good in the lives of other characters in the novel. She had been more of a victim than either Mrs. Penn or Tsui-O, but she forges an independence more victorious and more triumphant than do the two others. Although she was led to some extent by circumstances over which she had no control, and much of her self-esteem came from the radiating influence of Shug, her rebellion was total and final. Mrs. Penn's revolt was neither, and even Mrs. Freeman did not quite believe in it. Revolt for Tsui-O and Celia had to be determined and complete, for each endured unending toil and debasement in a type of cultural bondage. Tsui-O left home to a large degree against her will. She would have preferred to stay, but chose to leave as an act of defiance. Independence or self-determination, if it came at all, came after her abandonment of husband and family. Celia, however, developed a spirit of independence as a gradual learning process. There was nothing dramatic in her leaving the man who had married her only to exploit her—no external force, no marital crisis, no change in condition. She merely announced her decision and moved out. Among the three fictional characters, she has the most in common with Ibsen's Nora. Her lesbian relationship with Shug may seem to place her in a separate category, but this sexual element has no fundamental bearing on her psychological triumph. Mrs. Penn is the only one of the three heroines to remain in her original household. The local color genre had no place for extreme cruelty or suffering, whereas they are essential ingredients of most postmodern fiction. Tsui-O and Celia suffered greater repression but were fundamentally willing victims, if victims at all, until the final moments of their revolt. All three protagonists were basically mild and acquiescing, and they reached middle age before declaring themselves free. Sexual abuse and violence may have exacerbated the condition of the postmodern protagonists, but their liberation came through internal moral courage. Freeman's protagonist may shine as an icon of the local color school, but she lacks the conviction required for a feminist heroine.

Works Cited

Freeman, Mary E. Wilkins. *The Revolt of Mother and Other Stories*. Old
  Westbury, N.Y.: The Feminist Press, 1974.
Yu, Li-hua. *In Liu Village*. In *Chinese Stories from Taiwan: 1960–1970,*
  edited by Joseph S. M. Lau. New York: Columbia University Press,
  1976.

Tsuda Umeko as University Founder
and Cultural Intermediary

NAOMI MATSUOKA

Tsuda Umeko (1864–1929), the founder of Tsuda College in Tokyo and a pioneer in higher education for women in the Meiji period (1868–1911), is an exemplary cultural intermediary. Owing to her rare experience, born Japanese but brought up in the United States for eleven years, she had access to both peoples and cultures. Her self-effacing effort as an intermediary culminated in the founding of an English school for women in 1900 both with Japanese government recognition and with philanthropic financial support from America, which was quite unusual in Japan. At the present time, after one century, her school still maintains the fame of a good English school and stands as a symbol of higher education for women. Umeko herself, on the other hand, has been all but forgotten. Although her life and thought are praised in a more or less Christian context, she is not recognized in the history of the Japanese feminist movement; instead, she is sometimes criticized as conservative and elitist. Her role as a cultural intermediary, however, should be more thoroughly examined because cultural understanding is what Japan needs, now more than ever, in order to be understood in the international community. Therefore, this essay will focus on what Umeko accepted from America and introduced to Japan, what she chose to express in order to win the sympathy of Americans when she spoke for Japanese women, and how she survived with her school through a tumultuous era of rapid Westernization followed by a reactionary backlash and two wars, an era when Japan was not at all sympathetic to women or their education and when a highly specialized English education for women was least wanted.

The life of Tsuda Umeko was a very unusual one, starting in 1871, when she was just about to be seven and was sent by the Japanese government to study in America for ten years. She was separated from her Japanese family and brought up entirely in an American way. She was baptized and attained fluency in English at the cost of her Japanese. But since she was always conscious of being Japanese and of returning to Japan to work for her country, she was to develop a double identity. After she returned to Japan in 1882, she strove hard to be accepted into Japanese society in order to improve the education of Japanese women. At the same time, she kept close contact with the United States, writing several hundred English letters to her American "mother" over thirty years. Eager to learn Japanese customs and ways of thinking, she struggled to improve her Japanese language skills, and slowly and cautiously, she became acknowledged in Japanese society. In 1889, she went back to the United States to study at Bryn Mawr and organized, with American women, philanthropic activities to raise scholarship money for Japanese women to study in America. In 1900, after abundant teaching in various schools, she founded Joshi Eigaku Juku (Women's School for English Studies). The school was a place to realize the Western ideas she had absorbed and experienced, so in that sense her school was the embodiment of her entire life: higher education for women, the means to be independent, and sisterhood among women.

Umeko was one of the first five Japanese girls the government sent to the United States with the Iwakura Mission in 1871. The others were Ueda Tei and Yoshimasu Ryo, both fourteen years old; Yamakawa Sutematsu, eleven years old; and Nagai Shige, eight years old. Tei and Ryo went back to Japan before they had finished one year in America. Shige completed her ten years of stay. And Sutematsu and Umeko extended their stay one more year in order to complete their schooling at Vassar College and Archer Institute. respectively. They returned to Japan together in 1882. Shige, Sutematsu, and Umeko called themselves a "trio" and remained close friends for the rest of their lives.

Umeko, being a daughter of the samurai class, was trained in Confucianism and had a strong sense of loyalty, duty, and responsibility to the lord and to society. This same inclination made her loyal to the emperor and his government in the new era but also led her to the Christian faith during her stay in the United States. Although the object of her loyalty changed from the Tokugawa Shogunate to the Imperial reign and finally to Christianity, her sense of duty and responsibility culminated in her mission to work for her countrywomen.

Just before Umeko left Japan, she and the other girls were called to the court and received from the empress a document from the Imperial Order:

Your intention of studying abroad, considering that you are a girl, is admirable. When, in time, schools for girls are established, you, having finished your studies, shall be examples to your countrywomen. Bear this in your mind and apply yourself to your studies day and night. (Furuki, 12)

Later, after she came back to Japan, Umeko wrote this Order in her own words as "to go abroad to study for the good of our countrywomen." She was to follow the order faithfully for the rest of her life (Umeko, *Writings,* 79).

In a sense, Umeko spent the eleven years of her stay in the United States obeying this Imperial Order. She received family love from her foster parents, a good education, and instruction in the Christian faith, all of which agreed with her expected future. She had a fortunate encounter with her foster parents, for Charles Lanman and his wife Adeline, who did not have a child, loved her as their own daughter and at the same time treated her as an important guest student from Japan who would work for her country in the future. In Washington, Charles Lanman was then a secretary at the Japanese legation and, fortunately for Umeko, had many contacts with Japanese statesmen and students who visited and studied there. He was a man of letters all his life, publishing over twenty books, including *The Japanese in America* (1872), which he wrote with the clear intention of defending Japanese students from Americans' contempt (Rose, 28). He was a model for Umeko, who later became a spokeswoman for Japan. He showed her the learned and literary life, and, since we have the several hundred letters Umeko wrote to Adeline, we can see his strong influence on her.

In a recent study, Louise Dumakis discusses the influence of Adeline on Umeko in regard to her idea of a woman's life. This is easily understood when we consider the large number of letters from Umeko to Adeline and the amount of time they must have spent together as mother and daughter in the Lanman house. Dumakis points out that Adeline was very enthusiastic about philanthropic activities and the temperance movement. Also, as Barbara Rose explains, the domesticity of women was an ideal in America during Umeko's stay, incorporating the idea that women should be good teachers at home and in public. Umeko, living in Washington, D.C., must have been exposed to the idea and the movement (30). And she must have seen many good examples of women's work.

Another important influence was Christianity, which was a means for Umeko to obtain an American identity and to absorb American culture. Since she was a very moral and self-disciplined child, she was attracted to Christian ethical teaching. Later, she believed that education and Christianity would save Japanese women. It was a delicate issue because the Japanese government had forbidden students to convert to a foreign religion during their stay abroad. But in February 1873 this prohibition was canceled by the Japanese government. Under the influence of the Lanmans, who were Episcopalians, less than two years after she came to America, Umeko asked to be baptized. The Lanmans consulted with the Japanese legation, and in July 1873, she was baptized according to the rites of the Protestant Episcopal Church. In her private life, at every turning point she was supported by her faith.

The first three years back in Japan were for Umeko a period of adjustment and assimilation to her culture. As she recovered gradually from the first "counterculture shock," she observed Japan closely, compared it with America, and selected good and useful qualities for women's education from both cultures. During this period, writing her reflections and impressions on Japan to Adeline seemed to be an indispensable part of her daily life, a form of psychotherapy, especially since she could write only in English and conversing with Adeline in letters was the only real communication that satisfied her mind.

In a year or so, she was frustrated, depressed, and helpless. She was quite lost between the two cultures: "I wish I were able to do Japanese ways altogether, or else all foreign. I hate a mixture, but it is impossible for me to do so, and so I am afraid that I shall neither wear foreign dresses or do foreign ways well after I get out of the habit, and that I shall never do Japanese ways" (Umeko, *Attic Letters,* 50–51). Sometimes, she felt ostracized from both peoples: "We [the trio] have no friend—true real friend—but each other; our ways of thinking are very different from Japanese, very different from the foreigners here" (53). Or even paranoid: "You may laugh at me minding people here, but somehow everyone, both Japanese and foreigners, want to know always how we three girls take everything, life, and customs and ways, and they would criticize my criticisms and my language, etc." (93). In a sense, her life was spent negotiating between the two different cultures, enduring ostracism, and trying not to be attacked.

We can imagine how this state of mind eventually formed two personalities: one for Japan and the other for America. This was Umeko's way of surviving as well as her apprenticeship as a cultural intermediary. Eventually she seemed to attain a detached and humorous manner for describing herself acting like a Japanese: how she wore a kimono, how she cleaned her Japanese room, and so on. She describes some of these accomplishments with childlike pride and joy. It shows that she had little by little recovered from counterculture shock and gained some confidence in living as a Japanese woman.

On the other hand, this half-forced muteness provided her with opportunities to observe carefully Japanese people and their society without being criticized. In her letters, she often sounded overcautious, always afraid of being criticized. Many of the comments she made in her letters she could not utter to Japanese or Americans, and she often closed her letters urging Adeline not to repeat what she had written. To this seventeen-year-old girl who had returned from a progressive and industrialized country, Japan seemed far behind in every way. The more she tried to control herself in her letters, the more we see how stunned she was. She described the Japanese lifestyle in detail, but at the end she told Adeline repeatedly, "You won't like it," revealing that it was difficult for Umeko to accept it herself but necessary for her to conceal her feelings probably out of pride and embarrassment. She seemed obliged to defend Japan and to ask for approval from Adeline, who for Umeko represented Americans, a modern, civilized, and moral people. Although she herself was shocked at how primitive Japan must seem from the American point of view, she tried not to give the impression that Japan was a premodern country. She developed this attitude to win the sympathy of Americans, especially when she had to depend on them to found her school.

Having recovered from the first culture shock, she became a fair observer of culture. In the letter of 20 January 1884, she wrote: "I have gotten used to think of everything in both ways. And I take things very differently from what I used to" (130). In her letters, she compared Japan and America, their peoples and their ways of doing things. Her topics ranged from food, clothes, and houses to education, marriage, religion, and morality. She tried not to judge which culture was superior or more civilized, but she eloquently explained the circumstances of each issue. In the letter mentioned above, she wrote that she tried to explain to Mrs. Ito, wife of Ito Hirobumi, the freedom of young American women who had gentlemen visitors and went out with them—behavior that would be considered scandalous in Japan. In return, she admired Mrs. Ito for her gentle motherhood and her children's good manners and respect for their parents. Whenever she had to make a judgment, it was a moral judgment: for example, she criticized the missionaries for being narrow-minded and hypocritical, and she thought many Japanese statesmen were immoral for keeping mistresses.

As for her teaching career, Umeko tried out different teaching occasions as offered to her: a mission school, private tutoring, a private girls school, and the Peeress's school. She chose none of them as models for her own school. In 1883, she taught for two months in a Methodist mission school, Kaigan Jogakko, in Tsukiji. The result was her rejection of mission schools. In her letters, she strongly criticized missionaries for enjoying luxurious lives in Japan entirely supported by their organization while their schools and pupils were left in poverty and a Japanese teacher like Umeko was hired with a pay as low as one-fourth or even one-fifth of that of the missionaries. They were not devoted and always ready to leave Japan after a short stay (51). And they "can not reach any but the lower kind of people because they will not conform to Japanese ways" (64). In the same letter, she admired Japanese ministers and observed that the Japanese were more appropriate as teachers of English to Japanese, a view she restated when considering teaching English in Japan. She wanted to train Japanese teachers for Japanese students. But again she asks that her opinion be kept confidential and adds, "Don't let anyone know I have said all this, but it is true I find no congeniality with them at all" (ibid.).

For about a half year from 1883 to 1884, she was a governess in the household of one of the most prominent Meiji leaders, Ito Hirobumi, the minister of the Imperial Household and later prime minister. He invited her to live in his house as a guest and teach his wife and daughters English and Western manners. Umeko enjoyed the opportunity to look into Japanese high society and the life of the prominent statesman who was turning Japan into a modern nation with a constitution. But it seems to me that she was more of a governess to Ito Hirobumi than to his wife and daughters. She reminds me of those governesses who came from the West to one of the Asian countries and rather naively but sincerely tried to teach Western ideas and customs to a non-Western mind:

> Mr. Ito and I have had some very serious talks on all sorts of subjects. He seems very anxious to promote the interest of Japan in every way—socially, morally, politically, intellectually. (123)

Christianity was the most important thing Umeko wanted to teach. In the same letter, she was excited that she had had a chance to talk with Ito about religion:

> It was, however, only last night that he began to ask me about Christianity and we talked nearly two hours on it. He is in favor of it, acknowledged that its morals and teachings surpassed that of any other religion, and that for Japan, Christianity would be a good thing. (Ibid.)

Umeko was also encouraged and inspired by Ito Hirobumi. The words of encouragement from this prominent national leader must have sounded promising:

Sometimes when I tell him about many things, about books, or interesting things about women's work, he tells me I must tell Japanese ladies all these sorts of things about work and taking care of the sick, and the worth of knowledge, etc. He wants me to learn and to bring me forward so that I can, and he is very kind. (Ibid.)

Umeko witnessed in Ito's house the realization of the project for a new school. The original plan was a school "for the higher classes" and "a first-rate school." Ito and Inoue Kaoru, the minister of foreign affairs, had meetings with Sutematsu, now Mrs. Oyama, and Shimoda Utako. Sutematsu submitted information about Vassar College, but the school turned out to be quite different from that liberal and progressive American women's college. Umeko did not doubt, however, that this would be the best school and that she would teach English there (137).

While she lived in Ito's house, she also taught at Shimoda Utako's Toyo Jojuku, a private girls school for upper-class daughters. She taught just a few courses there and exchanged lessons with Utako: Umeko gave English lessons and Utako gave Japanese and calligraphy lessons. Teaching and studying at this school, however, were often interrupted by Utako's sickness, the death of her husband, and so on, and did not seem to be satisfactory. Umeko's encounter with Shimoda Utako, however, seems more significant than her teaching experience at the latter's school: Umeko learned an important lesson from Utako's situation. They were both Meiji female educators, although they represented two extreme cases. Utako, the model of a traditional Japanese woman, was one of the empress's favorite court ladies and established her fame in Japanese traditional poetry, while Umeko was a Westernized woman. Even after she left the court, Utako was among the circle of Meiji statesmen and received many favors from them. She was protected by Ito Hirobumi, as Umeko was. When she opened her private school, Toyo Jojuku, there were many students from high society. She was appointed a director of the Peeress's School. Later, however, she suffered from social scandals mainly because she was a capable woman and was too closely related to the power of the time, as Umeko pointed out in one of her letters. Umeko admired her intelligence and ability and defended her in her letters:

You see, Japan is in such a whirl now, and the question of women's education, etc. being so much agitated that any woman as Mrs. Shimoda or Sutematsu, who is in any way prominent or well known, is picked to pieces by the old school people, who are against the new code, and you see the dreadful stories they get up against them. (305)

Later, the paths of these two women departed further from each other. Shimoda Utako founded another private school, Jissen Jogakko, whose aim was to provide useful skills to young women to be good mothers and good maids. She went along with the national policy of expansion to Korea and China, and her school accepted many Korean and Chinese students. She tried to assimilate them into Japanese society while Umeko strove to raise the status of Japanese women to the Western level.

Ito Hirobumi's plan to open a new school was realized in 1885. The Peeress's school was founded under the guidance of the Imperial Household, and Umeko was appointed assistant professor of English. She was very excited, happy, and proud of her government appointment, especially because she was one of very few women appointed. She wrote in detail to Adeline about Japanese court rankings and the level of her own position. However, she was very soon worn out by being always busy with ceremonies such as the empress's visit to the school. Moreover, the students were too reserved and were not enthusiastic about studying. They also left school to marry at the age of sixteen or seventeen, carelessly giving up their educational opportunities.

A few years after her official status was settled, she had the urge to go back to the United States to attain a higher level of education. In Japan, the number of women who graduated from Normal School was increasing, and when she met these women in reading and study gatherings, she realized that she needed a higher degree of educational background than just a good knowledge of English. In her letters, she started asking Adeline to look for an appropriate school for her, while in Japan she in a reserved way requested a sabbatical from the Peeress's School. Mrs. Morris, the wife of a rich businessman in Boston and a devoted Quaker, knew Umeko from her Archer Institute days and asked her friend, President Rhoads of Bryn Mawr College, to help Umeko. In 1889, she was admitted to Bryn Mawr College as a special student exempted from fees for tuition, room and board. The Peeress's School agreed to give her a paid sabbatical leave of two years while keeping her position until she finished her study at Bryn Mawr.

She extended her stay one more year, and those three years were fruitful in many ways. At Bryn Mawr she majored in biology. The choice of study reflects her inclination toward science, and she proved that she was quite successful in the field. During her extended stay in 1891, she conducted research with Professor T. H. Morgan, and in 1894 she co-published the article "The Orientation of the Frog's Egg" in the *Quarterly Journal of Microscopical Science*. Umeko was asked to stay at Bryn Mawr to continue the research, but she declined, saying that she must return to Japan. By then it seemed that she had firmly made up her mind to devote her life to enlightening Japanese women.

In her private life, Umeko further developed a close friendship with Alice Bacon, the daughter of Reverend Leonard Bacon, Yamakawa Sutematsu's foster father in Boston. Originally Sutematsu and Alice planned to open a school for Japanese women, but, since Sutematsu was married, their plan was unrealized. Umeko and Sutematsu worked, however, to have Alice invited to teach English at the Peeress's School from 1888 to 1889. During that period, Umeko and Alice lived together in the same house, and Umeko enjoyed her company greatly. In summer 1890, they got together again. Umeko stayed at Alice's place in Hampton and helped her complete her book *Japanese Girls and Women*. Umeko was also acquainted with Anna C. Hartshorne, another Bryn Mawr student. Both Alice and Anna became faithful friends of Umeko. Alice came back to Japan to teach at Umeko's school when it was finally opened in 1900. Anna was Umeko's lifelong friend: after coming to Japan to teach at Umeko's school in 1902, she worked for Umeko and her school until 1940, when she was forced to leave Japan because of the war. At the beginning, she taught without pay, and when the school buildings were completely destroyed by the Great Kanto Earthquake in 1923, she went back to the United States to raise funds to rebuild the school.

Umeko was also active socially during her three years in America. She helped raise a fund of $8,000 to send a female student every four years from Japan to the United States for a higher education. The dean of Bryn Mawr at the time was Martha Carey Thomas, and she gave Umeko good advice on how to carry out the project. Mrs. Morris organized a committee and raised the planned sum of $8,000. The influence of Carey Thomas should not be neglected because she was an advocate of higher education for women, and of course there was the influence of Bryn Mawr, the ideals of which are openness, high standards, and diligent work. Umeko also observed that Mrs. Morris and other American women carried out philanthropic enterprises.

Supported and encouraged by these American women, Umeko spoke about Japanese women, appealing to their notion of sisterhood and enlightenment. One of her speeches, "The Education of Japanese Women," given in Philadelphia in August 1891, explained the situation of women in Japan in relation to that of women in the United States and asked for support to improve it (Umeko, *Writings,* 28–32). She assured the American women that Japanese women had the potential for advanced education but were just a little bit behind in time. Therefore, they needed education to find their role in the coming society "under the new and wonderful light of the nineteenth-century civilization" (29). She also reminded American women of their own recent past, when they had been completely subordinate to men. Thus she tried to place Japanese women's problems in the context of universal women's issues regardless of nation and race. Such a speech could only be made by a person familiar with both cultures and both societies, a person who had a profound sympathy and love for Japanese women and a firm confidence in and respect for American women.

She began her speech: "It is already true that 'the woman question,' which we cannot say has entirely ceased to be agitated in progressive America even, is now the great topic of the day in Japan." And she led her audience to her goal: "A number of American women with generous hearts, and sympathies not limited by country or race, and with, perhaps, some recollection of a somewhat similar struggle, on a different plane, for the better education of women in this country, have come to aid us in meeting the great want of well-educated women teachers." She clearly criticized the education so far available for Japanese women, saying that it "was too limited to fit them for other than lives of dependence." And she continued, "The training which they received made them gentle ladies and lovely wives" (30). She also clearly advocated independent womanhood, a goal which she pursued in Japan as we shall see later: "The new present time demands broader education for women, new avenues of employment and of self-support, so that it may be possible for a woman to be independent" (31).

In the same speech, Umeko also maintained that, in Japan, education for women should be intensified because men had already achieved progress under the flow of Western knowledge, leading Japan to be recognized in the Western world: "Real progress is impossible while the growth is all on one side, and Japan cannot take a high stand until the women, as well as the men, are educated" (32). This notion of balance between men and women, or equal opportunity between two sexes, was one of Umeko's main concerns, as she repeatedly expressed in her later speeches and writings. She keenly sensed that the government would not provide many education opportunities for women. She had learned this from her personal experience, and that was why she asked American women for help.

It is surprising to see that Umeko crossed all the boundaries so easily. Nations, races, religions, and languages seemed to be minor obstacles for her. Without hesitation, she directly sought for cooperation among women. Her contemporaneity should be remembered among us, especially when we witness that at the 1995 United Nations Conference for Women held in Beijing, women's groups from all over the world presented their problems in their respective countries and pledged cooperation among themselves.

Umeko continued to be a spokeswoman for Japanese women when she returned to Japan after her three years at Bryn Mawr. Just after the Sino-Japanese War ended in 1895, she published an article, "Japanese Women and the War," in the weekly periodical *The New York Independent*. She praised the contribution of Japanese women to the war—a contribution that was being underrated both inside and outside Japan:

> The following brief account may serve to give some idea of the intense patriotic feeling which prevails, and the hidden, tho' by no means unimportant, part which the Japanese women have wonderfully sustained from the beginning of the war. (49)

She explained in detail how mothers and wives endured the deaths of their beloved in the battlefields with a strong sense of patriotism and loyalty. She believed that Japanese women deserved equal honor with men:

> The women of Japan—it is not on the battle-field that they die; but their lives are sacrificed for their country in their silent homes and by their saddened experiences; and tho' no monument may be built to them, they have given their all willingly, and done their share for the nation's glory. (56)

The article no doubt has a pro-war tone, yet the readers are saddened by the tragic scenes of Japanese families and individuals, especially of women, Umeko described here. The more she emphasized the patriotism and self-sacrifice of Japanese women, the closer Umeko came to casting doubt on the war, which actually caused great loss of lives, poverty, and unbearable grief for women. By writing about families and women left in deep sorrow and despair, Umeko presented here a more humane image of the Japanese. This is what Japan needed. Japan needed more people like Umeko who could describe the more ordinary life and feelings of Japanese rather than their militaristic and patriotic zeal. Japanese military successes surprised many Western nations and won their admiration but at the same time it called attention to them as a threat. So Umeko was not only a spokeswoman for her women but also for Japan.

On the opening of her English school, Joshi Eigaku Juku, on 14 September 1900, Umeko was again facing both sides. In her opening speech in Japanese, she singled out one specific purpose of the school among many, that is, to provide a high level of training to women who wanted to obtain a teacher's license in English (3). Later, however, in her

report published in the *Bryn Mawr Alumnae Quarterly* (August 1907),
she maintained that English learning would promote understanding of the
West among the students:

> Apart from its usefulness and its commercial value, the thorough mastery of a
> Western language, especially a close study of the literature, gives to us of the
> East the key to Western thought, ideals and point of view. Often the simplest
> book or story gives us subject-matter for discussion because of the different
> mental attitudes of the East and West, an understanding of which helps vastly
> to bring our nations closer together. (96)

In Japan, she tended to focus on the more practical merit of teaching
and learning the English language, which was definitely needed and consequently an acceptable goal. Meanwhile, toward America, she explained
that the Japanese were making efforts to understand them better. Today,
approximately one hundred years after the founding of her English
school, Umeko's aim to promote understanding between the East and the
West through English study seems convincing and significant, while the
teacher-training program for women seems anachronistic and limited.

In both her opening speech in Japanese and her English report in the
Bryn Mawr Alumnae Quarterly, Umeko emphasized that it was the
enthusiasm of both students and teachers that formed a school, not the
school buildings and facilities:

> While fine class rooms, books, and other helps are not to be despised but to
> be made as perfect as possible, yet these material objects, or even any one
> fixed method or system of work are far from comparison with other and more
> essential things of a school. I mean by this, the qualifications of the teacher,
> the zeal, patience and industry of both teachers and pupils, and the spirit in
> which they pursue their work. (Furuki, 104)

But, at the end of her Japanese speech addressed to Japanese students she
added one warning that does not sound appropriate for an opening
address. From it, we can see that Umeko really feared social criticism of
women who sought higher education:

> And criticism will mostly come, not so much on our courses of study or
> methods of work, but on points which simply requires a little care and
> thoughtfulness on your part—the little things which constitute the making of
> a true lady—the language you use, your manner in intercourse with others—
> your attention to the details of our etiquette. So I ask you not in any way to
> make yourselves conspicuous or to seem forward, but be always gentle, sub-
> missive and courteous as have always been our women in the past. (Rose,
> 129)

Finally, in her English report, she emphasized that the educational environment was about the same all over the world. She showed the pride and confidence of an experienced educator and then invited Americans to understand the Japanese situation with sympathy. Again what we see here is her efforts to put the Japanese situation in a context familiar to Americans, rather than to emphasize Japan's backwardness and difference:

> I have come to believe that schools and students and a true teacher's work are about the same everywhere in the world, that most of the so-called national traits are not inborn, but develop from environment and education, and that in dealing with the young, our material, whether we are in the East or West, Japan or America, does not differ essentially. (Umeko, *Writings*, 93)

The strange mixture of content in the opening ceremony shows not only Umeko's cautious approach toward Japanese society, but also her double identity. The ceremony started with the reading of the Imperial Rescript on Education followed by a hymn in Japanese, psalms in English, and a prayer in Japanese. Umeko then gave her opening speech in Japanese from English notes in her hand. The ceremony was closed with the singing of the Japanese anthem. This mixture reflects the rather conspicuous position her school occupied in Japan. Joshi Eigaku Juku was a private English school, which was officially approved and recognized by the Ministry of Education as an institute for the higher education of women. The founder was one of five girls who had been ordered to study in the United States for the future education for their countrywomen, and she was pursuing this original Imperial order. The government actually was responsible for her and her school, although it did not really provide the opportunity for her to pursue her vocation. The founder was also a former English teacher at the Peeress's School and so was naturally loyal to the Imperial family and their peers as well as respectful of the Japanese traditional culture and customs. Although her school was not a mission school, it respected Christianity. Finally, the school was entirely supported by her philanthropic activities in the United States.

Umeko was a devoted Christian ever since she was baptized in America at the age of nine, and she was eager to guide the Japanese to Christianity. She was eager to talk about the subject with Ito Hirobumi, as we have seen, and she was willing to teach the religion to her students whenever they showed interest while she was teaching at the Peeress's School. Later on, after Buddhism and Confucianism declined into conventions that tended to be no more than social restraints, especially for women, she saw that it was more appropriate to introduce Christianity as a moral code . In 1905, the Japan YWCA was formed, and Umeko was elected its first president. In 1913, she read a paper, "The Presentation of the Gospel in Japan," at the World Conference of the Student Christian Federation, held at Lake Mohon. Her speech was published in the July issue of *The Student World* of the same year:

> Thus when young Japan is awakening to a realization of itself, when the emptiness and hollowness of the older teachings is becoming more and more apparent, in this age of greater freedom of thought for both men and women, a strong appeal can be made to our students through the ethical side of Christianity, the value of which is appreciated by all the thinking men of Japan. (499)

The school remained conspicuously bicultural. The teachers and students lived in the same school buildings, pretty much in Japanese style, but the courses were offered mostly in English, including one on current events. She invited distinguished scholars, thinkers, educators, and statesmen, who were all friends of the school. Seven years after its establishment, she wrote a report, "Teaching in Japan," which was published in *The Bryn Mawr Alumnae Quarterly:*

> As to the educational side, we have gained a corner for ourselves in the educational world, our school has government recognition as preparing teachers of English, and our graduates of the normal course receive the teacher's license in English for government High and Normal school without further examination, a privilege held by no other girls' school in Japan. (95)

Meanwhile, the financial support from America also continued. When the school moved from a rented house in Ichibancho, Kojimachi, to an old but spacious mansion in Motozonocho, Kojimachi, the land was bought by money raised in Boston.

Umeko's school, which was started with just ten students in 1900, grew rapidly; the number of students reached 170 in 1907 and almost 400 in 1910. Inevitably, Umeko had to worry constantly about school finances. Teaching, managing her school, and social duties, including writing numerous letters for the students, asking for financial support, exhausted her. She fell ill of diabetes in 1917 and resigned from the presidency in 1919. She had several strokes in the same year and was forced to spend the rest of her life in bed until 1933, when she died in her house in Kamakura.

In the rather short period of her presidency, Umeko firmly established her school. Even after she left office, the financial support from America continued, the school kept producing well-trained young women and sending them out into Japanese society, and it eventually became a university. Even when the school was completely destroyed in the Great Kanto Earthquake, Anna C. Hartshorn managed to raise money in America to reopen and enlarge the school. She organized the Philadelphia Committee to help Miss Tsuda's School, stayed in America for over two years until she was certain that the planned fund of $500,000 would be raised. Umeko wanted to make her school a university when the Japanese government acknowledged men's vocational schools as universities in 1918. After Umeko resigned, Tsuji Matsu, the acting president, added a liberal arts course to the school and prepared to have the status of the school raised from that of a vocational school to that of a university. In 1948, the Japanese government acknowledged the first six women's universities, and Tsuda Juku Daigaku Tsuda College was started. After World War II, the GHQ (General Headquarters)[1] had great influence on the improvement of women's education in Japan, and Hoshino Ai, the president of Tsuda College, spoke to the U.S. Education Mission, explaining that the Japanese government was slow to advance women's education and demanding that Japanese women be provided with equal opportunity for education. General Douglas MacArthur's advisor on women's education, Dr. Lulu Holmes, and then MacArthur himself heard this and responded. Like Umeko, Hoshino Ai did not hesitate to appeal to the American mind in order to utilize the current situation to the benefit of Japanese women.

Works Cited

Furuki, Yoshiko. *The White Plum: A Biography of Umeko Tsuda, Pioneer in the Higher Education of Japanese Women.* New York: Weatherhill, 1991.

Rose, Barbara. *Tsuda Umeko and Women's Education in Japan.* New Haven: Yale University Press, 1992.

Umeko, Tsuda. *The Attic Letters: Umeko Tsuda's Correspondence to Her American Mother.* Edited by Yoshiko Furuki et al. New York: Weatherhill, 1991.

———. *The Writings of Umeko Tsuda.* Rev. ed. Edited by Yoshiko Furuki et al. Tokyo: Tsuda College, 1984.

Notes

1. GHQ refers to the American military occupation government in psotwar Japan. In America, it is perhaps better known as SCAP, which originally referred to the position of General MacArthur as Supreme Commander, Allied Powers. In Japan, GHQ is widely known as the American Occupation Government.

List of Contributors

MASAYUKI AKIYAMA is dean and professor in the College of International Relations at Nihon University, Japan, and holds the offices of trustee and secretary general in the Japanese Comparative Literature Association. He has engaged in joint projects with A. O. Aldridge at both the University of Illinois and Nihon University as well as at various international conferences. He has published *Henry James: His World, His Thought, His Art*, 1981; *A Comparative Study of Henry James and Major Japanese Writers*, 1991; *Henry James's International Novels: Encounter and conflict with Different Cultures*, 1993; and *The World of Henry James: America, Europe and the East*, 1996.

KAI-CHONG CHEUNG received her M.A. and Ph.D. in comparative literature from the University of Illinois and is now chairman of the Department of English at Soochow University, Taipei, Taiwan. In 1996 she was awarded a Fulbright-Hayes grant for a year's research at the University of Illinois. Author of *The Theme of Chastity in "Hau Ch'iu Chuan" and Parallel Western Fiction* in the series Euro-Sinica, 1994, Cheung has published several articles on comparative literature and is now writing a book on Lin Yutang.

JOHN T. DORSEY is professor of English and American literature at Rikkyo University. He received the B.A. in comparative literature from Fordham University and the M.A. and Ph.D. from the University of Illinois, where he was a student of Professor Aldridge. He has published extensively on contemporary American, Japanese, and European fiction and drama.

EUGENE EOYANG, professor of comparative literature at Indiana University since 1980, has also served there as chairman of East Asian Studies. He is currently president of the American Comparative Literature Association. Author of many articles, he has most recently published *The Transparent Eye: Reflections on Translation, Chinese Literature, and Comparative Poetics*, 1993, and *Coat of Many Colors: Reflections on Diversity by a Minority of One*, 1995.

MATOSHI FUJISAWA is professor of English at Nihon University. He has published *A Critical Study of Modern Japanese Literature*, 1980; *A Study of Japanese Emigrant Literature*, 1985; and *A Study of Yasushi Inoue's Young Day*, 1996, as well as articles on Japanese-British relations.

MARIÁN GÁLIK, a sinologist specializing in modern Chinese literature, is a member of the Institute of Asian and African Studies at the Slovak Academy of Sciences, Bratislava. He has edited the proceedings of several international congresses and has published *Mao Tun and Modern Chinese Literary Criticism*, 1969, and *The Genesis of Modern Chinese Literary Criticism*, 1980, as well as several books in Chinese.

SHUNSUKE KAMEI, a well-known literary commentator on Japanese television, is Professor Emeritus at the University of Tokyo and Professor of American Literature at Gifu Women's University. His books include *Walt Whitman in Modern Literature* (Japanese Academy Award, 1971) and *The World of Mark Twain*, 1995.

KOON-KI T. HO, who holds a Ph.D. in comparative literature from the University of Illinois, is currently Lecturer at the School of Professional and Continuing Education, University of Hong Kong. He has published books on utopias and dystopias of the twentieth century and articles on modern and contemporary Chinese literature.

ADRIAN HSIA received a doctor of philosophy degree from the Free University of Berlin. Since 1968 he has been teaching German and Comparative literature at McGill University in Montreal, Canada. His main interest is cross-cultural studies. He has published seventeen books and more than sixty articles.

SEONG-KON KIM, professor of English at Seoul National University, Korea, obtained his Ph.D. from the State University of New York at Buffalo. He has also taught at Penn State University, Brigham Young University, Columbia University, and SUNY/Buffalo. His awards include a Fulbright Scholarship, a Fulbright Scholar-in-Residence Grant, and a Korea Research Foundation Grant. He has published ten books, including *Literature in the New Media Age*, 1996; *Words in the Labyrinth: Inter-*

views with American Writers, 1996; *Essays on Film*, 1994; and *Literature and Film*, 1997.

YIU-NAM LEUNG received his Ph.D. in comparative literature in 1987 with A. O. Aldridge as his dissertation director. Since 1987 he has been Associate Professor of English at Tsing Hua University in Taiwan. In 1993 he was awarded a Fulbright-Hayes grant for a year's research at the University of California, Berkeley, on the American Bildungsroman as well as a further grant from the National Science Council of the Republic of China for the same purpose. In 1996, he received a Mackay Canadian Studies Grant for research at the University of Alberta. He has recently been elected Secretary of the English Teachers' Association of Taiwan.

YOKO MATSUI is instructor at Seitoku University in Japan. She has published *Ruiko Kuroiwa's My Sin (Warawa no Isumi) as an Adapted Work of Bertha Clay* as well as articles on Japanese-Western literary relations.

NAOMI MATSUOKA is associate professor in the English Department of the Junior College of Nihon University. She received a B.A. degree from Tsuda College in Tokyo and an M.A. from the University of Illinois. She has published articles on contemporary fiction in Japan and America.

I-CHUN WANG, a Ph.D. from the University of Illinois, is associate pro-fessor of English and Comparative Literature at National Sun Yat-sen University in Taiwan. She is now working on a book tentatively entitled "Female Transgressions: Disciplining Women in English Renaissance Drama." She has published articles on English Renaissance playwrights and modern Irish dramatists.

WAI-LIM YIP, professor in the Department of Literature of the Univer-sity of California at La Jolla, has published several books in Chinese and English, including *Ezra Pound's Cathay*, 1969; *Chinese Poetry: Major Modes and Genres*, 1976; and *Diffusion of Distances: Dialogues between Chinese and Western Poetics*, 1993.

HEH-HSIANG YUAN, a reader in English at the New Asia College, Chi-nese University of Hong Kong, has published articles on comparative literature and English literature and a book entitled *Essays on Chinese-Western Comparative Esthetics and Literature*.

DAI-YUN YUE is a professor in the Chinese Department of Peking University, China, and head of the Research Institute of Comparative Literature. She has held the offices of president of the Chinese Comparative Literature Association and vice president of the International Comparative Literature Association. She has published widely on comparative literature, Chinese literature, Chinese literary theory, and modern literary theory.

Index

In this index, Chinese, Japanese, and Korean names, including those of contributors to this book, are printed in the oriental style, with family names preceding given names.